GRACE *and* TRUTH
in the
SECULAR AGE

GRACE *and* TRUTH *in the* SECULAR AGE

Edited by

Timothy Bradshaw

WILLIAM B. EERDMANS PUBLISHING COMPANY
GRAND RAPIDS, MICHIGAN / CAMBRIDGE, U.K.

© 1998 Wm. B. Eerdmans Publishing Co.
255 Jefferson Ave. S.E., Grand Rapids, Michigan 49503 /
P.O. Box 163, Cambridge CB3 9PU U.K.

Printed in the United States of America

03 02 01 00 99 98   7 6 5 4 3 2 1

Library of Congress Cataloging-in-Publication Data

Grace and truth in the secular age / edited by Timothy Bradshaw.
        p.   cm.
    Includes bibliographical references.
    ISBN 0-8028-4343-3 (pbk. : alk. paper)
    1. Anglican Communion. 2. Church and the world. 3. Evangelicalism
— Anglican Communion. I. Bradshaw, Timothy.
BX5005.G69   1998
283 — dc21   98-13685
                        CIP

Contents

93701

CONTENTS

Foreword

THE MOST REVEREND DR GEORGE CAREY, ARCHBISHOP OF CANTERBURY

In inviting the Bishops of the Anglican communion to meet together for the 1998 Lambeth Conference at Canterbury, one of my hopes was that it would provide a focus for many of the debates going on both within the communion and more widely in the church and society at present. I hoped too that those from the different traditions within our communion would be prepared to make their distinctive contributions to those debates in a spirit of being willing to listen to the contributions of others.

Grace and Truth in the Secular Age is one such contribution that brings with it the distinctive insights and concerns of Anglican Evangelicals. The essays themselves are far from monochrome and they reflect the lively debates going on within that constituency at present. Only some, even within the latter, will agree with everything each of the writers says, but the volume as a whole provides a useful guide outlining parameters and suggesting possible ways forward for our communion as a whole.

I welcome this vigorous contribution and commend it as a resource for study and reflection.

† George Cantuar

Lambeth Palace
London
December, 1997

Contributors

Rev Dr Peter Adam was a Lecturer in Systematic Theology at St John's College, Durham, and is presently Vicar of St Jude's, Carlton, a thriving inner-city church in Melbourne, Australia, as well as being a Chaplain of Melbourne University, Canon of St Paul's Cathedral and Director of the Timothy Institute, a training course for ministers.

Rt Rev Fitzsimmons Allison has been a leading conservative Episcopalian bishop in the US since 1980 and is the author of several books published by Morehouse and SPCK, including *Fear, Love and Worship; Guilt, Anger and God; The Rise of Moralism;* and *The Cruelty of Heresy: An Affirmation of Christian Orthodoxy.*

Rt Rev Dr Paul Barnett is Bishop of North Sydney, a distinguished New Testament scholar, Visiting Lecturer in New Testament and Church History at Moore Theological College and writer at both academic and popular levels.

Rev Dr Timothy Bradshaw, Dean of Regent's Park College, Oxford, is author of *The Olive Branch: an Evangelical Anglican Doctrine of the Church* and editor of the recent symposium of essays on homosexuality and the church entitled *The Way Forward?* He is a long-standing member of the International Anglican-Orthodox Theological Dialogue and chairman of the 1995 St Andrew's Day Statement on homosexuality and the church.

Rev Dr Gerald Bray is currently Professor of Divinity at Beeson Divinity School, Samford University, Birmingham, Alabama. He has written widely on doctrinal subjects for many publishers.

Dr Peter Brierley is Executive Director of Christian Research, a registered charity devoted to collecting and collating church information world-wide. He is editor of the *UK Christian Handbook* and a leading statistics expert on Christianity.

Rev Dr John Fenwick was formerly Assistant Secretary for Ecumenical Affairs for the Archbishop of Canterbury and on the staff of the 1988 Lambeth Conference in that capacity. He writes on liturgy and patristic theology and is now Vicar of Chorley, Lancashire.

Canon Michael Green is an Anglican evangelical scholar and missioner; former Principal of St John's College, Nottingham; Professor at Regent College, Vancouver; now co-director of the Archbishop of Canterbury's 'Decade of Evangelism' initiative.

Rev Dr Christopher D. Hancock has been Vicar of Holy Trinity Church, Cambridge, England, since 1994. Prior to that he was Chaplain of Magdalene College, Cambridge, teaching in the University Faculty of Divinity, and then Associate Professor of Theology at Virginia Theological Seminary, Alexandria, VA. He was co-founder of SEAD (Scholarly Engagement with Anglican Doctrine).

Dr Edith Humphrey received her doctorate in 1991 from McGill University, specialising in New Testament and early Christian origins, and has since lectured at various universities in Canada. She contributed a paper to the Montreal Declaration of Essentials in 1994 and has been involved in subsequent conferences. She has recently been appointed to the Primates' Theological Commission.

Professor Stanton L. Jones is Provost and Professor of Psychology at Wheaton College. A clinical psychologist by training, he has published books on such topics as the relationship of psychology, science and religious faith, psychotherapy theory, and human sexuality. In 1995-96 he was a Visiting Scholar and Fellow at Cambridge University.

Rt Rev Benjamin A. Kwashi is from Nigeria. He has written widely on pastoral and theological issues for that country and is an active member of several social welfare and educational institutions. He was consecrated Bishop of Jos in 1992.

Rev Dr Michael Lloyd wrote his doctoral thesis on *The Cosmic Fall and the Free Will Defence* at Worcester College, Oxford. He spent five years as a College Chaplain at Cambridge University and now serves as Curate to St James the Less in Pimlico, while continuing to write theological books.

Professor David Lyon is Head of the Department of Sociology at Queen's University in Kingston, Ontario. His research and writing focuses on long-term social, technological and cultural change, ranging from *The Steeple's Shadow: On the Myths and Realities of Secularisation* (1985) to *Postmodernity* (1994) and *The Electronic Eye: The Rise of Surveillance Society* (1994).

Professor J. I. Packer is one of the world's best known evangelical authors. He has held various positions in the United Kingdom including Warden, Latimer House, Oxford; Principal, Tyndale Hall, Bristol, and Associate Principal, Trinity College, Bristol, before becoming Professor of Theology at Regent College, Vancouver. He is Senior Editor and Visiting Scholar of *Christianity Today* and is currently working on a number of books.

Dr Vinoth Ramachandra, formerly a nuclear scientist, is Regional Secretary for South Asia for the International Fellowship of Evangelical Students (IFES) and is author of *The Recovery of Mission: Beyond the Pluralist Paradigm* published by Paternoster and Eerdmans in 1996.

Dr Chris Sinkinson completed his doctoral research into pluralism at Bristol University. He has worked as a pastoral asistant and is now on the staff of the Universities and Colleges Christian Fellowship in the south west of England where he assists Christian Unions in Higher Education.

Vivienne Stacey was a partner with Interserve in Asia and the Middle East for almost forty years and was Principal of the United Bible Training Centre in Pakistan. Residing now in Cyprus, she writes and lectures about Christian ministry and the world of Islam. Her most recent book, *Submitting to God,* was published in 1997 by Hodder and Stoughton as the first in a series on communities of faith.

Professor John Webster is Lady Margaret Professor of Divinity in the University of Oxford and Canon of Christ Church. He taught theology in Durham and was Professor of Theology at Wycliffe College, Toronto, for ten years. He also served the Anglican Church in Canada on a variety of ecumenical, liturgical and doctrinal commissions. His research and writing are in the area of dogmatics and the history of modern theology.

A Watershed Lambeth Conference

Lambeth 1998 has been called a watershed for the Anglican communion as it meets to discuss its chosen agenda, 'a call to full humanity'. It is a watershed because the agendas for revision of the structure and ethics of the church are proving so divisive as to threaten the integrity of the communion, focused by the issues of the ordination and consecration of women and homosexuality. These questions have raged particularly in the western provinces of the communion, especially in Canada and the United States. Most other provinces disagree with the drive to revision, but by virtue of academic, bureaucratic and financial power the minority have disproportionate influence in relation to the declining numbers in their local churches.

How is the Anglican family to respond? This book was written by loyal Anglicans in pastoral, missionary and theological posts who wish to address this Lambeth agenda beforehand and reflect upon the difficult questions involved. Formerly there was a natural agreement in doctrine and practice of an impressive sort, without any need for a central power to enforce it. The Bible, tradition, sacraments and episcopacy produced a loyalty to reformed catholicism, with the Book of Common Prayer as the world's finest English language liturgy. Rather like the Orthodox churches, doctrine and worship formed an unspoken centre, including the biblical and traditional ethical pattern of life.

The ferment in the late twentieth century English speaking culture has been generated in large measure by the rise of feminist criticism of the tradition, and now the rise of demands for sexual revision. Churches have sought to accommodate ethical demands for change, and this has

xiv

been done with great speed. Perhaps part of the problem is the demand for very fast revision, the lack of 'space' and time for long-term reflection and gestation of ideas. A Western sociological analysis has taken root whereby people are categorised into groups and allocated sets of 'rights', often with these groups adopting an injured stance over against the mainline tradition, a victim attitude which demands concessions. This consciousness has undoubtedly entered into the mindset of the intelligentsia of Western culture, which controls education, media and many professions, and it is mirrored in the bureaucracy of many Western churches.

One feature of this mindset is that doctrinal lines are avoided pending constant revision. Accordingly a state of uncertainty is produced, a state of instability in which change is sensed to be just around the corner. In the UK the media play their part in this, some simply ignorant, some actually mischievous and some apparently contemptuous of the Anglican church. The Lambeth '98 bishops will do well to pay scant attention to the writings of most of the religious correspondents for this reason, and will remember Lambeth '88 when the 'Lambeth Daily' was printed in protest at the distorting 'coverage' of the conference.

These essays, born out of deep affection and love for the church, are attempts to grapple with the serious issues to be discussed. They wish their church to remain catholic and reformed, holy and apostolic, scriptural and oriented by tradition, cautious and unhurried by strident demands arising from a sick Western culture. The essayists, drawn from around the globe, emerge with a totally natural sense of harmony in the gospel, to point to Christ as their focus. A wealth of experience and wisdom comes to these essays and is made available to the conference and to the Christian public who are interested in joining the discussions and in praying for the future of this great communion of Christians. The authors go to first order theological doctrines, such as those of the trinity, christology, image and fall, to address the current debates.

Readers will find an enthusiasm for the living biblical witness to the triune God, for the order found there to complement the fashionable calls for increasing freedom, for Christ and his teaching as the criterion by which 'a call to full humanity' should be judged. Irenaeus, in the second century, classically linked the doctrine of creation with that of redemption, the first Adam to the second, Old to New Testaments, so as to produce a theological framework for the gospel: this heritage must be continued by today's churches if major errors are to be avoided. In this way the present day semi-transcendent idols, such as consumerist relativism and hedonist sexualism, may be resisted and their grip on modern lives loosed.

Read these essays carefully. Use them in groups prior to Lambeth to pray and seek God's face for the church. Our prayer is that they will help to clarify the main contemporary problems in the light of the gospel. The watershed of Lambeth '98 is this: whether the Anglican communion chooses to mutate into an ethically liberal, non-doctrinal, 'free-wheeling' body of Christians, or to maintain its accountability to Christ as defined by Scripture and the historic tradition. This choice could hardly be of greater moment and, realising this, the authors offer their work.

Timothy Bradshaw   November, 1997
Editor

THE SCOPE OF CHRIST

The Scope of the Cosmic Christ

MICHAEL GREEN

A friend asked me the other day, 'Why is the Anglican church like a swimming pool?' The answer (which, needless to say, I did not get) was 'Because most of the noise and splashing take place at the shallow end!'

Anyone who reads the correspondence columns of the church press, or who absorbs the image of church and clergy presented in the soap operas, could be pardoned for thinking the church in this country is on its last legs, and its officers are unintelligent buffoons. To be sure, the church often majors on minor issues, and some of its episcopal pronouncements give the impression of owing more to the political correctness of the day than to the gospel we read of in the New Testament. As a church, we have been preoccupied with internal arguments over women priests, homosexuality, feminism, finance and the like. In our public utterances at least, we have not been notable for grappling with the issues which concern ordinary people. More importantly, we have not exhibited that quality of holiness, of likeness to Christ, which is the supreme commendation for the gospel. There has been a great deal of noise and splashing at the shallow end.

But that is far from being the whole story. When 90,000 Christians march for Jesus into Hyde Park and the police are in tears at the attitude of the crowd, not a mention of such a thing appears on the media. When a bishop gets 25,000 people to a marvellous event called 'Share the Feast', the climax of much dedicated work in the diocese and of more than a hundred Anglican clergy and lay people from South East Asia coming to help re-evangelise the Midlands, there is not a squeak on the

TV. People are, apparently, not supposed to hear good things about the church! The average media-man is as ignorant as the average church-man that upwards of 70,000 people are becoming Christians world-wide every day. That would disturb the politically correct view that Christianity is on the way out. Nobody hears about this sort of thing, because there is so much splashing at the shallow end of the pool.

This series of essays directs us towards the deeper end of the pool — the end of unashamed Christian belief as we find it in the first Christians; the end of fearless mission, such as they engaged in; the end of unity among real believers in Christ rather than obsessive denomi-national concerns. There is, in some minds, the suspicion that the Lam-beth agenda may be in danger of being somewhat anthropocentric. Seeking full visible unity, living as Anglicans in a pluralistic world, holding and sharing the faith, and the call to full humanity — all this is admirable, but without lifting the vision to the glorious Christ whose ambassadors we are, it could be in danger of relapsing into ecclesiastical tinkering. There is little in this agenda to raise the sights and give us a vision of the great Saviour we serve, the one God of the whole earth. If the apostle Paul were here today, I fancy his agenda might be rather different.

Indeed, we are not left to speculate on the matter. He wrote a letter to Christians in Colossae, an influential inland town in Asia Minor. His was, like ours, an age of much material prosperity. An age of varied pagan and pantheistic beliefs. It was an age highly pluralist in religion, with its fancied 'thrones, dominions, principalities and powers' that were as-sumed to get you into touch with the divine. It was a period when Christians were tempted to bow to the contemporary political correct-ness, and be conformed to the un-Christlike philosophies and ethics of the surrounding society. Significantly, when he writes to the Colossians, before moving into specific injunctions and warnings, Paul majors on the glory of the Christ who had given them a radically new life.

It could be helpful, therefore, to refresh our own vision, and to lift our sights to where Christ is, seated at the right hand of God. Where better to start than with the famous hymn of Colossians 1:15-20? Paul has just given us an example of the quality of his missionary prayer. He is so grateful that these Colossians, whom he has never seen, have been qualified by the Father to share in the inheritance of the saints in light. God has delivered them from the dominion of darkness and transferred them to the kingdom of his dear Son, in whom they have redemption, the forgiveness of their sins. There must be thousands of churches, at least in the Western part of the Anglican communion, where such directness and clarity is totally unknown.

He prays that they may know God's will, and live a life worthy of him by seeking to please him in all they do. He wants to find them fruitful in every good work, and increasing in the knowledge of God. He wants to see them strengthened with all the power of the resurrection so that they may live this quality of life, and endure to the end with joy and thanksgiving, never forgetting their conversion to Jesus Christ. Not many of our congregations are encouraged to pray in those terms, least of all for people they have never seen. We have a long way to go, if we are to return to anything approaching New Testament convictions and lifestyle.

But we have even further to go if we are to approach Paul's convictions about the gospel itself. Mention of redemption into the kingdom of Jesus and forgiveness through him leads him to an amazing paean of adoration. 'He is the image of the invisible God, the firstborn of all creation; for in him all things were created in heaven and earth, visible and invisible, whether thrones or dominions or principalities or authorities — all things were created through him and for him. He is before all things, and in him all things hold together. He is the head of the body, the church. He is the beginning, the firstborn from the dead, that in everything he might be pre-eminent. For in him all the fullness of God was pleased to dwell, and through him to reconcile to himself all things, whether on earth or in heaven, making peace through the blood of his cross.'

Ponder some of the phrases given here to describe a Jewish carpenter crucified some thirty years earlier.

First, he is the image of the God we cannot see. As Michael Ramsey used to say, 'God is Christlike, and in him is no unChristlikeness at all'. Judaism had, in Proverbs 8, Wisdom 7 and Philo, seen God's Wisdom and Torah as semi-divine pre-existent entities which did not compromise God's monotheism but manifested his character. What Judaism applied to Wisdom and Torah Paul now applies to Jesus. He is the one who existed before all time with the Father, and without in the least compromising monotheism, displays to perfection the wisdom and the will of that God whom we cannot see.

5

It is impossible to exaggerate the significance of this claim. Years ago C. F. Burney[1] showed that everything the Jews had claimed for Wisdom by combining Genesis 1:1 with Proverbs 8:22, is applicable to Jesus. God made us human beings in his 'image' (Gen. 1:26-27). Together men and women represented the climax of God's creation; but sadly, humanity disappointed. However, in Jesus we see both the image of man as he was intended to be, and also of the God whom he faithfully represents. So all discussion among Christians about what it means to be human, which is indeed an important part of late twentieth century perplexity, must be dominated by relation to Jesus. He is the norm of what it means to be a full human being.

Second, Jesus is the firstborn of all creation. That again was an Old Testament understanding of Wisdom (Prov. 8:22). 'Firstborn' indicates priority both in terms of time and of rank. Jesus embodies God's Wisdom. All we need to know about God is to be found in his revelation through Jesus. Christians cannot have any truck with a religious pluralism which suggests that Jesus has his contribution to make alongside the Buddha, Confucius, the Hindu Avatars, or the most recent theological guru. Christ is prior to them all, in virtue of his pre-existence, which is strongly underlined here. He is also supreme over them all, as 'firstborn'.

Third, Jesus is hailed as the agent in creation. He is not simply one among the many members of the created world. He is their source. All that is true within the various religions, the 'thrones and principalities' which govern human thought and aspiration, are made through him. There is much discussion about these principalities and powers. If they are seen as spiritual entities, then he is sovereign over them. If they are seen as power politics and economic structures, then once again Christ must be proclaimed as their ultimate source and the standard by which they must be assessed. Not much sign here of the apostle ranking alongside Jesus North American Indian spirituality or African religion! All that is good and true in them comes from him. All that is idolatrous is superseded by him. It is fascinating to see the almost impatient way in which Paul refuses to be drawn into discussion of these spiritualities so beloved by the proto-Gnostics at Colossae. He gathers them all together, as if in a waste-paper basket, and proclaims

1. C. F. Burney, 'Christ as the Arché of Creation', *Journal of Theological Studies* 87 (1925/26), pp. 160-77.

6

Jesus as their Creator and Lord. That is an important insight for the Lambeth fathers to maintain.

As if that was not enough, Paul hails Jesus as the source, the goal and the principle of coherence of the whole universe. No mere Jewish peasant, no wandering wonder-worker or witty rabbi, Jesus is the origin from whom the whole universe derives. He was there before the 'big bang' erupted in obedience to the Father's will. The laws of physics and chemistry to be discerned everywhere in the world are his laws; they are the principles of uniformity which derive from God himself. The Stoics maintained that Reason was the principle which kept the world together. Paul, consciously or unconsciously echoing their language, claims that place for Christ alone. Moreover, he is the goal of destiny for the whole cosmos. Jesus gave a lot of teaching when on this earth about his impending return, and this gives force to the point Paul is making. The world has not seen the last of Jesus Christ. It is moving on, not to chaos (as it might seem) but to Christ and his return at the consummation of all history. Such, and no less, is the Jesus we serve: he is the source, the goal and the principle of coherence for the totality of existence. No wonder Paul dismissed all other 'gods' as 'idols', which literally means unreal entities, nothings. We must not in this pluralistic age compromise, however tempting it may seem, on the crown rights of Jesus Christ as creator and redeemer.

It may appear arrogant to maintain that Jesus is the ultimate self-disclosure of God, but that has been the Christian claim from the outset. It is explicit in the earliest of all baptismal confessions, 'Jesus Christ is Lord' (1 Cor. 8:5, 6). If it is hard to maintain now, remember how hard it was when the gospel first burst upon the ancient world with its thousands of competing deities. The Romans had no objection to this pluralism among the peoples they conquered. They either identified a local god with one of their own who performed roughly the same function, or else simply added the new god to their pantheon. They maintained some unity in the religious life of the Empire by making it imperative for all to pledge loyalty to Rome and the emperor, with the words 'Caesar is Lord'. We sometimes forget that the first Christians refused to have their Jesus identified with any other deity. They refused to have him added to the pantheon: was he not Lord of all? They emphatically refused to bow the knee to Caesar and call him Lord. They kept that name for somebody else! Let us never run away with the naive idea that Christian particularity

7

about Jesus only became scandalous when writers like Hick and Knitter[2] drew attention to it. Our forefathers in the faith died for their witness to the uniqueness and supremacy of Jesus as Lord and Saviour. It is not for us to betray them and him in our generation.

And, wonder of wonders, it is this cosmic Christ who is the church's Christ. He and none other is the head of the body, the church in which we are all limbs, once we are linked to the head. He made possible this entry into his 'body', this 'redemption' and 'forgiveness of sins' (v. 14) by 'the blood of his cross'. The cross was the divine method of reconciling our alienated humanity back to himself. It is the centrepoint of all history, and its impact is truly cosmic. God plans for an eventual elimination of all evil and a complete restoration of the universe to his original purpose as its creator. How that will come about we do not know, and neither did Paul, but that did not prevent him from holding out the hope of complete restoration, and basing it not only on the redemption achieved by Jesus on the cross, but also on the firstfruits of the new creation demonstrated by Jesus through the resurrection. The firstborn of all creation is also the firstborn from the dead.

These are some of the aspects of the ascended Christ which make the apostle bow in awe and wonder. He is amazed that he and his Colossians readers should have been reconciled when they were estranged from God and hostile to him in their minds. He is profoundly determined that holiness must mark their lifestyle, for one day they will have to be presented before the holy God who is their Creator and Redeemer. He is determined not to compromise the gospel which alone brings hope in a dark world; and he makes it his priority — as he trusts they will — to proclaim this Christ to 'every creature under heaven' (Col. 1:21-23).

Significant pointers emerge from this passage — aspects of the glory of Christ which must not be cloaked by ecclesiastical concerns, however pressing. Here are some of the more obvious ones:

(1) There is a prevailing tendency today to see Christianity as just one of the religious aspirations of humankind. It is nothing of the kind. Indeed, it is strictly not a religion at all; for religions are human attempts, in all their variety, to pierce the incognito of the ultimate. No,

2. J. Hick and P. F. Knitter (eds.), *The Myth of Christian Uniqueness* (London: SCM, 1987). P. F. Knitter, *No Other Name?* (New York: Orbis, 1986).

the Christianity Paul proclaimed is not religion at all, but a revelation, a rescue and a relationship. It is God's own revelation of himself in the pre-existent Son who shares his nature. This Jesus is the very image of the God we cannot see. He shares in the divine work of creation, effects reconciliation with God and, by virtue of his resurrection, points to the final destiny God plans alike for believers and for the whole cosmos.

(2) Whatever pointers to God can be found in the Jewish speculation about Torah and Wisdom, or Greek speculation about a ladder of spiritual forces, thrones and principalities — they all find their consummation in Jesus who is the image both of what it means to be fully divine and of what it means to be truly human. He is supreme over all, and revealed his will in focused particularity in the life of Jesus who fully affirmed the Hebrew ethical tradition.

(3) Christians are people who were once alienated but are now reconciled, once in the dominion of darkness but now in the kingdom of God's dear Son, once lost but now redeemed. There was nothing automatic about this change of status. You do not become 'qualified to share in the inheritance of the saints in light' automatically. You have to choose. This can become obscured in an Anglicanism which suggests that baptism alone, without faith and without commitment, without nurture and without church-going, makes a person a Christian. The whole Bible sets its face against that type of nominalism. Any dispassionate study of the New Testament will show that baptism, repentance and faith, and the reception of the Holy Spirit constitute the triple cord which binds us to Christ,[3] and any tendency to identify Christian initiation with baptism alone, repentance and faith alone, or reception of the Spirit alone is a dangerous aberration. Anglicans are quite properly happy to baptise the children of believers, but recent recommendation in high quarters of the propriety of baptising all and sundry whether they or their sponsors believe anything or not, and whether or not they have any intention to live the Christian life, is consonant neither with Scripture nor with the tradition of the church, and prostitutes the sacrament which the early Christians were careful to safeguard as the gateway to Christian discipleship.

(4) The issue of other faiths has become acute and contentious in our lifetime. In many parts of the world it is pursued with violence.

3. See, for example, my *Baptism* (London: Hodder, 1987), esp. ch. 1.

9

Christians true to the Christ whom Paul worshipped will indeed maintain that the one Creator God has revealed himself fully and finally in Jesus Christ. But that does not in the least imply that there is no light in other faiths. There is. But any truth provided by whatever philosophical system, material discovery or correct religious insight, derives ultimately from the Christ who is the source and the fulfilment of them all.

(5) Christ and Christ alone is the head of the church. Great care must be taken in our synodical deliberations and clerical pronouncements never to go against the clearly revealed will of our founder, and to bring all doubtful matters prayerfully before him for determination, rather than being swayed by what is acceptable in contemporary society. Christianity stood out like a sore thumb in antiquity. In the West today it is often bland. The first Christians would not tolerate abortion, sex outside marriage, homosexuality, drunkenness, abuse of employees, etc. Much of that clarity is retained by the ethical teaching of the Roman Catholic church, but it could hardly be said to be a characteristic of our own Western Anglicanism.

(6) N. T. Wright, who has written a superb article on this passage entitled 'Poetry and Theology in Colossians 1:15-20',[4] as well as a valuable commentary, points out that this Colossian hymn has a strong bearing on the church's task in the world. Jesus is sovereign both in creation and redemption, so there can be no dualistic division between the areas where he reigns and where he does not. He quotes the perceptive words of C. S. Lewis, 'There is no neutral ground in the universe: every square inch, every split second, is claimed by God and counterclaimed by Satan'.[5] So the task both of evangelism and of social involvement is to see Christ as already Lord in every sphere of life, and to go and make him known. We do not bring Christ to people. We proclaim that he is there already, that every aspect of human life has been modelled by him, and that every human being can be redeemed through him.

Wright observes, 'Christians must work to help create conditions in which human beings, and the whole created world, can live as God always intended. There is a whole range of ethical norms which God built into his world: respect for persons and property, maintenance of

4. N. T. Wright, 'Poetry and Theology in Colossians 1:15-20', in *New Testament Studies*, 1990.
5. C. S. Lewis, *Christian Reflections* (London: Fount, 1981), p. 52.

family life and the ecological order of creation, justice between individuals and groups. Christians must be in the forefront of those working to promote such causes. Many opportunities to speak about Jesus will occur in the undertaking of such work, as it becomes clear that the gospel provides a coherent and satisfying underpinning for those standards which uphold and enhance a truly human life'.[6]

In recent years I have had the privilege of working as Adviser in Evangelism to the Archbishops of Canterbury and York. In the course of this work I have been travelling widely in this country and abroad. I have observed that not only do non-white Anglicans outnumber white ones, but that their vitality in proclaiming the gospel is normally much higher. One reason may be that they have never gone through the Enlightenment. Be that as it may, there can be no doubt that the massive growth of Christians, including Anglicans, is happening not in the West but in the Two Thirds World. There are, for example, more Anglicans in Nigeria than in the whole of Europe and North America combined. When the bishops come to Lambeth, those from these fast-growing parts of the Anglican communion must ensure that they make their voice heard and are not over impressed by the sophistication of their brethren from England and America. The latter may have more degrees, more finance, more learning, more managerial expertise, but their dioceses are less effective in bringing others to Christ. It is the churches from Asia and Africa that are in the vanguard of Christian advance today. They must be given respectful hearing, for they have more to teach us Anglo-Saxon Anglicans than we have to teach them.

It cannot be denied that it is those who have this high view of Christ and a passionate determination to proclaim the 'faith once and for all delivered to the saints' who are making such advances in the world today. I cannot help noticing that it is the Bible-believing evangelical and charismatic churches around the world which are growing so fast, and that this is as much the case in the Anglican communion as it is in other denominations. The plain truth of the matter is that reductionist 'liberal' reinterpretations of Christianity, based on the sufficiency of human reason, rather than on biblical revelation, have little to offer us, though they are still prevalent in many of our theological institutions and among many senior churchmen.

6. N. T. Wright, *Colossians and Philemon* (Wheaton: Tyndale Press, 1986).

There are several reasons why we should be slow to follow this agenda. For one thing it is intellectually dated and discredited. The high noon of rationalism has passed. The whole modernist liberal mindset is increasingly being abandoned with the erosion of the Enlightenment world view. This holds good in much secular academia as well as in ecclesiastical circles, where the strong churches are almost invariably those which believe and seek to practise unvarnished New Testament Christianity. A Christianity wedded to an empiricist rationalistic mindset is barren. It has nothing to offer us. The growth of the New Age, astrology and the new paganism is evidence enough that people today are not dominated by rationalistic considerations. Neither is New Testament Christianity — nor should we be.

For another thing, such liberalism is spiritually ineffective. It rarely wins people to Christ; indeed many adherents do not believe in conversion. Liberalism tends to grow parasitically through working on those who have already become Christians through commitment to New Testament gospel preaching, by persuading them that such naïve faith is impossible to hold with intellectual integrity in the late twentieth century. For all its attractive open-mindedness this revisionism is spiritually ineffective — and people realise it. A sociological study of the five mainline Christian denominations in America has shown that they have all been heavily influenced by anthropocentric liberal assumptions and agenda, and are currently all in deep trouble through a shortage of clergy, a shortage of money, and desertion by many of their members. It is well known that the Episcopal church in the USA is being torn in two by the split between the conservatives and the liberals. Under these circumstances it is hardly surprising that evangelism takes a low priority, and that money and members are flowing away from the Episcopal church at a record rate.

According to current statistics, Africa, Latin America, and South East Asia rather than England and America will carry the flagship of Anglicanism in the next century. Their bishops must be recognised as senior and not junior partners at the forthcoming Lambeth Conference.[7] Their unanimous view, expressed in the recent Anglican Encounter in

7. America has a disproportionately large number of bishops for a disproportionately small number of churchmen, and their sheer number at Lambeth, with their largely revisionist agenda, must not be allowed a disproportionate effect. See, for example, the table on p. 28 below.

the South,[8] reaffirmed the scriptural view of Christ, the gospel and ethics as normative for Anglicans. Alarmed at reports of sexual revisionism and lax pastoral discipline,[9] they wrote: 'While acknowledging the complexities of our sexual nature and the strong drives it places within us, we are quite clear about God's will in this area which is expressed in the Bible. The Scriptures bear witness to God's will regarding human sexuality which is to be expressed only within the lifelong union of a man and a woman in matrimony. The Holy Scriptures are clear in teaching that all sexual promiscuity is sin. We are convinced that this includes homosexual practices between men or women, as well as heterosexual relationships outside marriage. We believe that the unambiguous teaching of the Holy Scriptures about human sexuality is of great help to Christians, as it provides clear boundaries. We find no conflict between clear biblical teaching and sensitive pastoral care'.

In making this statement the bishops are, of course, representing not only the ecumenical consensus throughout the centuries, but the apostolic and catholic heart of the New Testament doctrine and ethics. Thus the stand they take is seen to be central to Christianity and not peripheral as is sometimes suggested in 'progressive' circles.

It is important to notice that this manifesto was agreed unanimously among all the Southern bishops: it is, of course, in the South that the strength of Christianity lies. Significantly, an archbishop from the South proposed, at a recent meeting of Anglican Primates, that the Episcopal church in the USA should be suspended from membership of the Anglican communion if they went ahead in ordaining practising homosexuals. This could equally apply to other churches so deeply affected by Western cultural hedonism.

It is high time that such a stand was taken. There are serious strains and stresses in the Anglican communion which could, if not handled wisely, spell its disintegration. The Southern bishops rightly observe: 'Diverging views of Scripture, different understandings of ministry, and a breakdown of discipline and teaching related to social ethics have all placed serious strain on the internal unity of the communion. There has been discussion about the permissible limits of diversity, but who sets these limits and according to what criteria? We

8. The Kuala Lumpur Statement is printed as an appendix, for reference.
9. Particularly the case referred to in Stanton Jones' essay, p. 83 below.

question the wisdom of retaining the complete autonomy of our many provinces and believe we should look for ways of strengthening mutual accountability and interdependence. It is vital for our mission that we have effective ways of seeking God's will together, of reaching a common mind, and of encouraging and admonishing one another'.

This indeed is a considerable challenge for the future. They go on to ask the Lambeth Conference to consider organisational and governmental changes to our communion, matched by spiritual reconstruction based on biblical renewal.

With them, I am persuaded that people will not see the glory of Christ in any individual or church which is deliberately in conflict with the teaching and ethics of the New Testament. That is why these matters are so important. In his second letter to Corinth, Paul had already written very movingly of the glory of Christ and his gospel. Paul is well aware of the 'god of this age', the devil, whose strategy is to blind the minds of unbelievers to the light of the glory of the gospel of Christ. He knows from joyful personal experience that 'the God who said "Let light shine out of darkness" has shone in our hearts to give the light of the knowledge of the glory of God in the face of Jesus Christ'. That glory and that biblical gospel are integrally connected. If secular and humanitarian issues dominate us so that we lose sight of the glory and greatness of Christ, there will be no glory in our church or in our message. We could deteriorate into just one more do-gooding society, intent on our own concerns — rather than constitute God's counter-culture, in all its richness and scope, in a desperately needy world. The call to full humanity will be realised in orienting our vision insistently towards the cosmic Christ whose holy love alone will transform ourselves, our congregations and our cultures. The authors of this book hope that its contents may help to lift the eyes of Christian readers to the glory and scope of Christ.

Questions

1. How are we allowing the cosmic Christ to renew our faith and our church, locally and nationally?

2. What areas of life are we closing off to the light of Christ?

3. In what ways does the cross of Christ impinge on our lifestyle in breaking down barriers?

The Anglican Communion and Christendom

PETER BRIERLEY

The Anglican communion is an important part of Christianity world-wide. This article explores how important and where it is important. In 1995 the estimated total number of Christians around the world (for which I use the term 'Christendom') was 1,614,000,000 people, or twenty-eight percent of the world's population. This is the number of adherents, or the Christian community, and includes many nominal Christians. It is, however, measured on the same basis as Muslims count the number of adherents to Islam, which Rev Dr David Barrett estimated at 1,057,000,000[1] or eighteen percent of the world's population, and which again includes many who are nominal. The third largest religious group is the Hindus, assessed by Dr Barrett at 777,000,000[2] or thirteen percent of the world's population. Three-fifths of the world, therefore, are either Christian, Muslim or Hindu, though these are not equally spread across all the continents.

The Christian figure is not the same as Dr Barrett's and is lower than his estimate, partly because he includes non-trinitarian churches like the Jehovah's Witnesses and Mormons which the above figure does not. It comes from the recently published *World Churches Handbook*,[3]

---

1. David Barrett, 'Status of Global Mission', *International Bulletin of Missionary Research* (Jan. 1995). This article is updated each year in the January issue.
2. Barrett, 'Status of Global Mission'.
3. Peter Brierley (ed.), *World Churches Handbook*, 1997, jointly published by

based on the data initially compiled by Patrick Johnstone for his *Operation World*,[4] but extensively updated and extended.

Population Comparison

If world Christendom was twenty-eight percent of the population in 1995, what was it in 1960 (the earliest year given in the *World Churches Handbook*)? The answer is thirty percent, so we have fallen behind in real terms and have not kept pace with our rapidly growing world population. The percentage is projected to fall to twenty-seven percent by the year 2010 (the latest forecast given in the *Handbook*). However, this fall has not been uniform across this fifty year period (actual and projected). Christendom's percentage rose in 1985 to twenty-nine percent and stayed at that level in 1990.

The declining percentage does not mean that the number of Christians in the world is decreasing; on the contrary, the number is increasing, but not quite as fast as the population. The following Table shows the average daily rate of increase in the two across the world:

TABLE 1
Average Daily Increase in Christendom
and the World's Population

Period	Christendom	World Population
1960-1965	+40,000	+175,000
1965-1970	+45,000	+199,000
1970-1975	+47,000	+208,000
1975-1980	+59,000	+201,000
1980-1985	+68,000	+219,000
1985-1990	+62,000	+231,000
1990-1995	+56,000	+245,000
1995-2000	+53,000	+240,000
2000-2005	+51,000	+238,000
2005-2010	+51,000	+239,000

Christian Research, London, UK, and the Lausanne Committee on World Evangelisation, Oslo, Norway.

4. Patrick Johnstone, *Operation World* (Carlisle: OM Publishing, 1993).

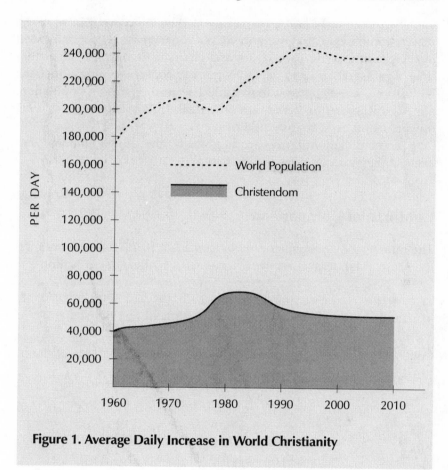

Figure 1. Average Daily Increase in World Christianity

These figures are interesting. They show that the *rate* of increase in the number of Christians rose very rapidly between 1975 and 1985, and since then has continuously declined, although not sharply. Looking at bar charts showing the number of Christians in each country in the world, as given in the *Atlas of World Christianity*,[5] one cannot but be struck by how the number jumped in this period, in country after country. If revival is defined as a rapid increase in the number becoming

5. Peter Brierley and Heather Wraight (eds.), *Atlas of World Christianity* (Hunt and Thorpe/Carlisle: Paternoster, 1997).

17

Christian, the world had a revival then! Why it occurred in so many places simultaneously is not known, but the increase is especially seen in the growth of the Pentecostal and charismatic movements at that time. Against the rise and fall in the rate of people becoming Christians is the slow, steady, almost inexorable rise in the world's population, although it seems as if the rate of increase has stabilised from 1995 onwards, and even slightly declined.

The population figures are as given by the United Nations,[6] but even so they include many estimates.

Continental Comparison

The number of Christian people by continent in 1995 was as follows, the continental definitions being those used by the United Nations:[7]

TABLE 2
Christian Community by Continent in 1995

Continent	Christian community	% of total	% of continent's population
Europe	434,900,000	27	60
North America	345,900,000	22	76
South America	308,100,000	19	96
Asia	262,700,000	16	8
Africa	243,700,000	15	33
Oceania	18,700,000	1	65
Total	1,614,000,000	100%	28%

This Table shows that just over a quarter of Christendom (27%) is in Europe, followed by a fifth in each of North (22%) and South (19%) America, with about a seventh in each of Asia (16%) and Africa (15%). The Table also shows that the proportion of a continent's population which are Christian varies greatly. Virtually everyone in South America

6. *E.g.*, World Population Data Sheet 1995, Population Reference Bureau, Washington, DC, United States, May, 1995.
7. World Population Data Sheet, May, 1995.

would say they are Christian (96%), and over three-quarters (76%) of those in North America. Oceania comes next with almost two-thirds (65%), followed by Europe with three in five (60%), along with a third of the African peoples. It is in Asia, where three-fifths (60%) of the world's population live, that the Christian percentage is lowest, and therefore where the priority of missions could be expected to focus.

The proportion of Christendom in the different continents is changing.

TABLE 3
Proportion of Christendom by Year

Continent	% of total Christians 1960	% of total Christians 1995	% of total Christians 2010
Europe	46	27	22
North America	23	22	22
South America	16	19	20
Asia	7	16	18
Africa	7	15	17
Oceania	1	1	1
Total (= 100%)	0.9b	1.6b	1.9b

These figures show the rapid advance of Christianity in both Africa and Asia in this fifty year period, the latter greatly due to the enormous increase in home meetings in China.

The plummeting drop in Europe is obvious; it is the only continent where the number of Christians has actually decreased over this period, from 426 million in 1960 to an estimated 422 million by 2010, against a population increase from 657 million in 1960 to an estimated 731 million by 2010. The churches in the other continents are sending increasing numbers of missionaries to Europe!

Denominational Comparison

The *World Churches Handbook* groups the many denominations in the world into ten broad groupings, of which the Anglican church is one.

19

The 'Catholic' group includes a few other than Roman Catholics, like the Uniates. 'Indigenous' churches are frequently individual churches which have formed within the culture of one particular country. They do not always group together into recognised denominations and rarely form congregations outside their own locality. There are none in Europe. They differ from the 'Other churches' which are mainly the smaller denominations, including, for example, the Salvation Army, Mennonites or Christian Brethren, which often occur in more than one country. The 'Pentecostal' churches are the world-wide mainline Pentecostal denominations plus other smaller groups. Independent churches, which may or may not be charismatic, are included under 'Other churches'.

The number of Christian people by these denominational groups in 1995, the percentage that number was of both the world's population and of total world Christianity, is given in the following Table:

TABLE 4
Christian Community by Denominational Grouping in 1995

Denomination	Christian community	% of Christian population	% of world population
Catholic	912,600,000	56	16
Other churches	142,500,000	9	2
Orthodox	139,500,000	9	2
Pentecostal	105,800,000	7	2
Lutheran	84,500,000	5	2
Baptist	67,100,000	4	1
Anglican	53,200,000	3	1
Presbyterian	48,000,000	3	1
Indigenous	35,200,000	2	–
Methodist	25,600,000	2	–
Total	1,614,000,000	100%	28%

This Table shows that five in every nine Christian people in the world are Catholic. The Orthodox and 'Other churches' groups account for a further nine percent each, or 1 person in every 11, followed by seven percent or 1 person in 14, who are Pentecostal. Of these ten groups, the Anglican church is seventh largest. These community figures will be defined differently for the various denominations. For the Anglicans and Catholics they seek to represent the number who have been baptised in a particular country, though few countries have reliable national figures; they are nearly always the best estimates that can be given.

Table 4 shows that the Catholic numbers dominate. Not only are they just over the half of Christendom, but they represent one person in six across the world as a whole (16%). When Cardinal Hume, the leader of the Roman Catholic church in Britain, speaks on television he typically says, 'The Church believes . . .', even though he has been introduced as 'The head of the Roman Catholic Church'. The next largest churches are the 'Other churches', Orthodox, Pentecostal and Lutheran, though each of these consists of several individual denominations. The Anglican church is one seventeenth the size of the Catholic church, but is it nevertheless a world church?

Just as the proportions in each continent are changing, so are the proportions for each denomination, as the following Table shows:

TABLE 5
Proportion of Christendom by Year

Denomination	% of total Christians 1960	% of total Christians 1995	% of total Christians 2010
Catholic	61	56	56
Other churches	4	9	10
Orthodox	10	9	8
Pentecostal	1	7	8
Lutheran	9	5	4
Baptist	4	4	4
Anglican	4	3	3
Presbyterian	3	3	3
Indigenous	1	2	3
Methodist	3	2	1
Total (= 100%)	0.9b	1.6b	1.9b

The denomination which is growing the fastest is the Pentecostal which increases dramatically in the 50 years 1960 to 2010, from 12 million in

1960 to an estimated 154 million by 2010. Indigenous churches are also increasing, as are the 'Other churches', largely due to the emergence of many new denominations, especially in Asia. The Lutherans and Orthodox decline most proportionately, though the Catholics also lose out. The Baptists and Presbyterians hold their own, the first by their growth in the United States, the second by their growth in South Korea. Anglicans decline slightly.

Denominations by Continent

Whether the world-wide Anglican communion is a world church depends on the definition! The spread of the various denominations across the continents is interesting because there are special dominances, as the following Table shows.

TABLE 6
The Proportions of Each Denomination in Each Continent in 1995

Denomination	Europe %	North America %	South America %	Asia %	Africa %	Oceania %	Total (=100%) million
Catholic	28	22	28	11	10	1	912.6
Other churches	3	15	4	55	22	1	142.5
Orthodox	54	6	0	19	21	0	139.5
Pentecostal	3	28	36	12	20	1	105.8
Lutheran	67	17	2	6	7	1	84.5
Baptist	4	66	4	12	13	1	67.1
Anglican	48	7	0	1	34	10	53.2
Presbyterian	26	17	2	30	23	2	48.0
Indigenous	0	1	0	26	73	0	35.2
Methodist	6	51	1	12	28	2	25.6
Overall	27	22	19	16	15	1	1,614.0

A third (34%) of the world's Anglicans are in Africa, ten percent in Oceania and virtually half (48%) in Europe. Over ninety-nine percent of those in Europe are in the United Kingdom. There are virtually none in South America. This geographical spread reflects the dominance of

22

the old British Empire rather than a true world-wide distribution, hence the continuation of the name 'Church of England'.

Almost two-thirds (66%) of the world's Baptists are in North America, with ninety-six percent of these in the United States. The Catholics are the only truly 'world church' in the sense that they are spread across all continents without any one dominating.

Almost three-quarters (73%) of the 'indigenous community' are in Africa, and of these twenty-nine percent are in Nigeria and twenty-three percent are in Zaire. Two-thirds (67%) of the world's Lutherans are in Europe, with fifty-nine percent of these in Germany. Just over half (51%) of the world's Methodists are in North America, and ninety-six percent again of these are in the United States.

Just over half of the Orthodox (54%) are in Europe. This figure was much higher in 1990 (70%) and the difference reflects the definitional change of moving most of the constituent countries of the old USSR, which was in Europe, to Asia. The Pentecostals are also well spread across the world but are relatively weak in Europe. More than a third of them (36%) are in South America, and eighty-one percent of these are in Brazil.

Nearly one-third (30%) of the world's Presbyterians are in Asia, forty-five percent of whom are in Korea. A further quarter (26%) are in Europe, found mainly as the Reformed Churches in the Netherlands (29%) and Hungary (16%), or the Church of Scotland and other Presbyterian churches in the United Kingdom (21%). Over half (55%) of those belonging to 'Other churches' are in Asia, with seventy percent of these coming from the estimated 55 million in home meetings in China.

These figures reflect the European origins of Anglicanism, Lutheranism and the Orthodox church. The Table shows the continental nature of many of the world's big denominations, almost their 'parochialism' or 'nationalism' if one can use these words in a continental setting.

In the 1990s the areas for growth are the increasing proportions of Anglicans in Africa (at the expense of Europe), Baptists in Asia (at the expense of North America), Methodists in Africa (at the expense of North America), and 'Other churches' in Asia (also at the expense of North America). Each of these movements represents a two or more percentage point change between 1990 and 1995.

Continents by Denominations

Table 6 looked at denominational spread across the world. Equally interesting is the spread of Christianity within each continent, and these figures are given in Table 7. Some percentages are very small, close to zero. These are given as '<1' but are counted as zero in the totals.

TABLE 7
The Proportions in Each Continent of Each Denomination in 1995

Denomination	Europe %	North America %	South America %	Asia %	Africa %	Oceania %	Overall %
Catholic	58	58	84	40	36	40	56
Other churches	1	6	2	30	13	11	9
Orthodox	17	2	<1	10	12	3	9
Pentecostal	1	9	12	5	8	4	7
Lutheran	13	4	1	2	2	5	5
Baptist	1	13	1	3	4	2	4
Anglican	6	1	<1	<1	7	27	3
Presbyterian	3	3	<1	6	4	5	3
Indigenous	0	<1	<1	3	11	1	2
Methodist	<1	4	<1	1	3	2	2
Total in millions (=100%)	434.9	345.9	308.1	262.7	243.7	18.7	1,614.0

Table 7 shows that the major denominations are present in every continent except South America, which is dominated by the Catholic Church and the Pentecostals. The Catholics account for over a third (36%) in Africa, their lowest proportion, and eighty-four percent in South America. 'Other churches' are especially strong in Asia. The Anglicans account for over a quarter (27%) of Oceania's small church community.

European Christianity is dominated by the Catholics (over a half of the community) and the Orthodox (a sixth), leaving only a quarter for all the others put together. In North America it is the Catholics and the Baptists which together account for over two-thirds (71%) of the church community. Each denominational group except the Methodists and Presbyterians are especially strong in at least one continent.

The relationship of denomination to continent is not often discussed, but these figures do show a correlation. This suggests that the cultures implicit in different continents are drawn to different forms of church life.

The Anglican Communion World-wide

In the 1990s the Anglican communion world-wide was growing at the rate of about 900 people per day, just under two percent or one-fiftieth of the total growth of Christianity. The world-wide communion figure in 1960 was 41 million, and it is estimated it will grow to 58 million by the year 2010, a growth of forty-two percent. This may seem small compared with other denominations, but at least it is growth, unlike the Lutheran church which actually declines in numerical terms in this period (from 82 million to 80 million). It is also a greater growth than the Methodist church which grows eighteen percent in this period (from 23 million in 1960 to 27 million in 2010).

It is, however, a smaller growth rate than was seen by the other denominations — the Orthodox grew fifty percent, the Presbyterians seventy-six percent, the Catholics eighty-eight percent, the Baptists 123%, whilst the 'Other churches' grew four-fold (442%), the Indigenous churches six fold (592%), and the Pentecostals twelve fold (1,162%) in this fifty year period. (It is interesting to note that the non-Trinitarian churches also grew four fold [396%]).

If, in growth terms, the Anglican church came eighth in the ten denominational groups being considered, in size terms it came seventh. Its 53 million in 1995 is greater than the 48 million Presbyterians, the 35 million 'indigenous church community', and the 26 million Methodists. It was a little smaller than the Baptists in 1995 (67 million), and behind the 85 million Lutherans, 106 million Pentecostals, 140 million Orthodox, 143 million in 'Other churches', and the 913 million Catholics.

Table 8 shows the growth of the Anglican community since 1960 with projections to 2010; these figures are graphed in Figure 2. The figure for 1980, 49 million, is considerably less than the figure of 64 million for 1978 suggested in the *Preparatory Information* booklet issued for the Lambeth Conference held that year but this larger figure is more comprehensive: 'all who claim to be Anglicans: baptised Anglicans, plus nominal Anglicans not known to the churches nor on its rolls'.[8] The column headed 'ratio' shows the proportion by which the figure for the particular years has increased, using 1960 as a base and equal to 100. 1995 has been added to show a more contemporary figure.

TABLE 8
Anglican and Total Christian Community and Population[9]

Year	Anglican community	Ratio	Total Christendom	Ratio	World population	Ratio
1960	40,892,000	100	924,263,000	100	3,040,955,000	100
1970	45,246,000	111	1,079,684,000	117	3,724,393,000	122
1980	48,920,000	120	1,273,665,000	138	4,471,080,000	147
1990	51,599,000	126	1,511,996,000	164	5,292,427,000	174
1995	53,217,000	130	1,614,069,000	175	5,739,642,000	189
2000	54,871,000	134	1,710,454,000	185	6,177,996,000	203
2010	58,027,000	142	1,897,239,000	205	7,047,971,000	232

The ratio figures for the Anglican community grew less between 1980 and 1990 (6 points) than they did in earlier decades or are projected to do so afterwards. The ratio figures for Christendom grew greatest in that same decade (26 points) showing basically that the competition between denominations was very intense in the 1980s. The fastest growth went to the non-institutional churches.

The Anglican Communion by Continent

Table 8 shows the growth in Anglicanism across the world, but how did it vary by continent? This is shown in Table 9 where, for simplicity in comparing figures, the ratio numbers are given for each decade, with

8. Preparatory Information, Statistics, Documentation, Addresses, Maps for the Lambeth Conference 1978 (London: CIO Publishing, 1978), data compiled by Rev Dr David Barrett and mostly taken from World Christian Encyclopaedia.
9. The Anglican figure for 1970 is 1 million less than that given in the World Churches Handbook due to a correction to the figure for Nigeria.

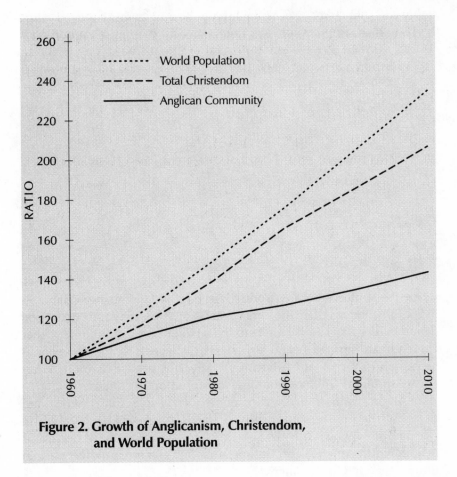

Figure 2. Growth of Anglicanism, Christendom, and World Population

the 1960 and 2010 figure in millions given at the foot of the Table. The final row puts these figures as percentages of the total, and these percentages are the ones used in Figure 3 (p. 29). It is obvious from Table 9 that the growth of the Anglican church in the latter part of the twentieth century, and projected into the twenty-first, is almost entirely because of the huge expansion in the African continent. This is in both the speed of increase (no other continent has a ratio as high as Africa in 2010) and in size of increase (no other continent has seen a 21 million person growth).

It can also be seen that Anglicanism is losing out in North America

TABLE 9
The Growth of the Anglican Communion by Continent since 1960

Year	Africa	Europe	Oceania	North America	Asia	South America	World
1960	100	100	100	100	100	100	100
1970	261	100	108	98	146	136	111
1980	395	97	106	91	195	161	120
1990	529	94	111	76	223	183	126
2000	679	90	112	68	254	197	134
2010	823	87	114	61	283	218	142
1960	3.0m	27.9m	4.6m	5.1m	0.2m	0.1m	40.9m
2010	24.7m	24.1m	5.3m	3.1m	0.6m	0.2m	58.0m
% of total	43	42	9	5	1	0	100

where the Pentecostals are strong (third largest denomination, Table 5), in South America where the Pentecostals are also strong (second largest denomination) and in Asia where the smaller non-institutional 'Other churches' are strong (second largest). This suggests that in these continents non-institutional Christianity is specially attractive, though Anglicanism might still have a unique contribution to make!

Anglicans have also grown quite quickly in South America and Asia, but the numbers are relatively small. Anglicans have grown in Oceania, slowly but with sizeable numbers. Anglicans have decreased in both North America and Europe, although at a much slower pace in Europe than in North America.

Anglicanism in Africa

As Africa is so important for the Anglican communion, details of the six countries where the *World Churches Handbook* forecasts at least 1 million Anglicans in 2010 are given in Table 10, again using ratios, with the remaining countries given in composite. These figures show the huge growth in the size of Anglicanism in Nigeria and Uganda, and the huge percentage increases in Tanzania, Nigeria and the Sudan. The importance of encouraging the church in Sudan, as typified by the two

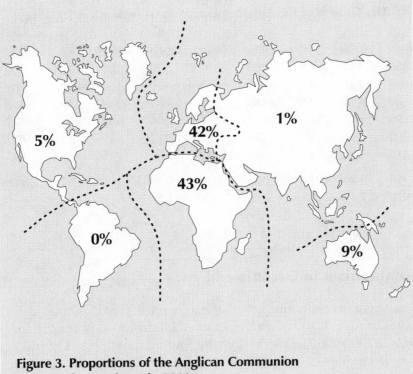

**Figure 3. Proportions of the Anglican Communion
by Continent in 2010**

visits of the Archbishop of Canterbury, can be seen from this Table. It is the second largest church in the country after the Catholics, and growing very quickly (actually faster than any other major denomination). One reason for the virtually static figure 1990 to 2000 in 'All others' is the many conflicts and civil wars which took place, and are taking place, in Africa in the 1990s.

The Table shows that there was almost an explosive growth of Anglicanism in Nigeria, Tanzania and the Sudan in the 1960s when numbers quadrupled. Presumably this is partly the impact of the East African Revival.

TABLE 10
The Growth of the Anglican Communion in Africa since 1960

Year	Kenya	Nigeria	South Africa	Sudan	Tanzania	Uganda	All others	All Africa
1960	100	100	100	100	100	100	100	100
1970	261	448	153	365	470	168	195	261
1980	455	889	186	600	769	339	308	395
1990	675	1039	248	974	1108	497	415	529
2000	890	1483	274	1145	1717	648	417	679
2010	1100	1811	311	1242	2180	795	517	823
1960	0.2m	0.4m	0.9m	0.1m	0.1m	0.8m	0.5m	3.0m
2010	2.2m	7.8m	2.7m	1.0m	1.8m	6.6m	2.6m	24.7m
% of total	9	32	11	4	7	27	10	100

Anglicanism in Oceania and Asia

The Anglican community in both these continents has grown since 1960, faster in Asia though the number of Anglicans there is much smaller than in Oceania. The two major contributing countries in Oceania are detailed in Table 11, together with the two countries with the largest Anglican communities in Asia — Malaysia and the Philippines. The decrease in the ratio between 1970 and 1980 in Australia, and consequently in Oceania, is due to the formation of the Uniting Church in Australia on 22 June 1977 between the Methodist, Presbyterian and Congregational Churches. Although this grouping excluded the Anglicans, the Australian Census figures (from which the figures are taken) showed almost a million decrease nationally between 1970 and 1980 as different groups re-aligned. Many more than usual did not record themselves as belonging to any denomination, some of which affected the Anglican church. The Anglican church has been growing steadily since then, if only slowly.

In New Zealand the reverse picture arises, with a constant decline since the high water mark of 1970. The striking growth in 'All others' comes from the highly contagious Anglicanism in the many Pacific islands where the Anglican community is sometimes the largest religious grouping involving a substantial majority of the population.

TABLE 11
The Growth of the Anglican Communion in Oceania and Asia

Year	Australia	New Zealand	All others	Oceania	Malaysia	Philippines	All others	Asia
1960	100	100	100	100	100	100	100	100
1970	108	107	127	108	175	125	145	146
1980	104	97	245	106	286	195	167	195
1990	110	88	326	111	377	204	184	223
2000	111	82	410	112	475	214	202	254
2010	112	76	499	114	570	223	219	283
1960	3.7m	0.8m	0.1m	4.6m	0.04m	0.05m	0.13m	0.22m
2010	4.1m	0.6m	0.5m	5.3m[10]	0.23m	0.10m	0.29m	0.62m
% of total	78	12	10	100	36	17	47	100

These populations are very small; the largest component of 'All others' (59% in 2010) is Papua New Guinea with a projected Anglican community of over 300,000 by 2010.

Throughout Asia the Anglican church has grown, and especially in Malaysia, where over a third of the continent's Anglicans can be found. It was already strong (and therefore an opportune situation in which to work) when the Overseas Missionary Fellowship made Malaysia their 'Anglican field' when the Mission spread into other countries of Asia after being forced to evacuate from China in 1952.

Anglicanism in North America and Europe

The Anglican church is declining in the continents of North America and Europe; details are in Table 12. The decline in the United States has not been uniform; Anglicanism grew there in the 1960s, but particularly declined in the 1980s. In Canada the 1980s were also a particularly disastrous decade with a drop of almost a quarter of the Anglican community. It was a difficult decade for most denominations in Canada,

10. The exact total of the three previous numbers is 5,259,542 which rounds up to 5.3 million even if the constituent numbers only add to 5.2 million.

TABLE 12
The Decline of the Anglican Communion
in North America and Europe

Year	USA	Canada	All others	North America	UK	All others	Europe
1960	100	100	100	100	100	100	100
1970	102	91	94	98	100	102	100
1980	93	83	93	91	97	105	97
1990	79	60	93	76	93	113	94
2000	68	54	93	68	90	116	90
2010	60	46	93	61	86	119	87
1960	3.1m	1.3m	0.7m	5.1m	27.6m	0.2m	27.8m
2010	1.9m	0.6m	0.6m	3.1m	23.9m	0.2m	24.1m
% of total	60	19	21	100	99	1	100

though the Catholics, Lutherans and Pentecostals all grew. The static numbers reflected in the 'All others' category show the steady contribution the Anglican church makes to the spiritual life of the many islands in the Caribbean.

In 2010, 97% of Anglicanism in Europe will be the Church of England in England. Unfortunately, the Anglican church in the United Kingdom has slowly declined, partly due to the decreasing number of baptisms which fell from 266,000 in 1980 to 229,000 in 1990 and is projected to fall further to 172,000 by 2010.[11] As a percentage of births, the 1980 baptisms represent forty percent of the total, and the 2010 figure thirty percent.

The Anglican church in the rest of Europe, though collectively small numerically, has, however, been slowly growing since 1960 and is projected to continue to do so. This is partly due to the work of organisations like the Intercontinental Church Society and the impact of increasing business in the European Community with many more English people at least temporarily resident in Europe and desiring English church services on a Sunday.

11. Peter Brierley (ed.), *UK Christian Handbook*, 1996/97 edition (London: Christian Research, 1995), Table 11, p. 244.

The Largest Anglican Countries

These continental figures show that there are just a few countries which account for the majority of the world's Anglicans. They are as follows, using the figures for the year 2010 as these already feature in the penultimate lines of Tables 9 to 12.

TABLE 13
The Key Anglican Countries in 2010

Country	Community millions	% of total	Cumulative millions	Cumulative %
England	23.9	41	23.9	41
Nigeria	7.8	14	31.7	55
Uganda	6.6	11	38.3	66
Australia	3.7	6	42.0	72
South Africa	2.7	5	44.7	77
Kenya	2.2	4	46.9	81
USA	1.9	3	48.8	84
Other 138 countries	9.2	16	58.0	100
Total	58.0	100	58.0	100

Five out of six Anglicans (84%) live in one of the seven countries listed in Table 13. Two in five of the world's Anglicans reside in England. The four countries of Africa in Table 13 account for a third (33%) of the Anglican community. The Table also shows how relatively thinly spread Anglicanism is in the remaining countries listing Anglicans in the *World Churches Handbook*.

Anglican Churches

According to David Barrett, there are about 25,000 denominations[12] world-wide. The *Handbook* gives the number of churches for many of these denominations each year.[13] It indicates that, in 1995, there were

12. David Barrett, *World Christian Encyclopaedia* (Oxford: Oxford University Press, 1982).
13. It also gives the number of church members, but since for Anglicans many

just over 80,000 Anglican churches world-wide, almost four percent of the 2.2 million churches. The Anglicans thus have proportionately slightly more of the world's churches than they do of the world's Christian community, meaning that the number of Christian people per church is lower for Anglicans than for other denominations. The following Table gives details for 1995, where the number per church is the size of the Christian community for each congregation:

TABLE 14
Christian Churches by Denominational Grouping in 1995

Denomination	Churches	% of total	Number per church
Other churches	613,000	27	230
Pentecostal	472,700	21	220
Catholic	386,400	17	2,360
Baptist	191,300	8	350
Indigenous	117,100	5	300
Presbyterian	109,700	5	440
Lutheran	108,100	5	780
Methodist	104,100	4	250
Orthodox	88,900	4	1,570
Anglican	80,300	4	660
Total/Overall	2,271,600	100	710

The distribution of denominational strength by the number of congregations is quite different from that given by the size of their community. Whilst the Catholics still show a substantial number of congregations — one church in every six in the world is Catholic — this is much less than the fifty-six percent of Christendom which is Catholic, shown in Table 4. The Baptists, Indigenous churches, Methodist, Pentecostal and 'Other churches' all have percentages substantially higher than those given as their 'share' of the Christian community. The Anglicans actually have the smallest number of churches of these ten denominational groupings: one church in twenty-five across the world is Anglican. One in five is Pentecostal.

---

of these are taken as a percentage of the community, in the absence of other data, these are not analysed here since they will show the same trends as the community figures.

The reason, of course, is that different denominations have structures and churches which vary enormously in average size. The five denominations just mentioned all, on average, have small congregations (there are plenty of exceptions to break the rule!). The Catholics and the Orthodox have much larger congregations. The Lutherans, Anglicans and Presbyterians are between these two groups, and, as it happens, the average Anglican church has a community proportion closest to the overall world-wide average for all denominations (660 to 710). Perhaps the Anglicans are the 'most average' church in the world!

It should be noted that the numbers per church relate to the community per church and are not the average membership or average attendance. Either of these will be considerably lower in many instances than the figures given in Table 14.

It is worth looking at how the Anglican figures vary by continent, and these are given in the final Table.

TABLE 15
The Number and Size of Anglican Churches by Continent in 1995

Feature	Africa	Europe	North America	Oceania	Asia	South America	Total
Number	42,500	19,500	12,300	4,200	1,200	600	80,300
% of total	53	24	15	5	2	1	100
Average size	420	1,310	300	1,230	420	350	660

Community v Attendance

The huge community figures in Europe and Oceania reflect the baptismal policies in England and Oceania. In turn they reveal the large numbers of nominal Christians implicit in these numbers. For example, in England in 1994 there were 896,000 adults in attendance on an average Sunday,[14] plus 273,000 children,[15] a total of 1,169,000 which is five percent of the estimated UK community, spread across 16,303 churches with an average attendance of 72 each.

14. Brierley (ed.), *UK Christian Handbook* (Item 11), Table 11, p. 244.
15. An estimate based on the proportions attending Anglican churches in the English Church Census 1989 in *Prospects for the Nineties* (London: MARC Europe, 1991).

This indicates the enormous gulf between community figures and actual attendance, requiring a focusing on the nominality of many. Nominalism is here defined as those belonging to a Christian community but not in regular attendance at a place of worship. In other places the term 'notional Christian' is also used for such people.[16] Anglicanism is not alone in having a great deal of nominality; the Catholics are the same, and in a number of dioceses, have undertaken special 'Renewal' programmes seeking to win back to regular attendance at Mass those baptised as Catholics. This is seen by them as primary evangelisation, winning their own back as it were, rather than new people.

However, total attenders are likely to be greater than the attendance on any particular Sunday because:

(a) Many who regularly came twice on a Sunday now attend only once or even less frequently. One vicar said, 'Many who came twice on a Sunday now come twice a month'.

(b) Visiting churches of other denominations, sometimes for extended periods, is becoming commonplace within suburban settings especially.

(c) The increasing pressure from Sunday working or leisure activities inhibits whole families attending together.

(d) The ease of travel to other towns to visit relatives, etc. means that Sundays are often used this way, with more 'casual' visitors in a congregation.

(e) The challenge of living the faith can easily mean that some people slip from the church altogether, not returning for several years — one study[17] found the average time out was eight years.

Conclusions

What are the implications behind so many figures?

(1) The Anglican church is significant in its virtually world-wide coverage, and is especially of key importance in Africa, Oceania and the United Kingdom.

16. Eddie Gibbs, *Winning Them Back* (Crowborough, UK: Monarch, 1993), p. 263.
17. Gibbs, *Winning Them Back*, p. 277.

(2) The growth of the Anglican church is slower in those continents where non-institutional denominations flourish (the two Americas and Asia). This suggests that it may be important to identify the primary characteristics of an Anglican church — what does it mean to be Anglican? Even, what are the benefits of being Anglican? Alternatively, the Anglican church could consider becoming less 'Anglican' and more 'national' in other cultural situations.

(3) The huge amount of nominalism in the Anglican community highlights the importance of tackling the problem. Whilst most obvious in England, the same issues are being found across the world, and suggest that this could be one of the key issues for the twenty-first century.

(4) That Anglicanism has followed similar trends to other world-wide institutional churches (like the Catholics mentioned above, but also the Lutherans, Methodists and Presbyterians) indicates that it is not alone in its problems, and working with others is likely to be of increasing importance.

(5) Anglicanism is growing in some countries but declining in others. What are the reasons for both, and what can those in the latter countries learn from those in the former? This suggests that increasing research is needed world-wide and increasing sharing of relevant information. Should an Anglican communion research officer be appointed?

CALLED TO FULL HUMANITY

God and Our Image

GERALD BRAY

Summary

The doctrine that we are all created in God's image is a crucially important truth to be emphasised today especially in the face of ideologies that seek to equate humans with the animal realm or the world of nature in general. This doctrine indicates a unique link with God and a unique calling to rule and exploit the creation in a proper way. Some contemporary ecological theory underplays the value of humanity and undercuts development for the poor. Human life is of supreme value, hence euthanasia and abortion are wrong, although hard cases will always arise. Humanity is creative, hence the wonderful culture we enjoy and for which we should strive in our worship. Relationships are rightly ordered according to the biblical pattern, male and female being equal but obviously distinctive. Modern professions, such as education and nursing, are rooted in the doctrine of the value of humanity, and the church must put her truth at the centre of advice she offers to society. Ethics, mission and society all need consideration through this doctrine of the image.

Introduction

In recent years there has been a considerable amount of new thinking about the doctrine of the image of God.[1] The apparent usefulness of

---

1. For a complete discussion see my paper, 'The Significance of God's Image in Man', *Tyndale Bulletin* 42.2 (1991), pp. 195-225.

this concept for contemporary theology is probably due to two principal factors. On the one hand, it is an inclusive term which transcends all distinctions of race, culture and sex ('gender'). Every human being, according to Genesis 1:27, is created in the image of God. At the same time, it is also clear, if only by implication, that the image of God is an exclusive term, in the sense that it separates out the human race from every other creature. This is important in a century which has seen widespread attempts to reduce people to the level of machines or animals. The image of God is a statement of human dignity which must be affirmed against any trend or ideology which would compromise the special place of the human race in the universe.

If this were all that Christians wanted to affirm by the phrase 'the image of God' what we have to say would probably be accepted by almost everyone, including those ecologists and others who lay great stress on the symbiotic relationship between our race and the rest of the created order. But general agreement on the practical consequences of the concept would probably not extend to the theological background which the term 'image of God' presupposes, and lack of consensus on this fundamental point would ultimately falsify superficial agreements at the practical level. In the secular culture of the West, mention of 'the word of God' would probably be regarded as a (potentially dangerous) irrelevance. But in the religious cultures of the rest of the world, where the relationship between God and man has until recently been perceived somewhat differently, it might well be the word 'image' which would cause the greatest offence. This is because 'image' might suggest that human beings are copies in miniature of the supreme Being, an idea which could tend to blur the absolute distinction between him (or it) and us.

It is because of these factors at work that modern Christians cannot rest content with general agreement about the practical consequences of our image of 'God' doctrine. We must not hesitate to go beyond them to matters of fundamental principle, and defend the appropriateness of the Biblical phrase as an expression of our belief about the meaning of human destiny. For it is this which gives Christian witness its distinctive flavour, and which alone will enable it to remain relevant, whatever ideology or tendency may surface in the years ahead.

The Doctrine of God

In sharp contrast to any secular, humanistic ideology, the primary focus of our concentration must be God, since it is he who provides the benchmark for our understanding of his image. What is there about God that we need to bear in mind when we consider the meaning of his image? The most fundamental attribute of God which we must remember is his absoluteness. Christians cannot accept that there is any power or ideology which is superior to God himself. Everything that is finds its ultimate meaning only in relation to him. Man is created with a special link to this ultimate reality, a fact which has the secondary (but still important) consequence of giving him another special relationship to the rest of creation.

This is spelled out very clearly in Genesis. To the human race is given the privilege and the responsibility of exercising dominion over the earth. This dominion is bound to be exercised through a process of 'exploitation', though we need not succumb to the negative connotations which that word has come to embody. The proper use of the creation means that the world's resources must be carefully husbanded, as well as employed in a way which brings out their maximum potential, and not in a way which merely destroys them, or renders them useless. In practical terms, this means that we must be committed to economic development for the benefit of as many people as possible, but at the same time that we must resist the overuse of scarce commodities and the pollution of the atmosphere in which we have to work.

On the other hand, it also means that we must resist the more extreme manifestations of the so-called 'green' or ecologist movement, which would have us treat the creation as a sacred entity, not to be touched any more than is absolutely necessary by human hands. Sacredness, let us remember, is a quality which belongs to God, not to the earth. Of course we must respect the trust which God has given us in his creation mandate, and not abuse the earth, but neither should we allow ourselves to fall into the trap of idolising it! This is very important, especially in the so-called 'under-developed' parts of the world, where improvement of the natural environment may not take place because of conservationist lobbying. It is easy to point to cases of destruction which could and should have been avoided, but the current danger is to go to the opposite extreme and turn large tracts of land into nature reserves for the benefit of Western tourists, when they could be used to boost the local economy and reduce poverty.

Second, there is God's creativity. Traditionally, this has been understood as applying to us in the commandment to be fruitful and multiply, and replenish the earth. Some Christians even use it as a pretext for attacking artificial means of birth control! Without going to that extreme, we can nevertheless affirm that the procreative role of the family, which has come under threat from many quarters, must be defended and preserved by the church's witness. In particular, we must combat the suggestion that it is somehow always better for a woman to have a career of her own than to bring up children inside the home. Some women may indeed be called to the single, career life, and they should be fully respected if that is indeed their choice, but motherhood must not be allowed to become defined as necessarily a part-time occupation, and one which is devalued because it is unpaid.

The future of our race depends on the careful nurture of the next generation, and only the family unit can supply this at all adequately. Faced with a rising tide of a kind of Western feminist ideology, which claims to 'liberate' women from their traditional roles as housewives and mothers, the church must take a firm stand in favour of procreation as a legitimate and indeed necessary application of the divine mandate in Genesis 1, without trying to impose this blindly on every woman. In particular, the church must look for ways of affirming the value of motherhood in a world where personal independence and cash income have come to be the main badges of self-esteem and self empowerment. That a woman should be made to feel inferior, or even penalised, for doing the most important thing any human being can ever do is intolerable, and the church must take the lead in restoring the honour due to the most basic activities of procreation and nurture within the marriage covenant.

At a different, but no less important level, the divine creativity must be reflected in human culture. Traditionally, the church has always been one of the principal sponsors of Western cultural activity, and most of the great works of art which we admire today would not have appeared if the church had not made it possible. Today, however, we are the victims of a cultural homogenisation which is rapidly reducing our intellectual horizons to the level of an immature adolescent, and there are disturbing signs that the church, in the name of 'outreach', is succumbing to it.

The Anglican church has been especially privileged, in that it has been the chief spiritual home for the flowering of the English language, and no student of our literature can hope to understand it properly without some understanding of our faith. It is surely time that we recognised that the so-called liturgical renewal of the mid-twentieth century has entailed much cultural loss, and that a great deal of what we encounter as 'worship' today is simply unworthy of our Christian profession. We have a duty to give of our best to God, and to encourage people to exert themselves to an extraordinary degree in divine service. To take but one example, the medieval cathedrals were built by illiterate peasants whose cultural awareness cannot have been very great, and yet they are masterpieces of art which have stood the test of time. Can this be said of modern church architecture, which has been built by the most educated generation in human history?

Thirdly, there is God's relational character. Our God is not a monolithic entity, but rather three persons who dwell in the most intimate communion of love and mutual affirmation. This must always remain an ideal for Christians, however little we may achieve it in practice. In the holy Trinity, each person fully respects the others, to whom he is united by voluntary bonds of love. In the church, this means that each human person must be respected and honoured, as an individual with specific gifts which should be used for the edification of the body of Christ (1 Cor. 12:14), and that conversely, each believer must commit himself to serve the interests of the whole community.

Despotic coercion from the top is just as damaging to the church's life as anarchic indiscipline from below, and we must confess that we have seen plenty of both in the past. Furthermore, whenever one of these extremes seems to be more prominent, there is a special temptation to try to solve the problem by unilateral recourse to the other. On the one hand, church leaders may seek to rein in their more enthusiastic followers by curbing their freedom to develop new types of witness and ministry. On the other hand, grassroots believers often thumb their noses at authority and claim for themselves a 'freedom', including theological heresy and liturgical aberration, which borders on anarchy. Here more than anywhere, there is need for a wise and responsible leadership within the church.

The Anglican communion puts great store by the institution of episcopacy, although sometimes failing to explore theologically the precise role of bishops. In many parts of the world they are missionary leaders, closely identified with their flocks and sometimes suffering on their behalf. In the developed world, however, it has to be asked whether the episcopal structure as we have it fully fuels mission rather than purely maintenance. Bishops can be tempted either to be swallowed up in administrative tasks which stifle their prophetic role, or occasionally to become media personalities and run the risk of appearing as eccentric. Furthermore, an episcopate which is seen to tolerate heretical beliefs or immoral behaviour among the church's authorised teachers, as is too often the case in the Western world, commands little respect if it then tries to enforce ritual or administrative conformity on lesser matters. The teaching role of the bishop, a preserver of the gospel rather than a radical critic, must remain an Anglican distinctive, given our commitment to both Scripture and the patristic tradition.

As Christians we do not have the freedom to violate the canon of God's revelation in Scripture, and as Anglicans we are further committed to the way in which that Scripture has been historically interpreted in the creeds and in the traditions of the church. In this respect, the recent decision of some provinces to ordain women may be seen as a risk since it conflicts with the historic *consensus fidelium* down through the centuries (as well as across cultural divides today). A particular onus lies on those who took this risk to demonstrate that they took it not as a deliberate break with Scripture and the ecumenical tradition, which would open the way for a radicalisation of doctrine, ethics and practice along the lines of modern Western cultural ideologies.

The church must strive for that harmony of mutual service and respect which the holy Trinity holds out to us. We are indeed equal, but we are also different — and different for a reason, according to the pattern found deep in Scripture and tradition. To say that a woman cannot be ordained to a teaching office within the church is no more a disparagement of her gifts than to say that the Father (or the Holy Spirit for that matter) could not have become a man and died for our salvation. Perhaps nowhere in the church today has greater harm been done to the long-term health of the body of Christ than by those well-meaning but misguided church leaders who have pushed their feminist convictions not merely to the point of recognising no distinction between the sexes, but to the point where they are prepared to discrimi-

nate against those traditionalists who cannot follow them in this matter
and indeed who represent the vast ecumenical consensus.

But the saddest aspect of the headlong rush towards a unisex
ministry, it can be argued, is that the gifts given to women are being
submerged. God created both male and female in his image, which does
not mean that male and female are identical, but that the particular gifts
given to each are equally reflective of the divine likeness. Women are
not called to be caricatures of men, nor are the sexes meant to combine
in some third entity. The Christian ministry ought to reflect the divine
order of different (not separate!) but equal in the way that it is structured, giving both men and women the freedom to be themselves in
the way that God intended them to be.

The Image of God

When we turn from consideration of God to the question of his image
in man, we come to an aspect of the question which may be more
immediately relevant to the concerns of many third-world church
leaders. Western Christians like to think that they have little difficulty
with the concept of the image; indeed, the principle of individual autonomy has been pushed to the point where in some cases it would
seem that every human person has the same freedom to dispose of
himself as God has! But if it is true that Western Christians need to
retreat from this extreme and rediscover those unitive and relational
aspects of our life which are best appreciated by theological reflection
on the word 'God', it is also true that there are many parts of the world
where 'God' presents little problem, but where human dignity is seriously undervalued. This can lead to an equal and opposite problem of
a crushing heteronomy, oppression by a rigid external law which takes
little account of the freedom of the human spirit.

In this respect, it is no secret that the greatest challenge to the
Christian church today is Islam. It may be true that we need to distinguish between a more moderate type of Islam, which still controls most
Muslim societies, and the fundamentalism which is on the rise in some
places but so far has taken over only in a very small number of countries
(Iran, Sudan). It may also be true that Christianity itself is having a
steady effect on the Islamic doctrine of God, leading to greater desig-

47

nations of God as compassionate and loving. But genuine and honest theological debate about God and the world is needed rather than incoherent statements that no important differences exist over the understanding of God. Such claims are not satisfactory to Muslims, as their rejection of the multi-faith syllabuses in British schools decisively shows.

If Western culture continues to fragment and reject its historic ethical base, a religion which offers firm revealed law, however heteronomous and regulative in character, will have an attraction, as indeed fundamentalisms of many kinds are showing widely. A vacuum of ethical norms is opening in Western society. God is no longer considered to be relevant to issues of public policy and discussions of value; rather God is relegated to the realm of purely private choice. Bishop Newbigin is to be thanked for much labour in making this point clear. Churches have colluded with this policy in the West, resigning any claim to speak with a distinctively theological voice to issues of public policy, in effect bracketing what most needs to be said in order not to offend the secular mind. This is done so as to gain a hearing, but it fails and merely discredits the church.

On issues such as divorce, education, and health care, the church often gives the impression of wanting to keep close to popular opinion, or expert secular opinion, in a mistaken effort to retain influence. In fact what the world wants to hear from the church is an intelligent application of gospel imperatives to the burning issues of the day. Such Christian ethics are grounded on our doctrine of the *imago dei*, which instantly underscores the sanctity of human life. Whereas other species are made 'after their own kind', we are made in the 'image and likeness of God', a huge discontinuity in the creation narrative and its theology.

Responsible to the gospel ethic and mode of life, what has the church to say to issues such as the crisis in nursing, the issue of 'care in the community' and the need to train teachers of religious education? Is the church interested in the public forum, for example, in vocation any longer? Nursing surely is one of the most Christ-like vocations imaginable: why has the Anglican church stepped back from encouraging and fostering a Christian vision in this area of public life? It is probably because God, and therefore the Christian anthropology of the image, is removed from the mouth of the church when she speaks to society: a kind of dual-speak is developing whereby we can preach about God, Christ and the image in church buildings, but must adopt the secular vocabulary in the public square.

The same has to be said about the colleges which are formally dubbed 'church' colleges for the training of teachers and now wider in scope, offering degrees for many professions. Dare these colleges offer a distinctively Christian track of preparation, incorporating gospel distinctives? Western church leaders need to face this question. There is no doubt that Islamic colleges will be glad to offer a religious base to courses they run, as do the Roman Catholics in their very successful and popular educational establishments. Does the Anglican tradition in the West dare to be an institution responsible to the message and ethical basis of Jesus, who fulfilled and restored the divine image? Will the Western Anglicans come out of the private closet and bring their faith and doctrine into the debates over social policies, so as to mitigate the managerial secularised understanding of humans so common in modern culture? Will the church, at every level, strive to offer an alternative to technological interpretations of the human being? The truth of the human condition is that it is made in the divine image, of infinite worth. Such truth is to be held aloft courageously and lived out sacrificially. Insisting on the universal truth claim of the Judaeo-Christian revelation of our identity as the image of God, in public debate as well as in private piety, constitutes a challenge to all churches, but especially to churches with political and social influence such as the Church of England.

Living the Image Today

One of the greatest misconceptions about the image of God is the belief that it was lost or corrupted by the fall of Adam. This belief is so ancient and so deep-rooted that it is taken for granted by almost everyone who thinks about the subject, even though the Bible says nothing about it. On the contrary, the few references which there are to the image (and/or likeness) of God after the fall all assume that it is still present. For example, murder is condemned in Genesis 9:6 on the ground that man is created in God's image, and in the New Testament we are all condemned as people who curse those who are made in the likeness of God (James 3:9). Neither of these verses would make sense as they stand if the image/likeness had been harmed or destroyed by the fall.

But if the Bible says nothing about the loss of the image, neither does it tell us much about what it means for Christians today. Jesus is frequently referred to as the image of (the invisible) God, and some theologians have assumed that he is the true image, the man that Adam was meant to be. But it is also possible (and probably better) to read these verses in a Trinitarian context, and interpret the 'image' as meaning that the Son is the divine replica of the Father. To call Christ the 'true image' in the Adamic sense would have the effect either of removing the image from the rest of us, or else of making us all little Christs, neither of which is true. For better or for worse, the image of God is present in fallen man, both Christian and non-Christian, even if it has not itself been materially affected by the fall.

What does this mean for us today? There are, I think, several points which can be made on the basis of the general witness of Scripture, even if it is difficult to find particular verses which state them clearly. First, it means that every person on earth has an in-built relationship with God. This does not mean that everyone will be saved, but it does mean that nobody can escape his responsibility for being in a state of rebellion against the creator. There is no human being to whom the call of the gospel to repentance and conversion is not addressed. In a day when the population of the world is exploding and when the message of tolerance threatens to produce a pluralism of indifference, the church must renew the message of Christ, that all men and women need to be saved in and through him. The concept of the image is therefore a missionary challenge to us, to go out and proclaim afresh the word of God's salvation to all mankind.

Secondly, the image of God in us is a reminder of the sacred nature of every human being. We live in a time when love and compassion are being used to further abortion, euthanasia, genetic engineering and other practices which are designed to eradicate the unwanted. But in God's eyes, no human being can ever be unwanted. There is a place for everyone, because everyone is made in his image. The doctrine of the image of God must therefore be the foundation of our ethical practice, and the chief justification for our insistence on the sanctity of human life. As Anglicans we do not accept that there are absolutes in this sphere in the way that Roman Catholics do, but although we are prepared to make allowances for the inevitable hard cases (such as abortion when the health of the mother is at stake), we are not prepared to sacrifice the basic principle that every human being has a right to life, even if this means that he or she will spend that life being cared for by others.

Thirdly, the image of God is the basis of our social existence. It is what unites us as human beings, whatever our race, gender, or colour. In Christian eyes it is the ultimate justification for a democratic form of government and for the right of every voice to be heard. But while it supports democracy, it also underscores responsibility, because as beings created in God's image we are responsible to him for what we think, say and do. This is the ultimate safeguard against tyranny and injustice, because it is when our consciences are open before God — and only then — that we shall be constrained to do his will in our lives and in the world which we have been entrusted with. It has been the foundation of the church's common life in the past, and it will protect us in the future, as we go forward in faith and await the coming of the Son of Man in his glory.

For all these reasons and more, the Christian doctrine that we are all, male and female, created in the image and likeness of God must remain central to our theological agenda, and guide our steps as we seek to walk in the way of Christ's peace. Let us pray that our Anglican communion will always hold this vision before us, and seek to share with other Christians the world over what it means to reflect God's image in a world as much in need of redemption now as it was when our Saviour walked this earth.

Questions

1. How can we maintain a fundamentally thankful orientation for our lives as made for fellowship with God, in the face of so much 'culture of complaint'?

2. Are we too individualistic in our mode of life? Are we too tribal?

3. Can congregational life interweave with family life in a real way? Here it would be interesting to compare experiences across the cultural divide of northern and southern hemispheres.

4. 'Care in the community': but if there is no 'community' to provide the care, what should Christians do?

5. Is a Christian hospice or school any different from a secular one? Should there be a difference?

The Trinity and Human Community

PETER ADAM

Summary

Human beings must look to God to find their meaning, especially because we are made in God's image. God is a model for humanity, especially for his covenant people, restored in Christ. The idea of God as a model for human community is problematic, but the triune God invites his people to participate in his life. This includes the imitation of Christ. The gospel of the Trinity, salvation through Jesus Christ, is the message of the Trinity to the world. The doctrine of the Trinity preserves the gospel, the message by which the world is invited to join the people of God, and to receive the gift of eternal life.

God and Humanity

1. Humanity in God's Image

It is right for us to look to God to find out how we should live as human beings. For God has made us and cares for us, and it is our duty and joy to be the kind of people he wants us to be. All through the Bible we find that God constantly tells us how to know him, how to serve him, and what patterns of living reflect his good purposes.

The Bible tells us not only how to live in order to please God, but also that there is a basic correspondence between ourselves and God, because God made us in his own image. In Genesis 1 we read 'Then

52

God said, "Let us make humankind in our image, according to our likeness. . . ." So God created humankind in his image, in the image of God he created them; male and female he created them'.[1] We would expect to find that there are at least some ways in which human beings are meant to reflect God's character and copy his actions. Barth writes that 'Man is the repetition of this divine form of life; its copy and reflection'.[2] This is the topic of this chapter.

But is it right to think that humankind as a whole is made in God's image, or that each individual is made in God's image? Different societies and cultures will tend to give different answers to this question. I think that the Bible teaches that both are true. In Genesis 1 the human race as a whole is described as being made in God's image, while in Genesis 9:6 when the writer gives the reason why the murder of an individual is wrong in God's sight, it is because of this feature of humanity. 'Whoever sheds the blood of a human, by a human shall that person's blood be shed; for in his own image God made humankind.' Similarly in James 3:9, we are told not to curse 'those who are made in the likeness of God'.

Thus human beings are meant to reflect God's character and to be like him. Because of this correspondence between God and ourselves, we would expect to find that our life would reflect God, at least in some respects. D. B. Knox has written 'Human relationships reflect the image of the Trinity. It follows that human language reflecting these human relationships is a suitable vehicle to describe God's relationships with Himself and with humanity, for we have been created in his image'.[3]

2. God as a Model for Humanity

The Bible tells us to imitate God. In the Old Testament, God is holy, and has created a people who are to reflect his holiness. God says 'the whole earth is mine, but you shall be for me a priestly kingdom and a

---

1. Genesis 1:26, 27. The New Revised Standard Version (New York/Oxford: Oxford University Press, 1989) is used throughout this essay.
2. Karl Barth, *Church Dogmatics*, Vol. iii, Pt. 1 (Edinburgh: T. & T. Clark, 1958), p. 185.
3. D. B. Knox, *The Everlasting God* (Homebush West: Anzea, 1988), p. 68.

holy nation'.[4] Holiness is the characteristic of the covenant-keeping God, and he makes his chosen covenant people a holy people: 'You shall be holy, for I the LORD your God am holy'.[5] As the people act in holy ways, as God has instructed them to act, they will imitate and share in his holiness.

So the covenant people of God imitate God's holiness. In particular the New Testament tells us to imitate both God the Father and also the Lord Jesus. Jesus says to follow the example of God the Father in loving our enemies. 'Love your enemies and pray for those who persecute you, so that you may be children of your Father in heaven; for he makes his sun rise on the evil and on the good, and sends rain on the righteous and on the unrighteous. . . . Be perfect, therefore, as your heavenly Father is perfect.'[6]

Paul tells us to follow the example of Christ. We must aim to please our neighbour, 'For Christ did not please himself; but, as it is written, "The insults of those who insult you have fallen on me"'.[7] We must follow Christ's example of humble obedience to God the Father. For Christ 'humbled himself and became obedient to the point of death — even death on a cross'. We too should look to the interests of others, and show the same obedience.[8]

The example of both the Father and the Son is set before us in Ephesians. 'Be kind and compassionate to one another, forgiving each other, just as in Christ God forgave you. Be imitators of God, therefore, as dearly loved children and live a life of love, just as Christ loved us and gave himself up for us as a fragrant offering and sacrifice to God.'[9]

We are not told to imitate or follow the example of the Spirit, though the same effect is produced if we are filled with the Spirit, and controlled by him, as in Acts 4:8 and Ephesians 5:18.

However, we are told to follow the example of God, especially the example of the Father and the Son, in love, care for others, obedience and forgiveness. God then is a model for human behaviour.

4. Exodus 19:5-6.
5. Leviticus 19:2; 11:44-45; 20:7; 1 Peter 1:16.
6. Matthew 6:44-45, 48.
7. Romans 15:3.
8. Philippians 2:8; also vv. 3, 4, 12.
9. Ephesians 4:32; 5:1-2.

3. Restoration in Christ

There is more to Christian living than imitating God. We cannot begin to follow God's example without dealing with the fractured nature of our relationship with God — sin. God's remedy for our sinfulness is to send his Son. He is 'the image of the invisible God' and in him 'all the fullness of God was pleased to dwell, and through him to reconcile to himself all things . . . by making peace through the blood of his cross'.[10] Our response must be to be reconciled to God through Christ, 'without shifting from the hope promised by the gospel'.[11] As we continue in that hope, and put off sin and put on godliness, our new self 'is being renewed in knowledge after the image of its creator'.[12] Our imitation of God, therefore, is an outworking of God's saving work in Christ, and his application of that work to our lives.

This restoration in Christ is in the context of the work of the Triune God for us and in us. Living as a Christian cannot be separated from experiencing and relating to God, Father, Son, and Holy Spirit. So Peter writes that we 'have been chosen and destined by God the Father and sanctified by the Spirit to be obedient to Jesus Christ and to be sprinkled with his blood'.[13]

The word 'gospel' is Bible code for the central message of Christianity. We cannot talk of God and humanity without talking of the gospel, for the gospel of Christ is the heart of God's work and message for humanity. The message of the gospel is that humankind is restored into the full image of God by Christ, and that when Christ returns 'we will be like him, for we will see him as he is'.[14] Jesus Christ is the message of God the Trinity to humanity.

10. Colossians 1:5, 19-20.
11. Colossians 1:22-23.
12. Colossians 3:10.
13. 1 Peter 1:2.
14. John 3:3.

PETER ADAM

God the Trinity and Humanity

1. The Trinity a Model for Human Community?

We have noted that God the Father and the Son can be models for us. Is it the case that the Trinity is a model for us? This is not a matter of imitating the actions of the Father or the Son, but of finding the way in which the Father, Son and Spirit relate together a model for our actions, and especially our inter-action with each other. There are a number of issues which we need to tackle in order to answer this question.

It is clear that in the Bible there are some aspects of the relationship between the Father and the Son which we should imitate. These are found most clearly in John's Gospel. For example, Jesus teaches that his response to the Father is a paradigm of how he expects the disciples to respond to him. 'As the Father has loved me, so I have loved you; abide in my love. If you keep my commandments, you will abide in my love, just as I have kept my Father's commandments and abide in his love.'[15] We can also infer from Jesus' words, 'As the Father has sent me so I send you',[16] that we should follow in the steps of Jesus' obedience to the Father, but this is still a long way from demonstrating that the basic model of inner-trinitarian relationships is an example for us.

One difficulty is that we do not have revealed to us a comprehensive picture of the inner workings of the Trinity. In this case it is difficult to explain how we can gain much from an unknown model. Of course the danger is that we will fill in the gaps by our imaginations, and then having described God in our image use the picture we have produced as a model for our own behaviour. We have some knowledge of what God the Trinity has done to objects or people 'outside' of God [ad extra], but much less knowledge about the relationships within the Trinity [ad intra].

What is called 'Rahner's Rule' attempts to remove this problem by asserting that God is the same in revelation as he is in essence, that the Trinity is the same in inner relationships [ad intra] as in revelation [ad extra].[17] If this is the case, then it is easier to find a clear model to

---

15. John 15:9-10.
16. John 20:21.
17. 'Rahner's Rule' was devised by Ted Peters as a description of an aspect

follow, though even this does not solve the problem of knowing which aspects we ought to imitate. It is hard to demonstrate that 'Rahner's Rule' is true, because we have such little evidence as to the inner life of God. It would be odd to be definite about an area of theology in which we do not have much evidence, when we are so often tentative in areas where we do have more evidence.

Those theologians who adopt a 'social' model of the Trinity provide an easy bridge for the development of the implications for human society. The 'social model' has been described as follows by Cornelius Plantinga Jr. 'Father, Son and Spirit are conceived as persons in a full sense of "person," *i.e.*, as distinct centres of love, will, knowledge, and purposeful action . . . and who are conceived as related to each other in some central ways analogous to . . . relations among the members of a society of human persons.'[18] L. Hodgson writes of the unity of God as 'a dynamic unity actively unifying in the one Divine life the lives of the three Divine persons' and then claims that this unity should inspire our attempts to find unity in the church and among the peoples of the world.[19] But the 'social' model by itself does not express the unity of God. Because it must be tempered by another complementary model, it is unwise to extrapolate from it to human behaviour, as the details of the analogy are not known.[20]

Surely we can say that the inner relationship of the Trinity is love, and that we too ought to live in love? Both statements are true, but it is the relationship between them which is the point at issue. For if we do not know the details of the type of love between the 'persons' of the Trinity, then we cannot apply this pattern in detail to ourselves. Indeed it is worthwhile to reflect that a large part of our love involves mutual

---

of Karl Rahner's teaching on the Trinity. See Ted Peters, *God as Trinity-Relationality and Temporality in Divine Life* (Louisville: Westminster/John Knox Press, 1993), p. 96.

18. Quoted from *The Thomist* 50 (1986), p. 325, in John L. Gresham Jr., 'The Social Model of the Trinity and Its Critics,' *Scottish Journal of Theology*, Vol. 46, pp. 327-28.

19. Leonard Hodgson, *The Doctrine of the Trinity* (London: Nisbet and Co., 1943), pp. 95, 187.

20. See Cornelius Plantinga Jr., 'Social Trinity and Tritheism', Ronald J. Feenstra and Cornelius Plantinga Jr. (eds.), *Trinity, Incarnation and Atonement* (Notre Dame: University of Notre Dame Press, 1989), pp. 21-47, for a Biblical defense of the 'social' model of the Trinity.

forgiveness: we have no evidence that this is part of the mutual self-love of the Trinity!

It is because we have such little knowledge of God's internal life that it is so easy to read into God what we want to find, and then find justification for our actions within the picture of God we have created. Barth's doctrine of the Trinity has been criticised by Moltmann for being hierarchical, for leaving little room for human freedom.[21] This is seen as a result of concentrating on the unity of God, on the rule of the one God.

If there is the danger of developing hierarchy from an over-emphasis on the unity of God, there is also a danger of reading a modern idea of equality into the three 'persons' of the Trinity. Peters comments, 'Moltmann asserts that the Trinity consists of three distinct subjects who are democratically and co-operatively organized'.[22]

While it is tempting to identify the rule of the one God with oppressive political systems, it is also simplistic to do so, for atheism, polytheism, and animism have also been identified with repressive and hierarchical societies.[23] In fact polytheism and animism seem to be naturally hierarchical systems.

L. Boff claims that in Moltmann's understanding of the Trinity the 'domination model is replaced by the communion model: production by invitation, conquest by participation. The Trinity understood in human terms as a communion of Persons lays the foundation for a society of brothers and sisters, of equals, in which dialogue and con-sensus are the basic ingredients of living together in both the church and the world'.[24] It is obvious that we must be opposed to domination in human life and in favour of consensus. The issue here is whether or not we find these democratic qualities in the life of the Trinity and can then retrieve them with divine affirmation for their implementation in human life. It may be how humans are meant to live: is it a true description of the life of God?

21. Jürgen Moltmann, *The Trinity and the Kingdom* (San Francisco: Harper and Row, 1981), pp. 139-44.

22. Peters, *God as Trinity*, p. 106.

23. I am grateful to Archdeacon John Harrower for this observation.

24. Leonardo Boff, *Trinity and Society* (Maryknoll, New York: Orbis Books, 1988), p. 120. As Peters points out, Boff is not consistent, and retains hierarchy within the Trinity. Peters, *God as Trinity*, p. 113.

It is very dangerous to identify a political theory with a theology, because it does not allow a diversity of patterns of society. It may actually produce the theological repression that Boff is trying to avoid!

If Moltmann and Boff are trying to produce a hierarchy-free and submission-free theological zone then they are much mistaken. For 'at the name of Jesus every knee should bend . . . and every tongue should confess that Jesus Christ is Lord, to the glory of God the Father.'[25] There is no disjunction in the Bible between loving God and submitting to him. In fact Jesus clearly combined the two, as we have already seen. 'I have kept my Father's commandments and abide in his love.'[26]

The idea that human beings are invited into the life of God the Trinity is an attractive one, and is held by many theologians. J. Torrance writes 'we are given the gift of participating in the [incarnate] Son's communion with the Father, in the Trinitarian life of God',[27] and certainly in John 17:26 Jesus' prayer is that 'the love with which you have loved me may be in them, and I in them'. But it is wrong to read that prayer as resulting in the inclusion of the disciples in the life of the Trinity. Jesus still distinguishes between 'my Father' and 'your Father', 'my God' and 'your God' (John 20:17).

Costa Carras writes that to 'mould God in the image of man would be to create an idol'.[28] He recognises the central point which I have been making in this section, that is, the great danger of reading what we want into God, and then thinking that we have achieved divine authorisation for the model of human society that we want to promote. We know so little of the internal life of God that we are unwise to build much on what we do know. The best course is to do what God says in Scripture, not more and not less.

It is important to remember that we can gain many ideas from the Bible about how we are to live, without having to find them in the

---

25. Philippians 2:10-11.

26. John 15:10.

27. J. B. Torrance, 'The Doctrine of the Trinity in our Contemporary Situation', Alasdair I. C. Heron (ed.), *The Forgotten Trinity* (London: BCC/CCBI, 1991), pp. 3-17. See also J. B. Torrance, *Worship, Community and the Triune God of Grace* (Carlisle: Paternoster Press, 1996).

28. Costa Carras, 'The Doctrine of the Trinity in Relation to Political Action and Thought', Heron (ed.), *The Forgotten Trinity*, p. 161.

model of inner-trinitarian relations. It would be a pity to not find them where they certainly can be found because we were looking for them where they may not be found.

In the Bible the call to be like God is given to the covenant people of God. They have been chosen by God to be in relationship with him, and they are called to be holy as he is holy. It is a call addressed to the church, not the world. God's call to the people of the world now is to join the covenant people of God, the church. People can join the church as they hear the gospel, and respond in obedient faith in Jesus Christ. As they believe in Christ they are incorporated into Christ's church, and can then receive the challenge and invitation of God: 'Be holy, as I am holy'. God's word to the world is not 'Be like me', but 'Repent and believe in the gospel of Christ'.

2. The Trinity as a Model for the Church?

As we have seen, God's people are called to be like God in some respects. Is the church called to imitate or reflect the inner life of the Trinity?

Moltmann writes 'Monarchical monotheism justifies the church as hierarchy, as sacred dominion. The doctrine of the Trinity consti-tutes the church as "a community free of dominion" '.[29] While it is simplistic to oppose love and hierarchy as we have seen, Moltmann is surely right in expecting that the church will reflect the fellowship within God.

According to C. Gunton, it is John Owen, the seventeenth century Puritan, who is one of the first modern writers to point to this theme of the fellowship of the church reflecting the fellowship within God the Trinity.[30] Gunton writes '[his] conception of the church as a community of freely relating persons must be accepted for what it is: an ecclesiology which echoes God's eternal being in relation'.[31] This is no surprise, for communion with the three persons of the Trinity is a key feature of

29. Moltmann, *The Trinity and the Kingdom*, p. 202.
30. Colin E. Gunton, *The Promise of Trinitarian Theology* (Edinburgh: T. & T. Clark, 1991), pp. 75-76.
31. Gunton, *The Promise*, p. 77.

Owen's spirituality.[32] The believer is in conscious fellowship with the Father, the Son, and the Spirit.

Believing in God involves trinitarian experience. I have written elsewhere 'Life caught up in God is more like relating to a loving community than it is like relating to a loving individual. We turn to the Father, and he gives us the Son and the Spirit; we turn to the Son, and he shows us the Father and breathes the Spirit upon us; we turn to the Spirit, and he shows us the Father and the Son'.[33] Yet this experience is also unitive, for in all of this we meet the one God.

Even this is not to say that the inner life of the triune God is a model for the church. Perhaps as far as we can go is to say that some aspects of the life of the Trinity are presented to us in the Bible for our imitation. These are characteristically, and predictably, those of Jesus' attitude to his Father, and Jesus' actions towards us. This is because 'it is in Christ that the character and purpose of God is focused for the benefit of man, and because the character and plan of God is conveyed through the Humanity of Christ'.[34]

Jesus provides for us a model of service (Mark 10:43-45 and John 13:15), love (John 13:34; Eph. 5:25-33), laying down our lives for others (1 John 3:16), generosity (2 Cor. 8:9), obedience and humility (Phil. 2:1-11), and forgiveness (Eph. 5:2; Col. 3:13). If we want the church to follow the model of God, we cannot by-pass these challenges.

We should not regard the call to imitate Christ as being anything less than trinitarian: for the Son has been sent by the Father, and is empowered by the Spirit. The example of Christ is an insight into the Trinity, and the imitation of Christ is a participation in the life of the Trinity.

D. B. Knox claims that the key to the life of the Trinity is what he calls 'other-person-centredness', or love. He writes 'This absolute other-person-centredness, which is the inalienable element in perfect, personal relationship, as in the Trinity, is the ground of our salvation', and

---

32. John Owen, 'Communion with God', *The Works of John Owen*, Vol. II (Edinburgh: Banner of Truth, 1965).

33. Peter Adam, *Living the Trinity* (Bramcote: Grove, 1982), p. 20.

34. Peter Adam, *The Practice of the Imitation of Christ with Special Reference to the Theology of Dietrich Bonhoeffer* (unpublished Ph.D. thesis, University of Durham, 1981), p. 177.

adds 'Thus the establishment and deepening of personal relationship between one another is also the true object of human activity'.[35]

Those who want to promote the idea that God provides an egalitarian model for the world should also be committed to the idea that the church should exemplify this in its structures and life. 'Relations in the church have often been construed in terms of the permanent subordination of one group to another, even though the superordinate group has for the sake of appearances dignified its position with the rhetoric of "service." '[36] It would be odd for a church to commend a non-hierarchical model to the world, based on the Trinity, while reserving hierarchical structures and patterns in its own life.

My own view is that the supposed dichotomy between love and hierarchy is a dead end. God is superior to us, but also calls us into loving fellowship through the Lord Jesus Christ. The church is called to be holy as God is holy. Now God invites people of every race, people-group and language to join his covenant people, summoning them to faith in Christ, the forgiveness of their sins, and the gift of eternal life. We can become holy with God's holiness if we trust in Christ and his substitutionary death for us on the cross: 'for our sake he made him to be sin who knew no sin, so that in him we might become the righteousness of God'.[37] As we turn to Christ, we see the glory of the Lord, and 'are being transformed into his likeness from one degree of glory to another; for this comes from the Lord, the Spirit'.[38] It is only by the gospel that human beings are summoned and enabled to share in the life and character of God.[39]

3. The Gospel of the Trinity for the Human Community

It has been a commonplace over the last forty years to assert that one of the characteristics of Anglicanism is its concentration on the incar-

---

35. Knox, *Everlasting God*, pp. 132, 134.
36. Gunton, *The Promise*, p. 80.
37. 2 Corinthians 5:21.
38. 2 Corinthians 3:18.
39. I have not discussed the feminist critique of the Trinity. See Torrance, *Worship, Community*, ch. 4, and D. G. Bloesch, *The Battle for the Trinity* (Ann Arbor: Servant Books, 1985).

nation. This is a misleading statement. It is only since the production of the set of essays called *Lux Mundi* (The Light of the World) in 1889 that some parts of Anglicanism have concentrated on the incarnation. Until this time Anglicanism had been resolutely trinitarian. For trinitarian faith was part of Anglicanism from its earliest days, and was obviously retained and re-invigorated at the Reformation, as is evident in *The Book of Common Prayer*, for example, in the Litany and the 'Athanasian Creed'. In view of the topic before us, it is worth remembering that Anglicanism is trinitarian.

While we have been considering the ways in which the Trinity may be a model for the church and for the world, it is worth remembering that these are minor themes in the Bible. The focus of the Bible is not on the model of the Trinity but on the message of the Trinity: and that message is the gospel of Jesus Christ. For 'God so loved the world that he gave his only Son, so that everyone who believes in him may not perish but have eternal life' (John 3:16). For 'there is one God; and there is also one mediator between God and humankind, Christ Jesus, himself human, who gave himself a ransom for all' (1 Tim. 2:5-6). And Jesus said of the Spirit 'He will glorify me, because he will take what is mine and declare it to you' (John 16:13). It is the gospel of the Trinity which must be our message to the world, as we 'make disciples of all nations, baptizing them in the name of the Father and of the Son and of the Holy Spirit' (Matt. 28:19) and teaching them the commands of Christ.

I have tried to show that the clearest call to be like God is the call to be holy, as God is holy. This is nothing other than a call to believe in Christ, as it is only through Christ that we can become holy. It is only as we through Christ join the covenant people of God that we can begin to exemplify the holiness of God in our life together.

Of what use is the doctrine of the Trinity? A number of recent writers have recognised that the doctrine of the Trinity is necessary to preserve the gospel.[40] Here are some of their comments.

> The function of trinitarian theology is to maintain . . . that the biblical story of God and us is true of and for God himself.[41]

---

40. I am grateful to Dr. Graham Cole for this observation.
41. Robert W. Jenson, 'What Is the Point of Trinitarian Theology?' in Christoph Schwöbel (ed.), *Trinitarian Theology Today* (Edinburgh: T. & T. Clark, 1995), p. 37.

. . . it is theological doctrine which defends the central faith of the Bible and the Church.[42]

The Trinity was crucial because it was a witness to the deity of Jesus Christ and thus to the certainty of salvation secured by him.[43]

No adequate distinction can be made between the doctrine of the Trinity and the doctrine of the economy of salvation.[44]

The purpose of the doctrine of the Trinity is to speak as truthfully as possible about the mystery of God who saves us through Christ in the Holy Spirit.[45]

[the Trinity is] the very grammar of the Christian Gospel.[46]

[the Trinity] is an immediate consequence of the gospel, because the revelation on which everything depends cannot be stated except in trinitarian terms.[47]

Jesus cannot be called Lord apart from the doctrine of the Trinity.[48]

To concentrate on the incarnation and neglect the Trinity will result in a Unitarian faith, an unsatisfactory christology, and a lack of confidence in the atonement. Anglicans need to catch up with the rest of the theological world[49] and rediscover the doctrine of the Trinity!

While it may be profitable to consider whether the Trinity is a model for the world, it is essential that the gospel of the Trinity, the message of salvation through Jesus Christ, is preached to the world. We may have a model: we certainly have a message, and we invite

42. Emil Brunner, *The Christian Doctrine of God*, Dogmatics, Vol. 1 (London: Lutterworth Press, 1949), p. 206.
43. Timothy George, *Theology of the Reformers* (Nashville: Broadman Press, 1988), pp. 200-201.
44. From Karl Rahner, *The Trinity*, p. 24, quoted in Catherine Mowry LaCugna, *God For Us* (San Francisco: Harper, 1991), p. 211.
45. LaCugna, *God For Us*, p. 320.
46. Torrance, *The Doctrine of the Trinity*, p. 3.
47. Claude Welch, *In This Name*, p. 238, quoted in Peters, *God as Trinity*, p. 87.
48. Knox, *Everlasting God*, p. 50.
49. For recent discussions of the Trinity in many traditions, see Gunton, *The Promise*, ch. 1, and Peters, *God as Trinity*, ch. 3.

everyone to receive and participate in the grace of the Lord Jesus Christ, the love of God, and the communion of the Holy Spirit.[50]

Questions

1. Is your experience of God positively trinitarian?
2. Is your corporate worship trinitarian?
3. How should we imitate God?
4. How can we continue to preach the gospel of the Trinity?
5. How can we avoid making God in our own image?
6. How does the doctrine of the Trinity help us to understand who Jesus was and what he did?

---

50. 2 Corinthians 13:13.

The Humanity of Fallenness

MICHAEL LLOYD

Summary

The church's most urgent theological task today is to recover the doctrine of the fall. This essay will seek to justify that bold claim by arguing that a loss of the doctrine of the fall, and in particular of the fallenness of nature, tends to lead to a loss of belief in the unambiguous goodness of God, a loss of soteriology and therefore of christology, a loss of any eschatology that is not abstract and anthropocentric if not anthropomonist, and a loss of pastoral and ethical resources at precisely the points where we currently most need them. It will argue that we cannot hope to address the issues — of genetic screening, abortion, homosexuality, animal rights, etc. — which face and divide us as a Christian community today, from a satisfactorily Christian perspective, unless we put a robust doctrine of the fall back in its rightful place within a Christian world-view. And, since many assume that it is simply not possible to hold on to such a doctrine in our post-Darwinian world, it will conclude by suggesting how such an enterprise might be achieved.

It should be observed at the outset that, since Darwin, the doctrine of the fall has, largely, been off the theological agenda. The discovery that pain, suffering, predation and death occurred long before the emergence of humanity (and could not, therefore, realistically be attributed to human agency) led most theologians to abandon the doctrine of the fall in any explanatory sense and to treat it, if at all, as a shorthand way of expressing the rather commonplace observation that human beings 'fall below the highest that they see and that they could achieve'.[1] Thus, the doctrine's scope was reduced from the cosmic to the merely human, and its nature changed from the explanatory to the merely paradigmatic — which, of course, leaves unexplained the facts of human 'under achievement' (or sinfulness) and of natural evil.

The Doctrine of the Fall and the Goodness of God

Human evil could continue to be explained by reference to the good of human freedom, but what explanation could be given for the natural evils of pain, disease, predation, disaster and death? If blame cannot be laid at the door of 'man's first disobedience', and if there is no hiatus between the world in the creational purposes of God and the world as it now stands, who can be responsible for the way the world is, but the world's creator? Believing there now to be no other, most theologians this century have gone the route of attributing to God the structures and necessities of a natural order to which ruthlessness and redness of tooth and claw are intrinsic. Killing others so that one may live oneself is thus enshrined as a principle upon which the whole natural order is founded. Disease and death are seen as built into the way things are, and into the way God intends them to be. Disability is thereby given a proper, if paradoxical, place in the purposes of God for some of his creatures. This position is usually justified by maintaining that such features of our world are either necessary (in the sense that a recognisably similar world to ours without such features would simply be impossible), or desirable, or both. I have argued elsewhere[2] that such attempts at justifying natural evil are not successful. What I want to do here is to demonstrate that in practice they tend to be accompanied by a severe qualification of the doctrine of the goodness of God. Let me give three examples.

Andrew Elphinstone's *Freedom, Suffering and Love*[3] dismisses the

1. Maurice Wiles, 'Myth in Theology', in John Hick (ed.), *The Myth of God Incarnate* (London: SCM Press, 1977), p. 160.
2. See my D.Phil. thesis, *The Cosmic Fall and the Free Will Defence*, Lloyd, 1997a, and my article, 'Are Animals Part of the Fallen Creation?', forthcoming in Andrew Linzey (ed.), *Animals on the Agenda* (London: SCM Press), Lloyd, 1997b.
3. Andrew Elphinstone, *Freedom, Suffering and Love* (London: SCM Press, 1976).

doctrine of the fall as 'a legend of long ago': 'Anthropology has long suggested that there was no height from which to fall, no perfection to disrupt, no relationship with the Creator to break, no tested morality to flout . . . no "primordial tragedy," no forfeiting of God's favour and no wholesale state of alienation.' He is therefore forced into, and does not shrink from, seeing pain as 'fundamentally good' and evolution as the unfolding of the Creator's purposes. This rejection of the concept of fallenness and the consequent acceptance of suffering as a God-given aspect of creation leads him to ask: 'Dare we discern anything so outrageous as the idea that here [on the cross] God is making an atonement towards man for all that his desired creation costs man in the making: that he was making amends to all those who feel, and have felt, that they cannot forgive God for all the pains which life has foisted, unwanted, upon them?'[4]

My second example is John V. Taylor's *The Christlike God*,[5] which attributes natural evil not (as in the doctrine of the fallenness of nature) to the reprehensible actions of free creatures, but to the God-given random indeterminacy of physical forces. Taylor agrees with Elphinstone that 'pain has been one of the most creative forces in the whole process' and quotes with approval his suggestion that the cross was God making atonement towards us. He justifies God's creation of indeterminate and therefore clashing forces and the suffering that it occasions as being necessary: 'the choice before God has been this or nothing. And, in a sense, that is the ultimate choice each one of us has to come to, for, as I have already said, "I believe in God" is a vote of confidence in the Creator and in the bloodstained enterprise in which willy-nilly he has involved us and himself.'[6] It is the doctrine of the fall which enables us to vote for the Creator without having to vote also for the bloodstained character of the creation.

My third example is Martin Israel's *Angels*.[7] Israel explicitly rejects any concept of the fall, be it human or angelic. He therefore sees evil as 'an integral part of creation', and defends Dr. Pangloss's dictum that this is the best of all possible worlds. Logically, he goes on to charac-

4. Elphinstone, *Freedom,* pp. 49, 100, 142, 147.
5. John V. Taylor, *The Christlike God* (London: SCM Press, 1992).
6. Taylor, *The Christlike God*, p. 196.
7. Martin Israel, *Angels: Messengers of Grace* (London: SPCK, 1995).

terise the Creator as 'necessarily the effector of evil also'. Not surprisingly, he ends up by asserting that we need to qualify the statement that 'God is light and in Him there is no darkness at all.'[8] It seems to me that a Christian theologian who finds himself saying that we need to qualify the goodness of God ought to ask himself where he has gone wrong. For that, according to the epistle, is our message, our gospel. Without the unambiguous goodness of God, we would have no better news to share with the world than does paganism, and in some ways it would be worse. The Greek and Roman gods were not good, but at least there was a whole pantheon of them to maintain some sort of balance of power. For all power to rest in the hands of one God, and for that God to be of ambiguous goodness and unreliable benevolence would be to return to a religion of fear.

The issue is simple. Either God has directly and deliberately set up a world of which disorder, disease and death are intrinsic and intended parts, or all such distortions of God's world are the consequence of wrongful choice by free creatures and have no planned place in the purposes of Providence. The fact that most theologians in the past century have given the first of these answers has, I suggest, led many intelligent and sensitive people to reject not only the doctrine of creation, but the whole concept of such a Creator.

The Doctrine of the Fall and the Erosion of Soteriology, Missiology and Christology

If there has been no fall, no disruption of the purposes of God for his world, no hiatus between the divinely desired plan and the *status quo;* if creation now is the sort of arena and battlefield[9] which God always intended and required; if joy and sorrow are truly so inseparable that 'when one sits alone with you at your board, . . . the other is asleep upon your bed';[10] if pain and suffering and predation and disease and death have a necessary niche in the natural order as God expressly

8. Israel, *Angels,* pp. 63, 79f., 85-86, 91-92; 1 John 1:5.
9. See Elphinstone, *Freedom,* pp. 4, 107, 142.
10. From Kahlil Gibran's *The Prophet* quoted with approval by John Taylor, p. 196.

established it, then why would he, indeed how *could* he heal it? And even if he were to heal it, how could we praise him for that, knowing that it was he who established it as a vale of tears in the first place?

What tends to happen, therefore, when the notion of the fallenness of nature is jettisoned is that salvation is either abandoned altogether, or restricted to the sphere of human sin, with or without the pietistic reduction in the scope of mission that that would seem to imply. Reduce the doctrine of the fall to a statement about human 'under achievement' and you reduce the doctrine of the atonement to a statement about human forgiveness (and not even that, unless the 'under achievement' is seen as culpable). Reduce the doctrine of the atonement to a statement about human forgiveness and you tend to reduce the nature of mission to the saving of human souls. An anthropomonist fall makes for an anthropomonist atonement, and an anthropomonist atonement makes for an anthropomonist mission such as fails to meet the aspirations or touch the concerns of socially and environmentally aware and embodied men and women.

The thought of John Hick is a good example of the links between fall, atonement and christology. He believes that man was created as a fallen being.[11] He does not shrink from seeing both natural evil and the human propensity to moral evil as the direct creations of God. He justifies both these moves with reference to the epistemic distance which (he claims) is necessary for the freedom of the human individual, and to the process of soul-making which is the purpose of human existence. 'Man's "fallenness" is thus the price paid for his freedom as a personal being in relation to the personal Infinite. . . . This means that the sinfulness from which man is being redeemed, and the human suffering which flows from that sinfulness, have in their own paradoxical way a place within the divine providence.'[12] This is another example of the logic we noted in the previous section, whereby a rejection of the fallenness of nature leads to God being seen as more directly responsible for evil, leaving his goodness correspondingly more compromised. The point here is that it leads too to a reduction in the scope of the atonement. Just as the fall becomes merely the virtually inevitable, and there-

11. John Hick, *Evil and the God of Love*, 2nd ed. (Basingstoke: Macmillan, 1985), p. 280.
12. Hick, *The Myth of God*, p. 323.

fore excusable, fact of individual human self-centredness,[13] so the atonement becomes merely 'the transformation of human existence from self-centredness to God — or Reality-consciousness'.[14] And for that transformation to take place, there is no need for any special act of God within the historical process. 'The father in the parable [of the prodigal son] did not require a blood sacrifice to appease his sense of justice: as soon as he saw his son returning he "had compassion, and ran, and fell upon his neck, and kissed him. . . ."' Thus the cross, in Hick's account, becomes 'an expression of the self-giving love that was incarnate in his [Jesus'] life'[15] — not even, notice, an expression of the self-giving *God* who was incarnate in his life. For this view of the cross, there is no need to see Jesus as divine. If the world is much as God wanted it, we don't have much need of a saviour. If the world doesn't need recreating, it won't take the Creator to do it. Jesus then can, without much loss, be demoted to the level of inspired human being, and inspiring religious teacher — a status much more amenable to accommodation within a pluralistic theology of religions,[16] which is Hick's stated motivation and intent.

If, therefore, we look for the root causes of that christological seepage which is one element of the contemporary church's loss of confidence in the gospel, we must look not only to the pluralistic context and to the task of interfaith dialogue which are the stated reasons for Hick's adoption and advocacy of this religious 'copernican revolution';[17] we must look also to the prior abandonment of a doctrine of the fall which made such a paradigm shift possible.

The Doctrine of the Fall and the Erosion of Eschatology

Again, if the world is now as God intended it to be; if the fall is to be seen as a shortfall within the minds of men rather than a downfall of

13. Hick, *The Myth of God*, pp. 279-80.

14. John Hick, 'The Non-Absoluteness of Christianity', John Hick and Paul F. Knitter (eds.), *The Myth of Christian Uniqueness* (London: SCM Press, 1988), p. 23.

15. Hick, 'The Non-Absoluteness of Christianity', p. 33.

16. 'Towards a Pluralistic Theology of Religions' is the subtitle of *The Myth of Christian Uniqueness*.

17. This is an image Hick himself uses to press us to move 'from Christian inclusivism to pluralism'; Hick, 'The Non-Absoluteness of Christianity', p. 23.

the cosmos; and if, in particular, suffering and death are to be seen not as a distortion of the purposes of God for his world but as part of those purposes — as intrinsic, God-given, *and necessary* aspects of the physical creation, then it is hard to see why God would want to, or how he could, bring about a healing of the whole created order so as to rid it of those aspects which so mar, constrain and negate our affirmation, enjoyment and celebration of existence.

Thus, the same tends to happen to eschatology as happens to soteriology. Once the fallenness of nature is jettisoned and the atonement atrophied, eschatology is either abandoned altogether or reduced to the notion of (individual or corporate) human persistence beyond death. An example of the former is Don Cupitt, who argues that 'we cannot look forward to any golden age in the future, because we cannot now look back to any golden age in the past.'[18] An example of the latter is the eschatology of John Hick. He certainly does not abandon the whole category of eschatology, for it is the focus of his entire theodicy. For Hick, it is the eschatological end which justifies the means of creating a world of which natural evil is a necessary element. However, it is definitely restricted to the notion of human persistence in a series of lives the other side of death. He recognises that 'in the end the individual cannot be saved in isolation from the society of which he is ultimately a part',[19] while insisting that 'society is composed of individuals and it is individual people who are to be saved'. Indeed, part of that salvation is the transcendence of egoity, culminating in a new corporateness. However, although he allows that salvation must be salvation of the individual in his or her *social* context, there is no corresponding inclusion of the individual's *environmental* context. Human beings seem, in Hick's thought, to be extractable or distillable without loss from the environmental context in which they are embodied. The children of God may be brought into

18. An answer given to a question at the Portsmouth Theological Society. The telling way in which he bases his abandonment of eschatology on the supposed impossibility of any concept of fallenness is perhaps not logically watertight — it would be possible (though, as I suggested above, not desirable) to see God as healing creational deficiencies for which he himself was originally responsible. It does, however, demonstrate that the abandonment of the doctrine of the fall has been an efficient cause, if not the logical ground, of the abandonment of eschatology.

19. John Hick, *Death and Eternal Life* (London: Collins, 1976), p. 455.

glorious liberty (though at the cost of their own individuality), but the creation itself is not going to be liberated from its bondage to decay.[20] And we who wait eagerly for the redemption of our bodies[21] will wait in vain. This hope in which we were saved has no possibility of fulfilment in Hick's eschatological scenario. As our individuality is to be transcended, and as our embodiment is a facet of our epistemic distance from the Ultimate Reality, so our continued embodiment in future lives would be incompatible both with our single corporate personhood and with our common vision of God, or nirvana. Embodiment will wither away.[22] It seems that the Good Shepherd brought back just a fleece after all.

If the world as it now operates is not in some ways a travesty and perversion of what it was intended to be in the creational purposes of God, and if the atonement was not in principle a radical and divine engagement with the world in its non-intrinsic pervertedness, 'healing and re-ordering it from its ontological roots and entirely renewing its relation to the Creator';[23] if, in short, the fall was not a distortion of creation and the atonement a healing of creation, then we may not look forward to any substantial *re*-creation. Those who, like Elphinstone, reject the fall, cannot see the atonement as either a rescue operation or the rebuilding of a shattered bridge.[24] Those who, like Hick, restrict the atonement to human transformation, truncate too the hope of our calling. For Jesus, by contrast, the hope was for resurrection[25] and the *re*newal of *all* things.[26] Peter's speech in the temple holds out the hope of an *apocatastasis*, a restoration of *all* things through Christ,[27] of which the healing miracles are just foretastes.[28] Revelation, too, proffers a cosmic and not merely human redemption: the whole of created reality

20. *Cf.*, Romans 8:21.
21. Romans 8:23.
22. Hick, *Death and Eternal Life*, pp. 463-64.
23. T. F. Torrance, *Divine and Contingent Order* (Oxford: Oxford University Press, 1981), p. 134.
24. Elphinstone, *Freedom*, p. 142.
25. *E.g.*, Luke 20:35.
26. Matthew 19:28.
27. Acts 3:21.
28. The word for 'restoration' comes from the same root as the word for 'restore' in the account of the healing of the man with the withered hand in Mark 3:5.

is to be made new.[29] To offer less is to short-change our hope-less contemporaries; to offer as much requires us to posit a cosmic fall.

The Doctrine of the Fall and Pastoral Truth Telling

If nature is fallen, then disease and disaster and death are extrinsic to the divine design; if nature is not fallen, then they are intrinsic — paradoxically intrinsic, or indirectly intrinsic, if you like, but intrinsic. Taking the latter route, therefore, leads to a pastoral impasse, for we instinctively and rightly shrink from telling anyone that their suffering or bereavement is the will of God. We long to tell them (verbally or perhaps just by our attempt to give and be to them the love of God) that God is not behind their suffering — he is against it. We want them to experience God, not as the instigator or inflictor of their pain, but as their co-sufferer. And we want to hold out to them the hope of a real future in which death and mourning and crying and pain are no more. What the doctrine of the fall does, at least in versions which include the fallenness of nature, is to put historico-mythical ground under the feet of such an instinct. For if there has been no fall, if the structures of creation are now as God wanted or required them to be, then suffering has a more direct place in his purposes than if there *has* been a fall and creation is now *far* from the harmless and harmonious environment he intended.

And if we wish to say that God suffers with his creatures, that in all our afflictions, he is afflicted, then we need to put distance between God and evil. We need to assert an hiatus between God's purposes and present reality. As Paul Fiddes writes: 'J. Moltmann perceptively remarks that the feeling of sorrow for suffering is in fact a protest against it, and so to believe that God participates in the sorrow of the world is to say that God himself is in protest against the conditions of natural evil. Thus the sorrow of the cross, no less than the glory of the resur-

29. Revelation 21:1-5; *cf.*, Isaiah 65:17, 66:22, 2 Peter 3:13. It may be that the traditional but wholly unbiblical language of 'heaven' as the locus of post-thanatical existence dug a channel down which the waters of a reductionist eschatology could flow. (See N. T. Wright's 1993 Drew Lecture, to be published in a forthcoming volume of Drew lectures.) I am suggesting that those waters flow, in part at least, from the spring of an inadequate account of the fall.

rection is God's contradiction of the suffering and death of the present world. With regard to pain, God is a protester rather then an educator. . . . A sorrowing God is in protest against natural evil, of which death as we know it now is the paradigm. If natural evil were a necessary consequence of creation, God could hardly protest against it or feel it as something "most alien" to his being; He would have planned it as an educational enterprise, and it would be altogether "most His own"'.[30]

Thus, if in truth we are to tell people that their suffering is not the will of God, that he shares in it and will one day eradicate all suffering, then for all of these pastoral assertions we need the undergirding of an understanding of creation as good but fallen, and of suffering as having no original nor ultimate place in the purposes of God but as assaulted by the healing miracles and, pre-eminently, the suffering and resurrection of Christ. If, as Fiddes suggests, death is indeed the paradigm of natural evil, and if, in the words of John Owen, we witness the death of death in the death of Christ, then God is the enemy of natural evil, both as its victim and as its victor.

The Doctrine of the Fall and Ethical Resources

If nature is fallen, then that transforms our view of what is natural. If the fall stands between creation and the present, 'then there is no straightforward line to be drawn from present reality to the purposes of God.'[31] If natural evil is extrinsic to God's purposes, then we are mandated to fight against it, where we can. If what is has not always been and will not always be, then that relativises the *status quo* — and gives us both a litmus paper by which to assess it and a fulcrum point from which to change it. If there has been an hiatus between the way God wanted his world to be and the way it now is, then ethics must take note of that hiatus, to avoid giving normative status to that which is a facet of our fallenness. Rumours of a different blueprint and

30. Paul Fiddes, *The Creative Suffering of God* (Oxford: Clarendon Press, 1990), pp. 223, 229, referring to Jürgen Moltmann's *The Crucified God* (London: SCM Press, 1974), pp. 225-26.

31. From my article on 'The Fall' in Paul Barry Clarke and Andrew Linzey (eds.), *Dictionary of Ethics, Theology and Society* (London: Routledge, 1996), p. 370.

glimpses of a healed future give us a different vision to see with and to work for. Whether we see nature as natural or as fallen will affect how we act towards it and within it. I want to argue that the eclipse of the doctrine of the fall has left us ethically hamstrung as we wrestle with the particular contemporary challenges which confront us as a church. Let me give four examples.

First, animal rights. If nature is not fallen, then God himself deliberately set up a system in which one animal has to kill another in order to live. Not only is this difficult to square with the God we meet in Christ (who gave up *his* life that *others* might live); it is also a difficult basis upon which to build a responsible ethic for our interaction with the animal world. To see the predatory chain as God-given would weaken any theological attempt to underpin and advocate the practice of animal welfare. To see nature as fallen, however, would enable precisely that re-evaluation of our exploitative dealings with the animal world which modern technology has made urgent and which our contemporaries demand.

Secondly, homosexuality. In his article, 'An Issue that will not go away',[32] Bishop Hugh Montefiore asks regarding homosexuals, 'Why cannot we accept that this is how God made them?' There are logical, psychological and sociological problems with the position implied in this question;[33] we are concerned here only with the theological problem. For Montefiore's question assumes that one may legitimately make deductions about the will of God from the way things are; that if this is the way things are, then this is the way God intends them to be. Yet that would imply that God always gets his way, and the very occurrence of sin should alert us to the fact that there are important senses in which this is not the case. If, as I have already argued, there has been an hiatus on the path from creation to present reality, then that would render illegitimate all attempts to argue back from the *status quo* to the creational intentions of God as if no such deviation from those intentions had taken place. Such reading back from the way things are to the will of God, which is rightly rejected in the pastoral context, should not be accepted in the ethical context either.

32. *Church Times* (1 Sept. 1995).
33. For a fuller exposition of this question, see my Latimer House Comment, '"God Made Me This Way": What Is Natural in a Fallen World?'.

Thirdly, genetic screening and 'therapeutic' abortion. The fact of spontaneous abortion (particularly where there is abnormality) is frequently used as a justification for therapeutic abortion: nature weeds out genetic abnormalities by spontaneous abortion, nature reflects the will of God, therefore it is right for us to weed out abnormalities ourselves. However, this is a dangerously de-humanising argument. Not only does it ignore the possibility that nature is fallen and does not unambiguously reflect the will of God; by doing that, it also risks justifying the unjustifiable. As it stands, it would seem to regard miscarriages as the will of God — which would not be acceptable within the pastoral context. And if some people were discovered to be genetically predisposed to violence or to uncontrollable and unwanted sexual imposition, would those predispositions not have to be seen as further instantiations of God's will? Would it not be simpler, and more undergirding of all that is truly human, just to deny that nature is unequivocally the outworking of God's design, and to posit, on the contrary, that division, disease and death are symptoms of the distortedness of creation?

Fourthly, the Nine O'Clock Service. In 1995, an alternative worship group, which had tried to utilise modern cultural forms and technologies in the service of Christian worship, had to be closed down due to abuse of power and sexual misconduct on the part of the group's (ordained Anglican) leadership. When nature is seen as unambiguously good, as it is in the theology of Matthew Fox which NOS espoused,[34] then, theologically, it is but a short step to the worship of nature, and, ethically, our every instinct and urge will be thought of as unambiguously good too, and the gratification of those cravings will be viewed, indiscriminately, as appropriate and liberating. When the fall is discounted, and creation is seen as good in such a flat and undifferentiated way that every aspect of our current existence is assumed to be underwritten by the 'very good' of God; if our physiology and psychology are thought to be much as God wants them, and if there is no concept of a blueprint by which to assess some forms of that physiology and some promptings of that psychology as distorted or distorting, then roadblocks are removed from the path towards the practice and approval of pagan spirituality and sexuality.

34. See Mark Stibbe, 'Seeds of Spiritual Decay', *Church Times* (1 Sept. 1996).

That such spirituality and sexuality are likely to take manipulative, exploitative forms is inevitable, given the cruelty of that very natural order which is being affirmed as good. Thus the abandonment of the doctrine of the fall tends to be accompanied by the removal of those very ethical constraints which subdue, purify and redirect our distorted impulses and yearnings, and which thereby buttress our humanity.

Towards a Post-Darwinian Doctrine of the Fall

If therefore we are to present God credibly to our generation, if we are to offer him as the cure and not the cause of the ugliness and brokenness of our world, if our contemporaries are to be able to overcome the understandable cynicism of our age and trust God when all else has proved untrustworthy, if they are to be able to rage rightly at death and the other distortions of the world without raging at the world's Creator, if we are to be faithful to one Lord in a world of many lords, if we are to have a mission to whole human beings and a cosmic hope, if we are to fight suffering and to assure those in pain that God is against their suffering but is for them and with them and shares their pain, if we are to live out and speak out an ethics which challenges and subverts the *status quo* rather than assuming it and acquiescing in it, if we are to discover what is *truly* natural and so act as signs of contradiction, going against the flow of the fallen world but with the grain of the coming kingdom, if we are to enjoy nature and work to protect and heal it without worshipping it or reflecting its violence, if we are to know and make known the beauty and freedom of purity and self-control, if we are to help people to see this world as the creation of a good God and to meet him within it, then we need to insist that it is not now as God made it to be. We need to see it as good but fallen. We need to find ways of continuing to proclaim, in a post-Darwinian world, a doctrine of the fallenness of nature.

But how is such a task to be accomplished? How can we maintain that this world is not now as God made it to be, how can we ascribe all that afflicts our world, not to the direct and deliberate intentionality of the Creator, but to the free and culpable agency of creatures, if many of the afflictions to which we and other creatures are susceptible

78

preceded our own emergence as a species? If Genesis 3 blames the present lack of sociological (3:12, 16; 4:8), psychological (3:7) and ecological (3:16-19) harmony in our world upon the historical loss of theological (3:6, 8) harmony between humanity and God, and if modern biological science insists that there was no creaturely harmony prior to the appearance of *homo sapiens* but that the very evolutionary development which led to humanity was itself the product of predation and pain — how can these positions ever be reconciled? The first step towards a post-Darwinian account of the fallenness of nature is to notice that the Genesis fall narrative does not, in fact, paint a picture of the prelapsarian cosmos in the colours of paradisal perfection. For one thing, we are presented, in the person of the serpent, with a part of the created order which is already operating in direct contravention of the Creator's commands, even before the disobedience of our first parents. For another, the human pair is commanded to 'fill the earth and subdue it' — even before the human fall, there is that which needs to be subdued. Third, the fertile and co-operative environment into which they are placed is only a garden — the narrative does not suggest that the whole of creation exhibits the harmonious *shalom* of the garden. Indeed, the garden may be seen as a restorative bridgehead within a fallen creation, the firstfruits of the Creator's re-creative determination.

If, then, creation had already fallen far from the harmonious purposes of its Creator even prior to the divisive and destructive disobedience of humanity, to what agency may that distance and disharmony be attributed? What creature or creatures could have caused that pre-human fallenness which the fossils evince? Three candidates have been put forward this century. First was the appropriation by N. P. Williams[35] of the Platonic notion of a World-Soul and his adaptation of it for post-Darwinian theodical purposes. Williams suggested that this World-Soul comprised in a unity all the personal and impersonal created entities of cosmic history, and that it should be seen as free, personal and self-conscious. It was thus capable of voluntarily veering away from the will and love of the Creator, and Williams posits a pre-mundane fall of the World-Soul as the cause of

35. N. P. Williams, *The Ideas of the Fall and of Original Sin* (London: Longmans, Green and Co., 1927).

the vitiation of the creative process. Second, exponents of process theology have proposed a metaphysic in which every level of reality — not just the human level — has freedom, and the currently competitive and predatory character of nature is the consequence of that freedom being used to go against the purpose and promptings of the Creator.[36] Third, Dom Illtyd Trethowan, Eric Mascall, Hans Urs von Balthasar, Alvin Plantinga, Stephen Davis and others have drawn on the Judaeo-Christian tradition of the fall of the angels, and suggested that such a deviation from the person and purpose of the Creator may have distorted the course and development of creation. I have argued elsewhere[37] that not only is this third proffered explanation of the fallenness of nature a logical possibility, as Plantinga has shown,[38] but it is also capable of theologically plausible exposition. Here it is only possible to sketch the briefest outline of this hypothesis's narrative framework. On this account, the enterprise of creation is not blood-stained by the will of the Creator, nor by some necessity which circumscribes his generative power, but by the voluntary defection of free creatures in the spiritual dimensions of God's world. Human beings thus emerge from a matrix of divided, violent and bloody interactions, but, having been stamped with the image of God, are called not only to relationships which reflect the character of their divine origin rather than of their evolutionary lineage, but also to heal the divisions and subdue the distortions of the already-fallen world in which they developed. Instead of following this therapeutic vocation, however, human beings used their freedom to join in the rebellion, to become distorted themselves in their turn, and to exacerbate rather than eradicate the evil effects of the demonic deviation.

That such a vocation was realistic and is conceivable may be seen by contemplating the life and ministry of Christ. There, at long last, a human being took up the human vocation, resisted the demonic beguilement, responded to the divine beckoning — with the consequence that creation began to be healed, and evil to be subdued, around him.

36. See especially David Ray Griffin, *God, Power and Evil* (Philadelphia: Westminster Press, 1976), and *Evil Revisited* (Albany: State University of New York Press, 1991).

37. See Lloyd, 1997a, and, more briefly, Lloyd, 1997b.

38. See, for example, A. Plantinga, *God, Freedom and Evil* (New York: Harper and Row, 1974).

Storms were stilled, illnesses were healed, death was reversed, the strong man bound and plundered. It took God to live a fully human life, but nevertheless it was a fully human life which finally began to undo the fallenness of the whole created order.

On this hypothesis, therefore, the fallenness of nature is the consequence of the angelic fall, but its continued fallenness is the consequence of human failure to play its proper rôle in the purposes of God, for if humanity had been obedient to its vocation, then creation would have been restored. This, I submit, maintains the appropriate balance between seeing ourselves as victims and seeing ourselves as culprits, enabling us to take responsibility for our world without having to shoulder, implausibly, the blame for evils which predated our emergence. Furthermore, it enables us to say what needs to be said theologically, scientifically and pastorally. It enables us to say what needs to be said theologically, that God is not the author of evil, but that all evil, all suffering, all disharmony is the result of free creatures using their freedom to contravene the purpose and calling of God, whose goodness is therefore not compromised. Second, it enables us to say what needs to be said scientifically, allowing and accounting for pre-human evil and suffering. Third, it enables us to say what needs to be said pastorally, that suffering is never the direct will or desire of God, but that, on the contrary, God is against it and calls us to fight it.

It is therefore possible, as well as necessary, to hold to the fallenness of nature in the post-Darwinian world. We are not forced to see God as responsible for the way the world is. We are able to hold, without inconsistency, that the atonement encompassed (and eschatology will embrace) the physicality of our humanity as well as of our world, and that our mission as a church should do likewise. We are committed to a high christology, for what is needed is not repair but re-creation, and the agent of re-creation must needs be the Creator. We are enabled to assure sufferers that God is not the inflictor but the sharer (and ultimately the transformer and destroyer) of their pain. We are forbidden to give normative status to the way things currently are. Our ethics are therefore to be based, not on what is, but on what was to be and what is to be, for which we are ultimately and utterly dependent upon him who is the Alpha and the Omega, the First and the Last, the Beginning and the End.

Questions

1. Is it possible to believe in the goodness of God without a doctrine of the fall?

2. What is lost if 'you reduce the doctrine of the atonement to a statement about human forgiveness'?

3. In what ways should mission be about more than 'the saving of human souls'? What kind of mission might 'meet the aspirations and touch the concerns of socially and environmentally aware and embodied men and women'?

4. Do you agree that there has been 'christological seepage' in the modern church? What other elements are there 'of the contemporary church's loss of confidence in the gospel'?

5. What sort of future hope should the church be offering the world?

6. In what ways, positive and negative, do our doctrinal beliefs impinge upon our pastoral care?

7. 'Our ethics are therefore to be based, not on what is, but on what was to be and what is to be, for which we are ultimately and utterly dependent upon him who is the Alpha and the Omega, the First and the Last, the Beginning and the End.' In what ways are we ethically dependent upon Christ?

Identity in Christ and Sexuality

STANTON L. JONES

Summary

Sexual conduct, particularly homosexuality, is hotly debated in the churches of the Western world. Behind this issue lies the truth of our creation and fallenness. Contested understandings of Scripture likewise are central, whether it is authoritative, irrelevant to modernity, simply wrong in places, or merely suggestive of a loving lifestyle. The future debate needs to address the correct ethical framework and heed the divine command ordering human sexual terms universally. Dialogue is good but has the problem of potentially eroding gospel 'common ground'. The deep questions of proper views of personhood and the goods of sex as created by God need careful attention. This debate may reflect Western cultural problems and we may need to listen carefully to African and Asian churches in considering which claims are truly divisive and unloving.

Introduction

Penthouse is not a frequent outlet for ecclesiastical news. Nevertheless, the December, 1996, issue of the raucously pornographic American 'men's magazine' contained a documented exposé of a purported clerical homosexual and transvestite sex ring in the Diocese of Long Island, New York. A number of clergy, it claimed, had regularly cruised Latin America, lured young men to Long Island with promises of good jobs, and then entrapped them in sexual servitude, even involving them in group homosexual orgies in a parish church sanctuary. *Penthouse* printed irrefutable photographs of the homosexual activities of one priest with a male partner.

In his official response to the *Penthouse* story, the accused priest denied many of the illegal or more grotesque *Penthouse* allegations (entrapment of international visitors, group orgies, desecration of the sacraments and of a church sanctuary, and so forth). In addition to his denials, this priest repented of an interesting catalogue of sins — of having let himself be used by others, of being self-deceived, of letting infatuation blind him to the reality of how nasty his young homosexual partner was, of not realising that age-disparate relationships cannot work, of the indiscretion of letting himself be photographed having sex, and of embarrassing his church. He did not, however, repent in his formal statement for any sexual sin. In his mind, and in the mind of many in the American Episcopal church, there was nothing wrong with his having had a homosexual relationship, nor with having this relationship outside of the bounds of holy matrimony.

Let us assume that his denials are substantiated, clearing him of any illegalities and of the more extreme allegations. With those allegations bracketed, we must ask, 'Did he do anything wrong?' 'Was his sexual behaviour godly?'

In both 1991 and 1994, the General Convention of the Episcopal Protestant Church in the USA rejected proposed canon laws declaring that Episcopal clergy should limit sexual intimacy to holy matrimony. The General Convention in 1994 passed a canonical statute declaring sexual orientation to be no barrier to ordination to the priesthood. In 1996, an Episcopal court exonerated a bishop who had knowingly ordained a practising homosexual man from charges of violating his consecration vows and the canons of the church. Without a firm definition of marriage as a union of one man and one woman, and a firm declaration of the immorality of full sexual intimacy outside the bounds of marriage, the American church appears to have no grounds on which to condemn the accused priest of sexual immorality. Many American Episcopal bishops are determined to export this 'enlightened, progressive approach' to sexuality to the world-wide Anglican communion. Roughly one quarter of ECUSA clergy are divorced and remarried. Is this the way of Christ? Is this a new message of the Holy Spirit of God to the church today?

The Past

In being called to follow Christ in costly discipleship, we are truly, in the words of one of the Lambeth themes, 'called to full humanity'. Our Lord said, 'The thief comes only to steal and kill and destroy; I have come that they may have life, and have it to the full' (John 10:10). In embracing the salvation offered to us through the life, death and resurrection of our Lord Jesus Christ, we are never called to cease being human, to despise our humanness, or to try to transcend our humanness. Rather, we are called to become the human beings we would have been had we not been marred and disfigured by the ravages of sin, and to become the human beings we would be were we able to be in full, complete and utterly unhindered communion with our maker and redeemer.

Our sexuality is a part of that humanness which we are meant to receive with thanksgiving, offer to God for his sanctification, and enjoy with gratitude as a gift from God (1 Tim. 4:1-5). What does it mean, with regard to our sexuality, that we are called by Christ to full humanity? This question is at the centre of the ecclesiastical debates about homosexuality and about how all persons are to experience and conduct their sexual lives. Fundamentally divergent and deeply incompatible understandings of the meaning of our sexuality, of what it means to be a person, and of the Christian faith, are resulting in divergent answers to this core question. Let us begin by looking to the past.

What is the Christian church's traditional view of sexuality? This is a difficult question to answer, as the views of Christians have, over the millennia, ranged from Corinthian sensuality and lasciviousness to the asceticism of the desert mystics and many of the second and third century patriarchs. Further, the Scriptures fail to present the kind of systematised treatment of sexual ethics and the reasoning behind those ethics that so many long for today. Nevertheless, the church, through much of its history, has regarded something like the following brief sketch as its core teaching on sexuality.

Our embodiment as physical beings, our differentiation into male and female, and our capacity for a loving physical union with a person of the other sex, including our capacity for sexual union in intercourse, were all created intentionally by God, and called 'very good!' on the sixth day of creation. Two of the prime purposes of sexual intercourse are mentioned in the early creation stories — procreation, and union where two become one flesh. Other purposes of sexual intercourse include pleasure and the satisfaction of what is regarded as a normal human desire (Prov. 5; 1 Cor. 7:1-5). It is the purpose or function of union that appears to be most central, as our Lord made this notion of union central to his teaching on divorce and the nature of marriage (Matt. 19), and Paul speaks of this purpose of union in describing the role which Christian marriage should play in instructing the world about the nature of the relationship between Christ and his church.[1]

Our sexuality was marred by the fall, along with all other aspects of life. What had previously been an unadulterated good was now, and forevermore, experienced as a battleground of twisted desires and motives, and an occasion for much suffering. Our sexuality became an arena in which many of the pathologies of human life are played out, and it became a focus for God's redeeming work. God's redemptive work began through the revelation of the outlines of his moral will for our lives in the Law of the Old Testament. In the moral law, God began to rein in the most offensive of human perversions of his beautiful gift of sexuality. Adultery, homosexual behaviour, rape, incest, bestiality were all condemned in harsh terms.

How did our Lord, in his earthly ministry, deal with sexual ethics? The topic was not a major preoccupation of his during his ministry in Palestine. Yet it is notable that, unlike his observance (or lack thereof) and teaching on the ceremonial law,[2] our Lord never modified any portion of the moral law dealing with sexuality other than to raise the expectations on us by expanding the domain of application of the law of God from what we do externally, with our bodies, to that *plus* what we do with our minds and hearts — this by condemning lust with the same vigour as any overt behaviour. Jesus himself lived a life of chaste singleness and commended that life as virtuous and a path pleasing to

1. Recent summaries of the traditional view in Anglican circles can be found in *Issues in Human Sexuality: A Statement by the House of Bishops of the General Synod of the Church of England* (Harrisburg, PA: Morehouse, 1991), and in Michael Banner et al., *The St. Andrew's Day Statement: An Examination of the Theological Principles Affecting the Homosexuality Debate* (released Nov. 1995, in response to the request of the Church of England Evangelical Council, PO Box 93, Newcastle, NE6 5WL UK).

2. Following the three-fold distinction of Ceremonial, Civil, and Moral Law as articulated in *The Thirty Nine Articles* embraced by all Anglican fellowships.

God, yet in his teachings on marriage continued the Jewish pattern of affirming marriage and the unifying gift of sexual intimacy as wonderful gifts from God. Paul and the other apostles continued this pattern of maintaining continuity with Old Testament moral law; we have no historical or textual indication of any fundamental revision of the Hebraic understanding of sexual morality in the life of the early church.

Christians have thus had good reason to regard a reasonable summary of Christian teaching on sexual morality to be that God commends chastity within marriage (the enjoyment of one's spouse and the shunning of all other sexual intimacies) and chastity outside of marriage (refraining from impure sexual relations); these have been the foundational sexual norms of our faith community. It is worth noting that the assumptions about the purposes of our sexuality mentioned earlier informed the Christian understanding both of what is moral and immoral, and of what is natural and unnatural. With regard to the latter, 'natural' was loosely understood as that which was in accord with God's purpose for our sexuality. Homosexual behaviour then was wrong: both because is was contrary to the revealed will of God as expressed in the moral law, and because it was unnatural, in that it could not well serve all of the purposes for which our sexuality was given.

The Present

These norms are no longer commonly shared or even widely upheld across the world-wide Anglican communion. While there is disagreement about all aspects of sexual morality, most of the energy and attention today is focused on the topic of homosexuality; it is here that this essay will focus.

Homosexual behaviour is addressed only briefly by the biblical authors. It assumes importance as a topic because real human beings struggle at this point and are either led towards, or away from, loving communion with our merciful God. It also assumes importance because it is here that the energies of the broader debate about sexual ethics are focused, a debate which is in turn a mere focal point for our most fundamental debates regarding the nature of God's revelation to us, of his claim over us, and of our very understanding of our natures and callings.

What are the terms of the current debate about homosexual behaviour? One way to understand the debate is to consider the different understandings of the meaning and relevance of the biblical texts on this topic. At the risk of oversimplification, four basic patterns of engagement with the biblical material may be discerned. First, that the moral evaluations of the Bible[3] and Christian tradition regarding homosexual behaviour are clear, relevant and binding today.

Second, that the moral evaluations of the Bible and Christian tradition regarding the particular types of homosexual behaviour known to the biblical authors are clear and binding today, but are not relevant to the present debate because homosexuality, understood today as an orientation and a consensual and loving lifestyle, is a different phenomenon than what confronted the biblical authors; in short, the biblical witness is largely irrelevant to homosexuality today.

Third, that the moral evaluations of the Bible and Christian tradition regarding homosexual behaviour must be balanced by other facets of God's equally authoritative revelation in church tradition and through human reason. It is through human reason, particularly through modern scientific discovery and our gradual emancipation from ignorance and prejudice, that we have become free to see homosexual lifestyle as a natural and normal and good human variant; in short, the biblical witness is wrong on this matter and has been superseded by a more authoritative human reason.

Fourth, that the moral evaluations of the Bible and Christian tradition regarding homosexual behaviour can provide only general moral guidance such as the imperative to love and to be just, and it is only the general moral guidance of Scripture which is clear, relevant and binding today.

3. The most commonly cited and most crucial texts that deal with the topic of homosexual behaviour are Leviticus 18:22; 30:13; Romans 1:26-27; and 1 Corinthians 6:9-10; other relevant texts include Genesis 19:4-11; Deuteronomy 23:17; 1 Kings 14:24; 15:12; 22:46; 2 Kings 23:7; Judges 19:22-30; 1 Timothy 1:8-11. For a helpful introduction to understanding these biblical texts, see Thomas Schmidt, *Straight and Narrow? Compassion and Clarity in the Homosexuality Debate* (Downers Grove, IL: InterVarsity Press, 1995).

1. The Bible as Authoritative

The first position is the traditional view of the church throughout its history. Given the seemingly clear words of Scripture and the consistent witness of the company of the saints on this issue, it would seem that we would need compelling reasons to depart from that witness, compelling evidence that we have received a 'new word from the Lord'.

2. The Bible as Irrelevant

The heart of the second position above is the claim that the scriptural injunctions against homosexual behaviour and its normative approval of celibacy and heterosexual marriage are somehow unclear or irrelevant to the present situation. It is often asserted that the Old Testament Hebrews may have known of such homosexual behaviour as the sodomisation of defeated armies by their conquerors, or of certain types of cultic homosexual practices associated with pagan worship practices, and the early Christians may have known about the paedophilic predilections of the Greek elite. But both were utterly ignorant of the type of stable preferential pattern of attraction toward the same gender that we today understand homosexual orientation to be.[4]

The problem with this argument is that we know beyond doubt that the Hebrews, from the earliest record to the time of the early church, were surrounded by alien cultures that practised every type of sexual practice imaginable to the sensualistic modern mind. In New Testament times, male and female homosexual behaviour was well known, being amply depicted on decorated pottery and described in many manuscripts known to modern historians and archaeologists. By reasonable inference, we may assume it to be well known to Paul, whose declarations of the sinfulness of homosexual behaviour in Romans, 1 Corinthians and 1 Timothy are so pivotal. Smith[5] notes that by the time of Paul, reports of pederastic practice were rare in the archaeological record of the era, while

4. See the widely cited books by John Boswell, *Christianity, Social Tolerance, and Homosexuality* (Chicago: University of Chicago Press, 1980), and by Robin Scroggs, *The New Testament and Homosexuality* (Philadelphia: Fortress, 1983).
5. Mark Smith, 'Ancient Bisexuality and the Interpretation of Romans 1:26-27', *Journal of the American Academy of Religion* 64 (Summer, 1996), pp. 223-56.

reports of a wide variety of other consensual homosexual practices, male and female, grow in frequency. He argues that Paul's inclusion of female homosexual practice in his discussion in Romans 1 obviates any interpretation that he is referring to Hellenistic pederasty, and establishes just how aware and knowledgeable of the wide array of sexual practices of his time the apostle was. Smith denies that there can be 'any avoiding the conclusion that Paul considers homosexual behaviour a sin'[6] and concludes that Romans 1 must be interpreted as Paul's declaration of the continuing moral relevance of the Levitical prohibitions on homosexual behaviour. He argues for the legitimacy of asking whether the situation in Rome at the time of the writing of Romans is sufficiently similar to our modern context to establish the relevance of the biblical pronouncements to our situation, and concludes that it is. So the core question is no longer 'Is Paul relevant?' but rather 'Is Paul correct?'. Is it any wonder then that some today denounce Paul's views, calling them 'texts of terror' and demanding their removal from the canon of Scripture?[7]

3. The Bible as Errant

If the scriptural injunctions against homosexual behaviour are not irrelevant to the modern situation, may we dismiss them as wrong? It might be argued that we have revelation not just in Scripture but also in tradition and reason, and that the evidences of science are so clear on this issue as to supersede the specific words of Scripture. I have argued elsewhere[8] (1) that the logic establishing the relevance of the scientific findings to the moral debate in most church documents is often unclear or simply missing; (2) that the supposed scientific findings are usually presented to discredit an impoverished caricature of the traditional view

6. Smith, 'Ancient Bisexuality', p. 247.

7. Robert Williams, *Just as I Am: A Practical Guide to Being Out, Proud and Christian* (New York: Harper Perennial, 1992), p. 53; G. D. Comstock, *Gay Theology without Apology* (Cleveland: Pilgrim Press, 1993).

8. Stanton Jones and Mark Yarhouse, 'The Use, Misuse, and Abuse of Science in the Ecclesiastical Homosexuality Debates', in D. Balch (ed.), *The Bible and Sexual Ethics* (Grand Rapids: Eerdmans, forthcoming). Stanton Jones and Mark Yarhouse, 'Science and the Ecclesiastical Homosexuality Debates', *Christian Scholar's Review* 26 (Summer 1997), pp. 446-77.

of sexual morality or to support the classification of homosexual behaviour as morally neutral rather than to advance a nuanced moral perspective; and (3) that the findings of science on this topic are much more provisional and sketchy than is commonly realised. Finally, I argue that while science can properly inform and contextualise good theology, the relevance of what we know about homosexuality from science to the Anglican moral debate is quite limited.

To expand on this last point, let us look at the four areas which are most frequently presented as relevant to the moral debate — prevalence, status as a 'mental disorder', etiology, and change.[9] Some suggest that homosexuality cannot be wrong if it is a characteristic of a large portion of people. The evidence suggests that homosexual behaviour typifies only a small segment of the population in the West — probably less than 3%. Prevalence, however, seems to have no direct relationship to morality; we can all think of frequent and infrequent sins which continue to be regarded as sins regardless of their incidence.

Some argue that we cannot regard homosexual behaviour as sin if it is one facet of what science declares to be a normal lifestyle variation. The evidence regarding the status of homosexuality as a 'mental disorder' is inconclusive. It is a matter of historical fact that homosexuality per se has been removed from the official diagnostic nomenclatures for 'mental illness' of the Western medical establishment, but this outcome appears to have been more a political than scientific necessity. It is often argued that research shows homosexuality to be a healthy and normal lifestyle variant, but this is a misrepresentation of the literature in this area. Neither the evidence that homosexuality is a normal variant nor that it is a mental disorder is convincing.[10] In any case, the value of the answer to this question for the moral debate is minimal. Many of what we commonly regard to be sins are not mental disorders (pride, greed, insensitivity to the plight of the poor, idolatry) and many of what we commonly regard to be mental disorders are not sins (anxiety, depression, paranoia).

Some argue that acting on homosexual desires cannot be wrong if homosexual orientation develops due to factors beyond the control

---

9. For more detailed argumentation and a review of the scientific evidence, see Jones and Yarhouse, 'Science and the Ecclesiastical Homosexuality Debates.'

10. Jones and Yarhouse, "Science and the Ecclesiastical Homosexuality Debates.'

or choice of the individual. Research on etiology or causation of the homosexual condition has made some striking advances. The current state of that research might be summarised in three key points — that biological factors may contribute to the development of this proclivity for some people; that there is credible evidence that psychological factors contribute as well; and that simplistic models of causation that focus only on one variable are inadequate. When we examine the research, we are forced to think in terms of multiple contributing causal factors. Similar research on other human problems, such as drunkenness and violence, which have clear moral implications has suggested that many different types of factors, including the genetic, can contribute to the development of these patterns. Such research does not answer the moral question — 'should a person who finds himself or herself with such proclivities indulge them?' We each may have received a genetic and/or biological and/or environmental push toward any number of unfortunate proclivities. Understanding those influences may increase our understanding and compassion, and may shape our pastoral response to those conditions, but knowledge of what causes homosexual orientation is irrelevant to the question of whether it is morally right to engage in homosexual behaviour.

Finally, it is often argued that since homosexuals cannot change their orientation, homosexual practice must be a valid life-style option. The premise is in error; the evidence suggests that some homosexuals can, and do, change orientation though this change is never easy and may be available to fewer than would be desired, perhaps even a small minority. Even if the premise were correct, though, the conclusion would not follow. The gospel does not promise healing in this life; rather, it calls us to a life of costly obedience to God's revealed will with the promise of God's companionship and strengthening while we are on that path. The call of Christ to the active homosexual is, most fundamentally, a call to godly chastity as a single person, and this is a call to which the statistics regarding the probabilities of conversion to heterosexuality are irrelevant.

4. The Bible as Merely Suggestive

I will address only briefly the fourth position on the relevance of Scripture to our sexuality debate which claims it is only the general moral guidance of Scripture which is clear, relevant and binding today. This view basically suggests that it is wrong to say 'God has spoken', and rather that it is more proper to suggest that 'God has hinted or generally suggested'. One can be a sincere follower of Christ and also take such a modest and low view of revelation, but such a view was certainly not the view of our Lord himself of the Scriptures, and is discordant with the church's historical understanding of God's revelation of himself and his will to us.

Proponents of this view do typically assume that there is an authority which can guide them in choosing given that Scripture is merely suggestive. That authority is that of their own experience or intuition, their own sense of inner 'rightness'. The logic might be summarised simply as follows:

- God has made me, and therefore made the desires I have.
- Everything God makes is good, and therefore my desires are good.
- Good desires deserve to be, even *ought* to be, fulfilled.[11]

A full answer to this logic would require compelling solutions to the problems of theodicy, of God's sovereignty, original sin, and the like. The Christian church, however, has never taught that all our desires come from God, nor that all our desires are good, nor that every good desire ought to be fulfilled. Further, such logic clearly presumes the individual to be in a God-like position of autonomy, perfection, and sovereignty, and that his or her personal inclinations are a reliable ethical guide. Such a view is highly discordant with traditional teachings on our depravity and capacity for self-deception.

The Future

Like the persistent widow seeking justice from the callous judge in the parable of our Lord, these issues of sexuality in general, and homosexuality in particular, are not going to go away. I turn now to the rhetorical frameworks in which the debate is likely to be continued in the next decade in the post-Christian West. The terms of these debates are likely to be exported to Anglican contexts around the world. In each case, we

11. My thanks to colleague Alan Jacobs for helping me clarify this logic.

must ask if these rhetorical frameworks are correct, whether they reflect the same understanding of our condition as that of our Lord himself. As in any debate, the person who sets the terms for the debate holds a decisive advantage in the subsequent discussion.

1. The Ethical Framework for the Debates

The first major dimension determining our approach to this ethical debate will be the ethical framework presumed as the ground for the outcome of the debate. The three great approaches to ethics have been (1) divine command ethics (reasoning from revealed and divinely sanctioned moral rules); (2) deontological ethics (reasoning from universally accepted ethical principles); and (3) consequentialist ethics (reasoning from the value of the consequences of acts). The traditionalist view has been defended in all three frameworks — it has been commonly held in the past that God has spoken decisively against homosexual behaviour as an abomination, that homosexual behaviour violates rational understandings of the natural use of the sexual organs and impulses, and that the consequences of homosexual activity are devastating for its practitioners and others.

A decisive moment in our ecclesiastical debates will be the decision on how to treat the scriptural message. I have already contended for the clarity and continuing relevance of the biblical message on this topic, and have done so presuming the foundational relevance of divine command to our moral reasonings. This view is under attack and actively derided in much of the Anglican West. Two underlying challenges seem in play.

First, there has been a steady loss of confidence in the reality and trustworthiness of revelation in the last two centuries. Just as the serpent caressed Eve with the words, 'Has God said?', so also are we caressed today.

This loss of confidence led originally to a greater trust in human reason and the fruits of the sciences, but in recent times has led to a willingness to trust our human instincts, including our sexual impulses, as revelatory. The body in orthodox Christian understanding is not viewed as evil and hence the source of necessarily bad guidance, but neither has it been viewed as itself a source of revelation. Yet it is common today for Western Christians to hold their own instincts and impulses as a more reliable guide in life than 'the dead myths of ancient peoples'.

The other challenge to taking divine commands as binding is a general unwillingness to commit to law that might be invariant. Rather, there is a taste for fluidity of judgement, one that ultimately places the individual moral actor in the role of the decisive moral judge. Ultimately, it is argued, 'only I can stand in judgement over myself'. Universal moral law is seen as an affront to the radical autonomy of the individual. And so it is. This has been one scandalous aspect of Christianity throughout history — its condemnation of our natural idolatry of the self and our deeply-rooted rebellion against our maker.

Cut loose from its anchoring in divine command, deontological and consequentialist ethics lead to varying outcomes as the participants in the debate take different starting points on the principles by which to evaluate sexual behaviour and on which consequences to examine (and their ranking) in determining the moral status of sexual behaviour. Is there a set of 'natural' sexual acts which stand in contrast to unnatural acts? Are all sexual acts to be evaluated only in terms of their contribution to the development of the person, their contribution to the stability of heterosexual marriage or their contribution to procreation? Which outcomes of sexual behaviour are to be weighed in evaluating sexual behaviour, and in what order of ranking? Some of these issues are dealt with below. For now the reader should note simply that there is no longer a universally recognised set of moral principles by which to evaluate sexual behaviour, nor a consensus on which consequences of sexual behaviour are germane to moral evaluation or on their relative 'moral weights'.

Much of the discussion about the moral valuation of homosexuality is conducted in terms of a laudable concern for basic human rights. Homosexuals should not, as a class, be denied access to basic human rights. But this truth does not determine what these basic human rights are, and particularly whether full moral acceptance of all homosexual acts by the church is a basic human right, along with the access to ordination and marriage that this would entail. Further, it has become commonplace in the West for homosexuals to claim class rights — homosexuals, it is supposed, are a class like racial and gender groups, and full acceptance is demanded just as we insist on the dignity of all persons regardless of gender or race.

This step in reasoning must be strenuously contested as it requires us to view sexuality, especially our sexual orientation, as being identified with the very core of the self. We generally tend to look at such categorisations as male and female, Asian and African, as identifying deep and enduring aspects of personhood, whereas we tend to see categorisations such as carpenter or juggler or socialist as descriptors of what one does or believes without enduring implications for who one is. Surely there are crossovers between who I am and what I do or believe (if I commit adultery, I am an adulterer), but when I cease that behaviour and am cleansed of it by the blood of our Saviour, that activity ceases to have its claim over my identity.

Are there really such things as 'homosexuals', as opposed to merely people who engage in homosexual acts? It would be foolish to deny that many people identify themselves as homosexuals, and to deny that for some the inclinations and passions that lead to homosexual behaviour are constant and intense. Still, should the core of those persons be identified by their sexual proclivities? Many say yes. Episcopal Bishop John Spong has said, 'Homosexuality is an issue of being itself'.[12] This view has been formalised in the academic debate over these issues as 'essentialism', a compound claim that (1) sexual orientations can be distinctly categorised into homosexual and heterosexual, or homosexual, heterosexual and bisexual; and (2) the person's sexual orientation constitutes an enduring, stable foundation around which a person properly, even necessarily, builds a core sense of self, of identity, and hence rightly describes his or her core identity as 'I am gay' or 'I am straight'. Essentialism has not gone uncontested even in the secular academy; in contrast, many propound constructivism, which argues that sexual orientation, rather like membership in a political party ('I am a socialist'), is a way of thinking about one's identity that is driven by changeable, socially determined thought forms and not by unchanging internal essences.[13]

For these and many other reasons, the move to ground discussion of the morality of homosexual behaviour in a presumption that homosexuals constitute a legitimate class such as gender or race on which to claim rights must be challenged. People who engage in homosexual

---

12. John Spong, *Living in Sin?* (San Francisco: Harper and Row, 1988), p. 72.
13. See Jones and Yarhouse, 'Science and the Ecclesiastical Homosexuality Debates.'

behaviour deserve the same basic human rights which all humans can claim, but this has little necessary bearing on the moral questions confronting the church.

Two final notes before leaving this issue of the fundamental ethical framework within which we grapple with this issue. First, it is important that those holding the traditional view do not deny that there is any good obtained in immoral sexual relations. In other words, we have little ground for claiming that homosexual relationships are utterly bereft of any type of good just because we judge homosexual acts to be immoral. The love exchanged by two homosexual men is no more devoid of all good than is that of the engaged couple who exchange sexual intimacies before marriage or the adulterous wife who finds pleasure and affection in an affair for which she is parched by an arid marriage. Homosexual apologists can rightly claim that many homosexual relationships are marked by considerable virtue. We can admit this point, yet deny its relevance to the claim that homosexual behaviour is therefore good or morally neutral.

Second, traditionalists must point out the lack of a coherent and consistent ethic among those promoting change. Proponents of change often subtly imply that the only difference between the traditional moral system and the new, improved alternative is a widened definition of the allowable genders of one's spouse; that in all other ways the ethic remains the same. The reality is more disconcerting. Monogamy is actually quite rare among male homosexual couples.[14] It is thus not surprising that we find in the writings of revisionist ethicists and theologians a striking lack of commitment to monogamy. Many are fairly explicit that nonmonogamous sexual liaisons are an ethical option for Christian homosexuals.[15] Further, it is common to find in the writings of revisionists a plea for blanket support for the 'rights' (meaning full moral acceptance and access to ordination and marriage) of other 'sexual minorities'. The concrete meaning of this phrase is full acceptance of bisexuality and other sexual 'variations' (pederasty? bestiality?), which by definition rule out monogamy. It is hard to construe a

14. See Jones and Yarhouse, 'The Use, Misuse, and Abuse of Science.'
15. For example, Chris Glaser, *Come Home! Reclaiming Spirituality and Community as Gay Men and Lesbians* (San Francisco: Harper and Row, 1990); Michael Vasey, *Strangers and Friends: A New Exploration of Homosexuality and the Bible* (London: Hodder and Stoughton, 1995); Williams, *Just as I Am*.

system that would embrace bisexuality as consistent or continuous with the sexual morality of our Lord and his apostles.

2. The Proper Process for Debate and Dialogue

The second major dimension determining our approach to this ethical debate will be defined by what we hold to be the proper process for these morality deliberations. Is it proper for the church simply to utter an authoritative teaching on sexuality generally and homosexuality in particular? In this age of democracy, does not moral proclamation require some degree of 'consent by those governed'?

The call in the Episcopal Church in the USA has been to 'dialogue'. Many believe that the church cannot pronounce teachings, but rather must accept discordant views within its midst, maintain fellowship with individuals holding wide variations in views, and continue to respect a wide variety of views as 'equally God's word for today'. We have been urged to hold the traditional moral teachings tentatively, to be cautious in pronouncing what was once taken to be 'the word of the Lord'. The articulation of the traditional view on sexual morality has been branded by some as repressive, dogmatic, and narrow. We have been called to seek 'common ground' with those who dissent from the traditional teachings of the church.

What are we being asked to do when we are called to dialogue? A Roman Catholic archbishop, responding to the call to dialogue with dissenters for the sake of establishing common ground and unity, said recently that 'the call to such dialogue obscures the true "common ground" for any effort to bring about unity within the Church. That true "common ground" is found in Scripture and tradition as handed on through the teaching office of the Holy Father and the bishops. . . . We cannot achieve Church unity by accommodating those who dissent from Church teaching — whether on the left or the right. To compromise the faith of the Church is to forfeit our "common ground" and to risk deeper polarization'.[16]

I concur. As a frequent participant in such ecclesiastical dialogues in the American context, I would offer the reader an encouragement

16. James Cardinal Hickey, reported in *First Things* 67 (Nov. 1996), p. 74.

and a warning about participating in sexuality dialogues. The encouragement? Our Lord was in constant and loving dialogue with every sort of person; we should follow his model. Further, unlike him, we are fallen and can be sadly deluded in our pronouncements of truth; dialogue is necessary as we seek truth and acknowledge that our knowledge of God's truth and will is ever partial and distorted. Dialogue can be a way of teaching and of learning how to articulate the teaching of the church in a manner relevant to the contemporary context. We should be in dialogue.

The warning? Much of the push for dialogue comes from those who presuppose that the truth is not fixed, that no one group has a corner on the truth, and that a firm judgement that certain acts are immoral is an arrogant and rejecting and hateful act. Others suppose truth in religion only to be visible from some putatively neutral vantage point outside of traditional religion. Further, radically incompatible fundamental views of the faith — of revelation, salvation and sanctification, ecclesiastical authority, our shared human nature, ethics — are in play in these dialogues, so that there is, in fact, no hope for reaching common ground unless fundamental shifts in these theological foundations take place.[17]

How is unity then to be obtained? Is it through compromise issuing from dialogue with those who disagree with core historic teachings of the church? Or should it be from gathering under the teaching of our Lord as bequeathed to his people through the faithful teaching of the apostles and their successors, recognising that we are one family through the work of the Holy Spirit, sharing one bread and wine, and sharing the life and walking the path of obedience and submission to the Father that Jesus himself walked, bearing his cross as we go?

Those who articulate the traditional view of sexual ethics will be labelled divisive, hateful, and disordered. We will be labelled divisive because we will be seen as driving a wedge between the homosexual and God, and between the homosexual and the church. Traditional Christians are charged with being divisive because they do not welcome homosexual practice; in fact they believe it to be most *unloving* to do

17. John Milbank, 'The End of Dialogue', in G. D'Costa (ed.), *Christian Uniqueness Reconsidered: The Myth of a Pluralistic Theology of Religions* (Maryknoll, NY: Orbis, 1990), pp. 174-91.

so since it welcomes what is damaging and wrong for the individuals concerned. Further they believe that covering up sinful practise is simply covering up the truth about the division revealed by the gospel, that of our sin and need for repentance, transformation and paths into newness of life, visibly enacted at baptism.

If we collude institutionally with patterns of life which are wrong at the behest of those who use the term 'inclusiveness' to warrant certain behaviour patterns, we deceive ourselves and the truth is not in us. This also applies to other wrongs which we may be tempted not to exclude, but this particular one is being pressed on the church by able campaigners who are well meaning but deeply misled. The appeal not to 'define' (literally meaning draw a line round) homosexual patterns of life as conflicting with the plain teaching of the Old and New Testaments, leads to deeper separation from God by structurally conniving with a clear symptom of sin. To affirm the line drawn by the apostolic testimony is ultimately to take the loving and most deeply inclusive option.

Further, in terms of the world-wide ecumenical church, we are in danger of dividing ourselves from the Roman and Orthodox communions and millions of evangelicals. We are also in danger of excluding the many in our congregations who have been faithfully dealing with desires for the same sex according to the plain teaching of Scripture. Such people feel driven out of revisionist churches for fear of once more being drawn back into the gay scene.

This relates to traditionalists being labelled 'hateful' because we will be caricatured as pushing some of God's children out of the church. In many circles, any principled opposition to the revisionist agenda is regarded and stigmatised as a hate crime. For instance, David Norgard wrote, 'I am convinced that the time has come when the church will have to cease its self-defeating practice of consoling those who hate, and to start embracing those whose only conspiracy has been to love'. Perhaps the only effective rebuttal of this is to point out that if clear condemnation of sinful behaviour is a hate crime, then our Lord and his disciples were among some of the worst perpetrators in their intolerance of immoral behaviour.

Finally, we will also be labelled, not just as divisive and hateful, but as disordered. In America, any criticism of homosexual behaviour is often caricatured as the product of 'homophobia', a term which suggests the offender to be neurotically afraid of homosexuals, possessed of a form of mental illness. The informal claim is clearly that objection to the gay-affirming agenda cannot be reasonable, but must be the product of an unjustifiable fear. But this clearly must be regarded as argument by name-calling, as by this logic one could counter that all who advance the acceptance of homosexuality are being disordered by the condition of homophilia — an irrational attraction to homosexuality. Such a sacrifice of rational content in our discussions would be regrettable indeed.

3. The Proper Views of Sexuality and of Persons

The third major dimension determining our approach to this ethical debate will be the fundamental views of sexuality and persons which we bring to the table. Let us begin to return full circle. In discussing 'the past', we examined the historic conceptions of the purposes of sexuality — unity, procreation, pleasure. Today, however, it is common to argue that the only foundational purposes of our sexuality are pleasure and affection. The key shift, unnoticed by many, is from a view that there are certain purposes, and hence certain goods, which are unique and inherent to sexuality, to a view that claims the purposes and goods connected to our sexuality are no different than those attached to all general forms of human interaction. In other words, we are divided on the question, 'Is there anything special, even sacred, about human sexuality?' Episcopal ethicist Philip Turner[18] discusses this brilliantly and incisively. He notes that in the discussions of revisionists there are no 'goods' of sexuality that are peculiar only to sexuality, but only those sorts of generic goods common to shared and bodily life,[19] and hence it follows that sexual acts of any kind must be judged in a manner similar to all other acts (which always works out to a deontological or consequentialist assessment and never an assessment that might presume that God really spoke for all time millennia ago). One might in response point out the incongruity of making sexual orientation the bedrock of identity, on the one hand, while on the other

18. Philip Turner, 'Sex and the Single Life', *First Things* 33 (May, 1993): 15-21.
19. This is clearly the view of James Nelson, *Body Theology* (Louisville: Westminster/John Knox Press, 1992).

making sexuality so inconsequential as to judge it ethically by the same standards or grid by which we judge table manners. But more importantly, Turner asks whether our sexuality has any pre-existing purposes which place a moral claim on how we understand and respond to our sexuality, purposes which are more fundamental morally than the easily understood human purposes of pleasure and affection. In our debate about homosexual morality, *everything hinges on our starting assumptions about what sexuality is for and about.* If sexual acts have nothing distinctive to them, then moral evaluation of them must be grounded in the same evaluative standards we use for all other forms of human interaction — was the act loving, fair, kind, and so forth. But if sexual acts are different, if they have inherent qualities that are fundamentally different in some ways from all other types of acts (and this is what we claim when we speak of the capacity of sexual acts to foster unity and to yield procreation), then we must use different standards to evaluate them.

Not only are fundamentally different visions of sexuality in play, but so also are fundamentally divergent visions of the person. At particular issue is the question of where the physical life fits into our understanding of personhood. Traditionalists can and must acknowledge the centrality of our embodiedness, our physicality, to what it means to be a person. The great doctrines of creation (God made us physical, sexual beings), incarnation (Christ became flesh and dwelt among us), and of our resurrection (we will be restored to permanent bodily existence for eternity) combine to affirm our embodiment. But an affirmation of bodily existence is not the same as asserting that full sexual expression, access to full sexual intimacy, is essential either to full humanness or to sanctification.

Nevertheless, such extreme claims are made frequently by authors who ground their theology in the concept of 'incarnation'. Traditional theology has emphasised the one unique incarnation of the one true God in the person of Jesus, but also has recognised secondarily the broken and fallible way in which God is incarnate among his people; this is part of the meaning of the doctrine of the church as the body of Christ. Revisionists take this much further and invert it in a curious way; instead of God invading and redeeming our humanity, they take incarnation to mean that everything human is godly. All of human experience is an incarnation. James Nelson goes this direction in declaring that our bodies, including their untidy functions (specifically mentioning urination, defecation, and the sexual functions), 'are the central vehicles of God's embodiment in our experience'.[20] Neither revelation, prayer and contemplation, nor even complex human emotional responsiveness (including our capacity for love) are deemed the primary vehicles in which we encounter God. The body, particularly the sexual body, is, in Nelson's analysis, the primary conduit of knowledge and revelation and guidance. To deprive oneself of any aspect of sexual experience is to lose part of what it means to be spiritual. It is no wonder then, that working from this theological base Nelson argues that all persons, including homosexuals, must be able to revel in sexual gratification, albeit in a loving and faithful way, in order that they might be fully human.

Similarly, American Episcopal theologian, Carter Heyward, argues very much in the style of the psychological reductionist, that our sensual relational experiences are the foundation for our experience of both our very selves and of God.[21] To deny oneself sensual experience is tantamount to cutting off one's experiencing of God. Thus, she terms the exercise of her lesbian sexuality as 'godding'. This seems remarkably similar to the worship practises directed toward Baal in the Old Testament where sensual experience was viewed as a means of experiencing and participating with a god. These were practises deplored and condemned in the Old Testament. We must not forget the distinction between a human characteristic as a means by which we, however dimly, reflect or manifest the *imago dei*, the image of God, versus a tendency to see our exercise of those human capacities as entirely an act or facet of godliness itself. Our sexuality is a part of the way we manifest the image of God; our sexuality shows our fundamentally relational nature in our desire for union, reminds us of our creatureliness, and connects us with God's transcendent and creative character through our desire and capacity for procreation and pleasure. But sexuality is not to be equated with the image of God, and full exercise of our capacity for sexual intimacy must not be seen as necessary for full humanness or godliness; if it were, our Lord himself in his earthly life must have been neither fully human nor fully sanctified.

20. Nelson, *Body Theology*, p. 31.
21. Carter Heyward, *Touching Our Strength* (San Francisco: Harper and Row, 1989).

4. *The Proper View of the Gospel*

Finally and briefly, fundamentally differing visions of the very nature and character of the Christian faith are at play in this debate. The very words of the Lambeth theme I have focused on here — that we are called in faith by Christ to 'full humanity' — are used to justify full acceptance of homosexual behaviour by those pressing for alteration of the church's traditional teaching. We are told that the call of Christ is a call to self-actualisation, fulfilment, a full experience of that which is at the core of our humanity, to a full experience of incarnation, to freedom from guilt and shame, and so forth. We are also told that morality is much less clear than we have believed, and that generally speaking, individuals must be left to judge for themselves on very general principles whether their behaviour is moral or not.

When one stands back from these portraits of the nature of our faith and examines them anew, it is quite striking the degree to which they are depictions simply alien to the biblical depiction of the faith. Absent are passionate calls to righteousness and to obedience to God's revealed will. Gone is the New Testament repugnance for sexual immorality and an alternative passion for purity. Gone is a vision for the chaste life of singleness as a lifestyle of dignity and delight. Gone is any sense of how our sexuality, and indeed our faith, can serve purposes beyond meeting our own needs. Absent is a vision for how our sexuality must be harnessed and channelled to serve higher ends. Absent is a cautious awareness of just how contaminated our lives are by the fall and by sin, and of how profound is our capacity for self-deception and desperate need for God's guidance in how to live our lives. Missing is any deep awareness, to paraphrase G. K. Chesterton, that no restriction God might place on how we should experience our sexuality is as incredible as the raw awareness of what a miraculous gift our sexuality is.

Conclusion

Why is the church in the Christian West racked by these debates over sexuality at this time? Revisionists would say it is the predictable result, much as the Jewish community in the time of the book of Acts was torn over the identity of Jesus, of hearing a new word from God which corrects our bigotry and intolerance. Traditionalists have other hypotheses — perhaps it is simply the natural outgrowth of our loss of centredness on biblical revelation; perhaps we have simply lost our first love; perhaps we are intoxicated by the desire to be relevant and inoffensive to moderns; perhaps we are suffering from widespread moral compromise in the lives of our leaders and laity; perhaps we have been deceived by the beguiling and false promises of the sexual liberation movement; perhaps in our embrace of individualism we have failed at achieving any sense of real community in our congregations, of connections between people that meet our needs and give real enduring satisfaction; perhaps we have been judged by God, weighed, found wanting, and given over to our own immorality. Whatever the reason, it is my hope that our non-Western brothers and sisters in Christ do not follow us down the path the Western church has been treading.

Why should faithful Christians continue to stress traditional moral norms, insisting on full sexual intimacy as a gift to be shared in heterosexual marriage alone? To paraphrase Philip Turner once more, we Christians are asked to say 'no' to certain types of sexual activity in order to say 'yes' to a certain ordering of our lives which is ordained by God to be a moral good. Such a life involves many elements alien to the modern mind — self-denial, sacrifice, openness to the possibility of self-deceit, but above all a willingness to admit our guilt and unworthiness before God, a willingness to plead for mercy and forgiveness, and a willingness to follow Christ in obedience to his revealed will. Our goal must be an unending pursuit of holiness of life. What is the core business of the faith? After loving and giving glory to God, is it not the transformation of the human character from its fallen condition, in which nothing good dwells, into the likeness of Jesus Christ himself? And is not sexual purity an integral part of loving and giving glory to God and of the transformation of our character, an integral part of being called to full humanity?

Questions

1. How can the church act more lovingly to those who perceive themselves as homosexual?

2. Are we potentially capable of being socialised into a ho-

STANTON L. JONES

mosexual lifestyle, given certain conditions, *e.g.*, long-term imprisonment?

3. Why has modern Western culture seen the phenomenon of various kinds of homosexual or gay culture?

4. Does constant dialogue erode the church's capacity to draw definite ethical guidelines?

CALLED TO LIVE AND PROCLAIM THE GOOD NEWS

What Is the Gospel?

JOHN WEBSTER

Summary

The gospel is the good news of Jesus Christ, who is its sum and substance. In Jesus, God intervenes in human history, putting an end to the disorder of sin and reconciling all things to himself. The gospel is good news because it is God's action of disorienting goodness. It is good news because it is God's act of eschatological deliverance. And it is good news because in its particularity it is comprehensively true and meaningful. The church is what it is because of the gospel. The church is assembly around the gospel, a spiritual event and not only a structure of human society. As assembly around the gospel, the church's most characteristic activities are praise, prayer, hearing the Word of God, celebrating the sacraments, proclamation and service. The church's vocation is to hear, and then live and proclaim, this good news.

The church is not called first of all to live and proclaim the gospel, but to *hear* the gospel. Of course, if the church really is to be a hearing church it must also live and proclaim the gospel — otherwise it will fall into a hopeless self-deception about its own hearing (James 1:22, 25). But only because it has heard, and continues to hear, the gospel is the church called to testify to what it hears in life and proclamation and; however indispensable the work and speech of the church may be, they are what they are only because they emerge from the unending attention to the good news.

What is involved in hearing the gospel? The church hears the gospel as it reads Holy Scripture in the context of the assembly of the people of God who gather to praise the Lord Jesus in sacrament, fellowship and service. But this 'hearing' is much more than indolent passivity; nor can it be made a matter of comfortable routine. The church hears the gospel in the repeated event of being encountered, accosted, by the word of the gospel as it meets us in the reading of Scripture in the midst of the community of faith and its worship. Hearing the gospel in this way involves repentance and faith, that is, constantly renewed abandonment of what the gospel excludes and embrace of what the gospel offers. Such hearing can never be finished business. Hearing the gospel is not a skill we may acquire nor a material condition in which we may find ourselves, but a spiritual event which happens in prayer for the coming of the Holy Spirit, and in which we are always at the beginning.

What does the church hear when it hears the gospel? When we try to define the gospel, we need to resist the temptation to make it into a manageable and relatively tame message, something which can perform useful functions in our religious world, and which we can make our own by annexing it to our own viewpoints or projects. The gospel cannot be owned, or even 'known' in any straightforward way, as if it were simply one more helpful piece of religious information. This is not to say that the gospel is vague or indefinite — nothing in the New Testament suggests that the gospel is other than something clearly expressible, with a sharp and perceptible outline and content. But what is perceived and expressed in the gospel is mystery. It concerns God and God's actions, and so is known only in the miracle of revelation and faith, and present among us after the manner of God, that is, spiritually, and not as some kind of religious or ecclesiastical possession. In one real sense, the gospel is not 'observable'. Once we lose sight of this, and convert the gospel into just another bit of Christian culture, then the gospel very quickly becomes 'something which would survive as Good News apart from faith and without God'.[1] Thus, 'We do not have the Gospel, but we hear it. We do not know it as we know other concepts, but we receive it anew again and again'.[2]

1. K. Barth, *The Epistle to the Romans* (London: Oxford University Press, 1933), p. 368.
2. E. Schlink, *Theology of the Lutheran Confessions* (Philadelphia: Fortress, 1961), p. 7.

Once again, we ask: what does the church hear when it hears the gospel? The gospel is 'the gospel of Christ'.[3] Jesus himself, the proclaimer and embodiment of God's good news, *is* the gospel. He is not simply its bearer, the instrument through which the good news reaches us. To say that, would be to reduce him to the status of prophet or herald, and reduce the gospel to some theory or message separable from Jesus. But Jesus is not a function of the gospel; he is its sum and substance. His person and acts, his proclamation, his humiliation and exaltation and rule over all things constitute and do not simply illustrate the gospel. 'If we were to sum up the content of the Gospel in a single word, it would be Jesus the Christ.'[4]

Jesus is the gospel because in, and as, him God intervenes decisively in the history of sin and death. In and as Jesus, God reconciles all things to himself, putting an end to our hostility and alienation and restoring us to freedom, fellowship, and hope. In and as Jesus, God makes all things new, and ensures that the creation, broken by disorder and condemned to perish, will attain its true end and be glorified. In and as Jesus, the 'gospel of God'[5] becomes reality, and because of this, the gospel is good news, in three senses.

First, the gospel is good news because in it we encounter God's action. Both the act and the content of proclaiming the good news set before us God's gracious work for us and our salvation. The heart of the gospel is not a piece of human religious teaching, or a pattern of human spiritual experience or a call to human moral commitment. It is *God's* gospel: originating in God himself, it concerns his presence and action, and points human life to its true fulfilment in fellowship with God. Moreover, because the gospel is the gospel of God, then encountering the gospel is, or ought to be, a confrontation with something deeply disturbing, something which is even, as one great Anglican theologian put it, 'a thing of terror'.[6] If the gospel is the place where we find ourselves face to face with the sovereign presence and activity of God in a way which is ultimate and unqualified, then the gospel is

---

3. 1 Thess. 3:2; Gal. 1:7; Phil. 1:27; 1 Cor. 9:12; 2 Cor. 2:12; 9:13; 10:14; Rom. 15:19.

4. G. Friedrich, 'Euaggeliov' in G. Kittel (ed.), *Theological Dictionary of the New Testament*, vol. 2 (Grand Rapids: Eerdmans, 1964), p. 731.

5. 1 Thess. 2:2, 8f.; 2 Cor. 11:7; Rom. 1:1; 15:16.

6. D. M. MacKinnon, *The Church of God* (London: Dacre Press, 1940), p. 26.

always against the grain of our expectations. It will not occupy a place which we reserve for it in a scheme of our own devising, for the gospel 'is not a truth among other truths' but that which 'sets a question-mark against all truths'.[7] If this is true, then the gospel sits rather uneasily with those styles of church life and theology which make a comfortable home for themselves in a particular culture (whether radical or traditionalist), putting down roots and setting themselves the task of confirming, and perhaps ameliorating or even transforming, their environment. The sensitivity, good will and cultural and social scrupulousness with which such projects are undertaken may make it difficult for us to see how they always lie exposed to the very considerable danger of making the gospel about something less than God — and therefore something less than good news of God's utterly transformative action.

Second, the gospel is good news because in it we have set before us God's act of eschatological deliverance in Christ. The intervention of God which is the content of the gospel is not merely one further factor in the history of the world, one more matter to be borne in mind as we adjust ourselves to reality. It is *the* factor, that which establishes the entire renewal of human life and history. The gospel concerns God's achievement and manifestation of radical newness. This re-ordering of human life from the very roots is accomplished by God in and as Jesus, whom the gospel declares to be 'Lord' (*cf.*, 2 Thess. 1:8) — that is, the one in whom God's irresistible and wholly good purpose for the creation is effected. In Jesus, the gospel tells us, a fundamental break has been made in the human situation, in view of which scepticism, vacillation, indifference, uncertainty, fear, hopelessness and joylessness have all been taken care of, set aside as things which do not match up to the new situation in which all things have been placed by God in Christ. For the gospel is the presence of salvation, the freeing of all things from disorder and confinement and the gift of life in fellowship with God. The gospel is the active reality of God's grace, God taking up the cause of those whose sin has eaten away at their humanity. It is the undefeated reality of the blessing of God. Certainly, the gospel constitutes a judgement of human life in its fallenness; but it does so only because it is the unsurpassably good news of the grace of God in Jesus, the one in whom all God's promises find their 'yes' (*cf.*, 2 Cor. 1:19f.).

7. Barth, *Romans*, p. 35.

Third, the gospel is good news because it is comprehensively true. All human reality is what it is in the light of the gospel. The gospel is not a partial truth or message enclosed by a larger reality such as history or culture or morals or religion. On the contrary, by the gospel all history and culture and morals and religion are to be evaluated. The gospel is thus both particular and catholic. It is *particular* because it is tied to the career and name of Jesus. The word 'gospel' acquires a singularity and exclusiveness of reference in the New Testament precisely because it is wholly defined by the coming of God in the ministry, suffering and glorification of Jesus.[8] The gospel is thus inherently anti-mythological. It cannot be reduced to something generic, for Jesus, who is the content of the gospel, is simply himself. He is not a condensation of some larger truth, but the concrete realisation of all God's saving purposes. It is not possible to avoid a stubborn exclusiveness at this point. In considering the gospel, we may not substitute one of its terms and still hope that we can have the same reality. The fierceness with which Paul asserts that there can be 'no other gospel' (Gal. 1:6-9) has to be understood, not as intolerant (and intolerable) partisanship in favour of one particular *version* of the gospel, but as a very basic claim that as there is only one Jesus, so there is only one 'grace of Christ' (Gal. 1:6). But in all its particularity, the gospel is *catholic*. The events of Jesus and the new life which they generate and sustain furnish the overarching context in which all human life and relation to God take place. Because the gospel concerns a 'power that determines life and destiny'[9] its scope cannot be in any way restricted. In its very particularity, therefore, the good news is universal in reach, since it is the good news of the one in whom God gathers up all things (*cf.*, Eph. 1:10).

If all this is true, then the gospel is a great deal less serene than we may be tempted to believe. Because it is good news of salvation setting before us the drama of our deliverance by God from darkness and death, it is more than anything else a matter of disorientation. A church which is seriously engaged by the gospel will have to be ready

8. See G. Ebeling, *The Truth of the Gospel: An Exposition of Galatians* (Philadelphia: Fortress, 1985), pp. 49-51.

9. E. Käsemann, *Commentary on Romans* (London: SCM, 1980), p. 9. On the universality of the gospel in Paul, see J. Becker, *Paul, Apostle to the Gentiles* (Louisville: Westminster/John Knox Press, 1993), p. 402.

for the instability which the gospel's presence provokes. What does this mean for how we think of the church?

Most fundamentally, it means that the church is what it is because of the gospel. Priority has to be accorded to the good news, so that we begin our talk about the church indirectly, by talking of the gospel which calls it into being and which remains its essential theme and source of vitality.[10] This does not simply mean that the gospel provides a rather remote background or context for our understanding of the church. Talk of the gospel here must be direct and operative. We can, that is, speak properly of the church only if we are very strict to allow the gospel to exercise in an immediate way a controlling and critical influence. The gospel constitutes the environment of the church, the field within which it has its being, the space within which it undertakes its mission, and so the gospel acts as the ultimate critical point of reference for the church's life and proclamation. Here at one and the same time the church is exposed to judgement and blessed beyond measure.

At its most basic level, therefore, the church is to be defined as assembly around the gospel. 'Church' is the event of gathering around the magnetic centre of the good news of Jesus Christ. Its dynamic is derived not primarily from human projects, decisions or undertakings, but from the presence of the breathtakingly new and different reality which is brought about by Jesus himself, the good news of God. The church exists because of a decision which has already taken place and which the good news declares — the divine decision to reconcile and glorify all things in Christ. 'Church' is not a struggle to make something happen, but a lived attempt to make sense of, celebrate and bear witness to what has already been established by God's grace. The gospel is 'the making known of that which can only be addressed to us affirmingly, God's determination that man is to be the creature who belongs to him'.[11] Whatever else we may go on to say about the life and proclamation of the church must be rooted in a deep sense that, more than anything else, the church must allow the divine decision to stand,

10. *Cf.*, J. Fitzmyer, 'The Gospel in the Theology of Paul', in *To Advance the Gospel. New Testament Studies* (New York: Crossroad, 1981), p. 155.
11. O. Weber, *Foundations of Dogmatics,* vol. 2 (Grand Rapids: Eerdmans, 1983), p. 438.

letting that decision manifest itself and work its own work. There is, therefore, a proper 'emptiness' about the gospel community in its refusal to derive its impulse from anything other than the sheer self-gift of God in the good news. '[T]he activity of the community is related to the Gospel only in so far as it is no more than a crater formed by the explosion of a shell and seeks to be no more than a void in which the Gospel reveals itself.'[12]

If the church is what it is because of the gospel, then it is primarily a spiritual event and only secondarily natural history and settled structure. Put in negative terms, this means that the church cannot rely on its history or its external forms (doctrinal, sacramental, ministerial, political) as somehow guaranteeing its existence as church. Put positively, this means that the church has true form and continuity in so far as it receives the grace of God through the life-giving presence of the Spirit of Jesus. Settled structures, such as patterns of order or doctrine or cult, serve to promote the life of the church; indeed, if the life of the people of God is to have identifiable continuity and some definite boundaries, a measure of institutional shape is a requirement. But institutional shape promotes the life of the church only as it is an instrument of the gospel's work among us, and a proper account of the ordered life of the church will, therefore, be gospel-centred, 'evangelical'.[13] Like the gospel, the church has a 'mysterious' character — the conditions under which it exists lie within the miracle of its occurrence, and not in any prior forms through which its existence might be secured.

If the church is what it is because of the gospel, it will be most basically characterised by astonishment at the good news of Jesus. What will lie at the heart of all its undertakings will be the primitive response to Jesus' presence and proclamation — 'they were all amazed' (Mark 1:27). What is this amazement? It is being held by a reality — the reality of Jesus — which presents itself as pure gift, without desert or expectation; it is letting ourselves be taken up by that reality and its inherent authority, worth and persuasiveness; it is having settled ideas and routines ruptured and transcended; it is being disconcerted by what is at

12. K. Barth, *Romans*, p. 36.
13. See M. Ramsey, *The Gospel and the Catholic Church* (London: Longmans, Green, 1936), pp. 8f.

115

once a matter of bewilderment and delight. The life and proclamation of the church are again 'evangelical' in so far as they are captivated in these ways by the good news. This captivation is to be permanent; it cannot be left behind us as we move on to our own preoccupations or interests, and so 'only as there is this astonishment . . . can there be serious, fruitful and edifying Christian thought and utterance in the Church'.[14]

If the church is what it is because of the gospel, then its basic activities will be those which manifest its 'ecstatic' character. That is to say, the definitive activities of the church are those which most clearly betray the fact that the origin, maintenance and perfection of its life lie beyond itself, in the work and word of God which the gospel proclaims. The church's true being is located outside itself. It exists by virtue of God's decision and calling; it is nourished and sustained by the ever-fresh gift of the Holy Spirit; its goal lies in the definitive self-manifestation of the Lord Jesus at his appearing. What activities testify to this?

We may conveniently distinguish these activities into acts of the church in gathering, and acts of the church in dispersal, that is, the acts of the church in its internal and its external orientations. The acts of the church in gathering are those acts by which the church is drawn towards the source of its life, and reinvested in the truth and goodness of the gospel. The acts of the church in dispersal are those acts in which the church follows the external impulse of its source of life, and is pushed beyond itself in proclamation and service. It is crucial that neither the acts of gathering nor the acts of dispersal are somehow to be considered as independent, free-standing operations which we may talk about without reference to the action of God. The gospel is not inert; it does not merely furnish the occasion for the church to get busy. Whatever the church does about the gospel is always response to the fact that God has already taken matters into his own hands.

The acts of the church in gathering include praise and prayer, attention to Holy Scripture, and the celebration of the sacraments of the gospel. Praise and prayer are delight in God and appeal to God for God's renewed presence and activity. They display most clearly the proper passivity which characterises the being of the church, even in its most strenuous activity. In praise as celebration of the divine goodness and beauty, and prayer as invocation of the mercy of God, the

14. K. Barth, *Church Dogmatics* IV/3 (Edinburgh: T & T Clark, 1961), p. 287.

church manifests what makes it into itself — dependence upon God's gift of himself. Furthermore, the public reading of Scripture as the address of God to the community of faith underlines that the church does not make up its own understanding of itself but receives it in the struggle to listen faithfully to the divine word. The sacraments, similarly, point the church beyond itself. Baptism and eucharist are not first and foremost the acts of the church, but the acts of the living Lord Jesus in which the Christian life is begun and sustained through the proclamation and sealing of the promises of the gospel. Praise, prayer, hearing the word, and sacraments, are thus fundamental public manifestations of the fact that the church, governed by the gospel, is characterised by faith. As God's 'faithful people' the church is neither self-generating nor self-defining; the community of faith is rather that form of human life which is what it is by virtue of the miracle of God's condescension in Jesus, and which allows God to do his work among us and in the world.

The acts of the church in dispersal include proclamation and service. Proclamation and service are not about striving to make the gospel real but about demonstrating that it is already indefatigably real. The gospel goes ahead of the church. Proclamation and service are the testimony borne by the community of faith to the progress of the gospel, a progress in which the community is always and only a distant and not very wise or powerful follower. 'Christ always leads us in triumph' (2 Cor. 2:14). Both proclamation and service emerge from a deep delight in the gospel, and from confidence in its capacity to look after itself. That is why proclamation is not a matter of tense polemic, anxious to win a hearing and persuade, but celebration, excited description of the world of the gospel in its compelling force. Such celebration certainly entails protest (against the rebellion, ignorance and half-heartedness of sin); but such protest is properly rooted in an abiding trust in the gospel's truth and effectiveness. Similarly, service as a following of Jesus is not the church making Christ real by doing in his stead what he has not yet done, but rather a 'showing' of his accomplishment, a manifestation of his diakonia.

In sum: in proclamation and service, as in praise, prayer, attention to Scripture and the celebration of the gospel ordinances, the church lives from the achievement of the good news of God in Jesus. Two lessons may be drawn by way of conclusion. First, Anglican Christians

117

are no different from any other Christians. We are called to hear the good news, to live in its world and to bear witness to its utter goodness. Of us, as of every Christian community, it is to be said that the 'singular occupation of the church is the holy gospel of our Lord Jesus Christ, that is, the true treasure of the church is the message that one, this one, Jesus the Son of David, the strange rabbi, healer and prophet from Nazareth, is risen from the dead, so as to live and reign for all eternity'.[15] Renewal in the church is renewal in the gospel, and we do well to be much about the business of meditating on, talking about and celebrating the gospel if we would learn how to live and proclaim it. Second, we need not feel excessively responsible for the gospel or for the church's life in the gospel. A church which feels that the gospel needs looking after (whether in doctrine, or evangelism, or the struggle for justice) has not really understood what is meant by 'the defence of the good news' (Phil. 1:7). The triumph of the gospel is God's affair, and God will reign. The task of the people of the gospel is to hear the good news, and so gladly, cheerfully and freely live and proclaim.

Questions

1. Why is the gospel good news?

2. What signs of astonishment at the gospel do you see in the life of the Anglican communion?

3. How do settled forms of order, worship and institutional life promote or inhibit the centrality of the gospel in the Anglican church?

4. If the gospel is catholic, how does this shape attitudes to culture, other religious traditions, and the struggle for just human societies?

---

15. R. W. Jenson, 'What Is the Point of Trinitarian Theology?' in C. Schwöbel (ed.), *Trinitarian Theology Today. Essays on Divine Action and Being* (Edinburgh: T & T Clark, 1995), p. 31.

Evangelism:
The Transformation of Trivialisation

FITZSIMMONS ALLISON

Summary

Evangelism and the truth about God are deeply integrated. If we forget God's majesty and awe, we sentimentalise and reduce him to our own lax standards of righteousness. The Bible is clear about divine transcendence and about our access to God as Father, the Father uniquely revealed at Calvary as righteous love. Evangelism cannot customise God to make for easier sales, and in fact people are glad to hear the real truth, the depth of our need and the strength of God's love. Expiation and propitiation must be retained as biblical truths showing how God deals honestly with sin. We are 'in Christ' because of God's sacrifice for us, the basis of our hope.

Authentic evangelism must restore the justice of God in the church's witness. There can be no justification by Christ, no forgiveness, no hope of reconciliation without recovering the majesty and justice that is God's revealed nature. The forfeiture of this understanding of God is at present so egregious, no statement on evangelism — its methods, rationale, or goals — can be undertaken until the problem is displayed in all its foreboding reality. It was once announced that 'God is Dead'. Now culture has exhumed God for further abuse.

A spate of books, a deluge of writings, shows the extent of the trivialisation of God.[1] In spite of all the imperfections in previous pe-

1. K. Armstrong, *A History of God* (Colchester: Ballantine Books, 1994). J. Miles,

riods of church history, no other is as guilty as ours is of Reinhold Niebuhr's dictum that 'in the beginning God created us in His own image and ever since we have attempted to return the compliment'. The recovery of God's righteousness is not only necessary to the good news of his mercy in Christ, but also is the sole antidote to the world's pathology.

The great themes of redemption from bondage, the Lamb who takes away our sin of scapegoating and victimising, the radical monotheism that frees us from idolatries of nation, tribe, family and self, the commandments that proclaim the righteousness of God by which all are condemned that he might have mercy upon all, the law like the schoolmaster that purges self-righteousness and gives us the easy yoke of Christ's righteousness, the Christmas revelation of tenderness and love in the very personal substance and very essence of God, the unique bonding hope of Good Friday and Easter that is neither condemnation nor sentimentality, and the gift of the Holy Spirit to judge and transform the virulent spirits of the age; all depend upon the revealed majesty and righteousness of God.

The majesty of God, especially in Western culture, is assaulted on many fronts. Every discipline by which the Bible has been studied in the last 150 years comes with a hyphenated partner: higher-, lower-, form-, textual-, redaction-, historical-, and literary-criticism. The very word 'criticism' has the inescapable connotation that we are the judge of Scripture and not vice-versa.

This is not to say that endeavours to find the earliest sources of texts and the dates and authorship of the writings are unworthy exer-

---

God: A Biography (Vintage Books, 1996); D. W. McCullough, The Trivialization of God: The Dangerous Illusion of a Manageable Deity (New Malden: Navpress, 1995); W. C. Placher, The Domestication of Transcendent Thinking About God (Edinburgh: John Knox Press, 1996); E. Brooks Holifield, A History of Pastoral Care in America: From Salvation to Self-Realization (Nashville: Abingdon Press, 1983); P. Vitz, Psychology as Religion: The Cult of Self-Worship (Grand Rapids: Eerdmans, 1977). Both Armstrong and Miles write as if God were an object for us to study, whose actions and 'growth' are evaluated by our standards. Vitz and Holifield show what is happening to reduce Christianity to a religion to meet modern persons' perception of their psychological needs. McCullough gives us a bracing criticism of the 'trivialization' of God in the current search for a 'manageable deity'. Placher traces the roots of this reductionist tide to the seventeenth and eighteenth centuries. Without a radical dissociation from the arrogant hubris of our present age any evangelism is a stillbirth.

cises. The overwhelming focus on the Bible as the object of criticism, however, carries with it the inevitable loss of the verifying experience of the reader's being an object of the Scripture's revelation. No wonder that many have found David Steinmetz's 'The Superiority of Pre-Critical Exegesis'[2] a refreshing liberation from the dogmatic claims of the historical-critical method. 'Until the historical-critical method becomes critical of its own theoretical foundations and develops a hermeneutical theory adequate to the nature of the text which it is interpreting, it will remain restricted — as it deserves to be — to the guild and the academy, where the question of truth can endlessly be deferred.'

Evangelism's authenticity is dependent upon a sound basis for biblical authority or it degenerates into getting members for an organisation or customers for a product. That God reveals himself as creator, redeemer, and sanctifier is indispensable to any firm ground for evangelism. Such scholars as N. T. Wright, Luke Timothy Johnson, Brevard Childs, and John Stott provide scholarly grounds for trusting canonical Scripture in the face of its many current detractors. Able younger but less famous scholars in the two-thirds world have been encouraged and supported by John Stott, as well as by Billy Graham. Brevard Childs of Yale has been a remarkable influence on many brilliant younger American scholars who give eloquent testimony to faithful biblical grounds for evangelism and mission. Two recipients of Yale's doctorates, Ephraim Radner and George Sumner, not only publish faithful, scholarly works, but have served as missionaries in Africa as well.

A clergyman in this diocese has a brother-in-law who is a Moslem. When he comes to visit the two sit up into the night arguing passionately their respective faiths. After one visit I asked the clergyman how it went. He replied, 'It was wonderful!' 'You made an impression on him?' I asked. 'No, not at all, but he made an impression on me.' The brother-in-law had insisted that the weakest and flabbiest thing about the Christian faith is that we call God 'Father'. He claimed that this hopelessly diminishes God's majesty, his awe and transcendent eminence. No Moslem, he insisted, would even think of diminishing the awesomeness of Allah by calling him 'father'. 'I realised for the first time why we say in the communion service: And now as our saviour Christ has taught us we are bold to say, "Our Father. . . ." I realised

2. *Theology Today* (1980), pp. 27-38.

more fully than ever before that the Christian God is every bit as transcendent and inexpressibly awesome as Allah — yet Jesus Christ showed us that in such unutterable eminence was a love he expressed in suffering for us which gives us this undeserved and unique access.'

The Old Testament refers to God as Father eleven times and virtually nowhere in prayer or as his name.[3] It is like calling George Washington the 'father of his country' which is not to be confused with his name. But in the New Testament 'Father' is used one hundred and seventy times both as his name and in prayer. It is crucial to appreciate that this intimacy with majesty is a costly gift given us in Christ. It is not our right or God's lowered familiarity. The failure to appreciate the substantial unity and distinct persons of Father and Son in Scripture, and proclaimed at Nicea in our creed, leaves us justifiably vulnerable to the Moslem charge of having a less majestic and a weakly accessible god.

Evangelism must at all costs keep this biblical and credal identification (and distinction) of, and between, Jesus and the Father in order to counter the widespread trivialisation of the Father and retain the acknowledgement of this costly accessibility of the saving agent. The failure to see that '. . . in Christ God was reconciling the world unto himself . . .' (2 Cor. 5:19) is a current cause of paralysis in evangelism.

A cleric, writing in *Episcopal Life*, stated that she hated the story of the crucifixion because it seemed to be nothing more than a terrible example of 'child abuse' for the Father to send his Son to be an innocent victim for the sins of others. Bishop John Spong likewise writes: 'The idea that somehow the very nature of the heavenly God required the death of Jesus as a ransom to be paid for our sins is ludicrous. A human parent who required the death of his or her child as a satisfaction for a relationship that had been broken would be either arrested or confined to a mental institution'.[4]

In classical Arian assumptions this minister and this bishop have separated the Father and Son and then attacked Christian teaching as if it were Arianism. The inevitable logic is to keep a sentimental Father without acknowledging God's own cost in making himself accessible

3. The exceptions in Isaiah 9, 63 and Jeremiah 3 are prophetic pre-figurations of a new dispensation.
4. *The Voice* (Oct. 1996), p. 2.

in Christ. Almost invariably, the widespread currency of this sort of misapprehension of God infects national church structures and its agencies, including those directed to Christian education, evangelism, and mission. Budgets in these areas are the first to be cut in fiscal tightening.

The awesomeness of God is reflected in religious reverence for his law (*cf.*, Pss. 1; 119:33-40; 97-102). I once preached what I thought was a very effective sermon on the woman taken in adultery. 'Has no one condemned you?' She answered, 'No one, Lord.' And Jesus said, 'Neither do I condemn you; go, and do not sin again.' This seemed to be overwhelmingly well-received as good news by the congregation.

However, a young man greeted me at the door with a quiet but disturbing request. 'Would you someday preach a sermon for me?' Sure, I thought with pride, not anticipating his next statement: 'I am the husband of an adulterous woman'. This laid open to me the cost of forgiveness. Consistent with this, though impossible to verify, is the suggestion that what Jesus wrote in the sand was the ten commandments and that those who had brought her to be condemned watched as he wrote. We recall his proposition that any without sin could throw the first stone. '. . . they went away, one by one, beginning with the eldest . . .' (John 8:9).

What happens to the law when no one can enforce it? In the American Supreme Court the rule for enforcing laws against pornography is tied to 'prevailing community standards'. When prevailing community standards become as unstable as white caps on the sea, the law is powerless. The solution to this dilemma is not that of the proverbial warden to whom the vicar appealed for forgiveness because 'didn't Jesus forgive the woman taken in adultery?' 'Yes,' the warden replied, 'but I don't think any more of him for having done it!'

No. The majesty and integrity of the law is not established by going back and denying forgiveness but by going forward to Good Friday and Easter. There is a problem here where resolution cannot be found in the schemes, even laudable, of mankind. The answer lies in the fact that this story is found in chapter eight of John's Gospel. It is not the whole story of the Gospel's good news. There are thirteen more chapters culminating in Good Friday and Easter. Someone must pay the price of sin. Jesus' 'it is finished' (John 19:30), as classic evangelism has always heard it, might just as well be rendered 'paid in full'.

The law as it expresses the will of almighty God cannot be lowered or erased to accommodate forgiveness. It is humanly impossible to erase murder by forgiveness. One cannot unslap a face, unsay a thoughtless and hurtful word. Sinful deeds cannot be undone. You and I can forgive each other but we cannot wipe away sin.

This is why evangelism cannot lower the law to effect 'acceptance' (the sentimentalised substitute for forgiveness) and why even statements like 'whose property is always to have mercy' without the righteousness of God will become empty bromides. The gospel is not only for the woman taken in adultery but for her hurt and offended husband as well. This is why the contemporary Jews were so offended by Jesus' claim to forgive sins. They knew that only God could forgive sins and they were right. In the sentimental religion of a trivialised god one can easily set aside his law to escape condemnation. The only laws to be taken seriously are those which protect self, property, or current politically correct issues. The Jews had no such deity. Their reverence for the law was never condemned by Jesus. 'Think not that I have come to abolish the law and the prophets; I have come not to abolish them but to fulfil them . . . not an iota, not a dot, will pass from the law until all is accomplished. Whoever relaxes one of the least of these commandments and teaches men so shall be called least in the kingdom of heaven . . .' (Matt. 5:17-19). If forgiveness of sinners were the whole gospel, John could have ended his Gospel with the eighth chapter, but the husband of the adulterous woman would have no good news.

There would be no good news for the past and present wrongs to Jews, Palestinians, Armenians and the sixty year old mother deserted by her husband for a 'trophy' wife. But John gives us thirteen more chapters, culminating in the Lamb that takes away the sin of the whole world, past and present, something only God could do. By *his* wounds, not by our endeavours or by our being victims, we are healed (1 Peter 2:24). 'For our sake he made him to be sin who knew no sin so that in him we might become the righteousness of God' (2 Cor. 5:21).

These so called 'hard texts' are hard in the sense of being foundational. They are the essence of good news when the law has been neither relaxed, abrogated, or adulterated, nor God's righteousness trivialised. Any lowering of God's majesty to shield sinners, any reduction of his righteousness to accommodate evil is what Dietrich Bonhoeffer called 'cheap grace'. On a more popular level, J. B. Phillips' *Your God Is Too Small* shows the emptiness of paying God's greatness as a price for reconciliation. Such domestication of God is a sentimentality of long-range cruelty. It deprives us of the hope of ultimate justice, makes irrelevant the cross and Easter and leaves us sinners with the unrelieved bitterness of sin and injustice.

Such trivialisation of God's majesty also undermines Christian duty and contribution to civilisation. It is ironic that Sigmund Freud saw something of this dynamic more clearly than many theologians. At the end of his *Civilization and Its Discontents* he laments the fact that guilt is 'the most important problem in the evolution of culture, and . . . that the price of progress in civilization is paid in forfeiting happiness through the heightening of the sense of guilt'.[5] He shows that a civilisation's height is in direct proportion to its engendering of conscience and its capacity for guilt. The latent aggression in human nature is inhibited by a strict conscience and a sense of guilt. Without internal restriction it is useless to attempt external control by police and armies. The latter are human, too, and cannot be successfully controlled except by the inner restrictions of a conscience capable of guilt. Being bereft of any sense of God's will behind the law that produces guilt and, especially of any benevolence in that will, Freud sees the necessity of guilt for civilisation. Yet he is pessimistic regarding civilisation's ability to endure the amount of guilt which is necessary to prevail against the aggressive self-centredness of human nature.

The Christian confidence that all history is subject to the justice of the last word (Omega), and the Christ-inspired hope of mercy in that judgement, impels Christians into the world with a capacity for guilt that is essential for responsible citizenship. 'Let all the world become guilty before God' (Rom. 3:19). Evangelism must proclaim in baptism, the 'in Christ' comfort of God's tender mercy that enables the Christian to endure without lowering or weakening the Father's majestic and perfect righteousness (*cf.* Rom. 3:5f.). The resulting gratitude for this mercy produces in Christians' witness the joy and delight that are indispensable to effective evangelism. Projects of transferred enlightenment or ingenuous claims to hear the innate goodness of another culture are poor substitutes for the good news.

The currently unfashionable biblical term 'expiate' deserves serious contemporary attention. No matter how essential and wonderful

5. S. Freud, *Civilization and Its Discontents* (London: Hogarth Press, 1957), p. 123.

forgiveness is, it is not the whole gospel. Forgiveness can restore relationships but it cannot wipe away sin. What John the Baptist announced, 'Behold the lamb of God who takes away the sin of the world' (John 1:29), is so crucially important in a world where humans try to do their own expiations. The hatred and revenge for long remembered injustices among nations, tribes, clans, families and individuals are symptoms of the human thirst for a justice that will 'right past wrongs' to expiate sin.

No nation, tribe, family or individual is bereft of some real or perceived injustice, some terrible wrong that tempts us to bitterness, suspicion, anger, and revenge. Much hostility and violence is a human attempt at justice, to right real or perceived wrongs. Surely this temptation is universal. 'Beloved, never avenge yourselves, but leave it to the wrath of God; for it is written 'vengeance is mine, I will repay, says the Lord' (Rom. 12:19). For one under the law this text is a command. For one under grace it is a promise. This is where the freedom to learn in evangelism gains its inner nerve and rationale.

It is a part of the Christian's blessed liberty to relinquish such burdens to God's providence. This freedom is an essential part of evangelism. We cannot legitimately tear away the graceful aspects of the good news, such as justification by faith, forgiveness, and reconciliation, from the Agency by which these experiences are possible. The essential foundation for these aspects of evangelism is the death of Jesus as sacrifice and propitiation.[6]

Propitiation is a particularly unfashionable term in an atmosphere of trivialising God's righteousness. It certainly carries no notion of sycophancy, apple-polishing, or of changing God's will as is the case with pagan deities and human relations. It is, on the contrary, essential to the consistence of abiding justice that forgiveness does not adulterate.

If a new puppy messes up the living room it can be forgiven but someone must clean up the mess. If we sinners are forgiven, when we are justly condemned by the law, only God can effect reconciliation without damaging the integrity of his justice. This he has done in Christ. Propitiation means nothing less than God's looking on the perfection of his Son and choosing, by that Son's offering, to see us reflected through him.

6. G. Kittel, *The Theological Dictionary of the New Testament*, Vol. 3 (Grand Rapids: Eerdmans, 1965), pp. 300-326.

Unless we perceive this essential sacrificial act as part of our evangelical proclamation we will be powerless to address the prevailing attempts to quench our thirst in human blood rather than in the blessing of Christ's blood. We must, however, recall that when Jesus stated what is pointed to above in John 6:54-56, '. . . he who eats my flesh and drinks my blood has eternal life. . . . He who eats my flesh and drinks my blood abides in me, and I in him', many of his disciples responded, 'This is a hard saying, who can listen to it?' (v. 60). 'After this many of his disciples drew back and no longer went about with him' (v. 66).

Yet it is through the eye of this needle, through the narrow gate of this 'hard saying', that one passes to joys ineffable, won by Christ for us and our salvation. Because many turned away, Jesus did not turn from Calvary, but set his face all the more firmly. The truth of evangelism's central message is a truth that inheres with God's very character as God. Let us embrace and hold fast the hope of our calling in Christ Jesus.

Questions

1. How is our local church in danger of trivialising God in its message? Can you think of some key passage of Scripture relevant to this problem?

2. Does the modern Western consumer society lead us to package God and his message, to make it less demanding? In what ways and how might we personally respond?

3. Is the sacrifice of Jesus sufficiently prominent as a focus of our worship, to humble us and bring us to fresh repentance and adoration?

4. Discuss the relevance of Isaiah 6:1-8 to evangelism and worship now.

Christian Community and the Gospel

PAUL BARNETT

Summary

The challenges facing the church in its mission may seem particularly vast in the late twentieth century, but in many ways the Christians of the New Testament age faced very similar issues in the Graeco-Roman culture of their day. Yet the church grew. How and why? A focus on the short epistle of 1 Peter reveals the importance of local evangelism (not dependent on apostles or 'clergy'), of Christians' lifestyles being distinctive from their neighbours, and of the congregation's corporate life pointing attractively to the values of God's future kingdom.

All ebb is flow; the continental shelf has tilted. The light of Christ is flickering and all but extinguished. Before it is too late we Christians need to go back to our historical roots and to theological basics. We can be inspired, informed and directed by a brief epistle like 1 Peter, a glittering gem in the jewel box of the New Testament. There we see the existence of vital Christian faith and dynamic church life arising out of the gospel which had come in the recent past to various Gentiles scattered across Asia Minor. All local churches need to have a working strategy to bring the gospel to the neighbourhood and community. Like those Christians, we need to be committed to a distinctive interface with the unbelieving community. Our 'good works' will be the replication of the very witness of Jesus among them. The 'Gentile' is to meet Christ in us. We must not shirk from testifying to the hope that is in us, that is, the confidence that death does not circumscribe and contain us.

Introduction

Even in the so-called 'Christian West' a crisis is upon us. Whether in the United Kingdom, for example, where the Church is established, or in the United States where it is not, Christianity is in decline. The continental shelf has tilted under the weight of secularism, affluence, multi-culturalism, political correctness and incessant sequence of clergy sex scandals. The tide is in full ebb. Our numerous now empty and crumbling churches are mocking reminders of an age of faith that has now passed.

However, we should pause before blaming our contemporary world's indifference to the faith once delivered to the saints as the explanation for the approaching eclipse of Christianity. It is important to recognise that in many ways our era has come full circle back to apostolic times. Apart from dazzling technological change there is little now that has not already been. Western culture has swung around and back to the Graeco-Roman milieu. Those times, too, were pluralist and multi-cultural, and like ours, overarched by a form of political correctness.[1] Theirs, too, was an age of anxiety, sexually decadent, preoccupied with entertainment, plagued with alcoholism and gambling, accepting of foetus terminations and suicide. Our deconstructionist anti-rationalism and new age mysticism find counterparts in their gnosticism, astrology and mystery cults, our environmentalism in their naturalism, our drug and alcohol dependency in their alcohol dependency, our gambling in their gambling, our abortion, euthanasia in their abortion and acceptance of suicide, our angst in their despair.

The Christian gospel did not find easy response in that culture. Jews were despised by Gentiles. Crucifixion was unmentionable in polite circles. Resurrection of a man from the dead was laughable. The proposition that God's anointed king was a Jew who had been crucified to death, but who had been raised from the dead was regarded as plain stupid in the cultivated salons of the Graeco-Roman cities where the apostles preached their message. Evangelism and apologetics are diffi-

---

1. The Roman world was overarched by Roman 'civic religion' which liberally embodied local cults within a broader emperor cult, but which illiberally attacked as a 'superstition' the Christians' proclamation of 'another king' (*cf.* Acts 17:7).

129

cult tasks for us, but they were no less difficult for Christians of the first century.

Our societies need to be re-evangelised. Humbly we need to return to our historical and theological roots and re-learn how to do it. This means nothing less than a radical re-reading of the New Testament. The gospel of Christ triumphed in just such a world. We must ask what they believed and did differently from us. Both historically and theologically we must learn from that body of literature that relates Christian origins, the New Testament.

In this paper I will focus our attention on one brief piece of that literature, the First Letter of Peter.[2] From 1 Peter let us learn three things for our edification and encouragement: (1) the readers became Christians through evangelism; (2) their witness in the wider community was to be distinctive; (3) their church life was to be distinctive.

Christians through Evangelism

Dramatic change of life direction is what marks Peter's readers. Perhaps the most critical word in the entire letter is the pronoun, 'you.' His opening 'we have been born anew,' in which Peter refers both to him and to them, immediately becomes '[for] an inheritance kept in heaven for you.' Thereafter Peter repeatedly addresses them as 'you.' He reminds them that Christ's 'sufferings and glory' have 'now been announced to you by those who preached the good news to you . . .'.[3] The entire letter resonates with a sense of immediacy and newness. These readers are recently converted people.

But who brought the good news to these readers in Pontus, Galatia, Cappadocia, Asia and Bithynia, that is, in a region approximating modern Turkey? 'Those who preached' puts them at arm's length from Peter. Apart from some awareness of their sufferings Peter appears not to know much detail about them. He mentions no one by name among them. It does not appear that Peter has been their evangelist. So who might it have been?

---

2. My working assumption is that 1 Peter arose out of the apostolate-mission of Peter, under his dictation or supervision and it was written sometime in the fifth to seventh decades of the first century.
3. 1 Peter 1:12.

Perhaps they were local people who, in the course of their travels, had brushed against Paul or Peter in Corinth, or against Paul in Ephesus? Or had Christian traders or soldiers or officials passed through,[4] preaching the gospel as they went? More probably, however, they were evangelists from churches in adjacent regions.

We know of Paul's ministry in several of the provinces mentioned by Peter, that is, Galatia and Asia, from the late forties until the midfifties. It is possible, too, that Peter had passed through the general region as he travelled from Antioch to Corinth.[5] Then, it is held, evangelists converted through Paul, and perhaps Peter (why else would *Peter* be writing to these people?), went to neighbouring regions preaching Christ, issuing in a number of conversions and the consequent creation of churches. So the gospel would incrementally spread in that region by local extension.

This, certainly, would be consistent with what we learn elsewhere of the growth of early Christianity. The ministry of the apostles was only part of the story.

1. The Spread of Early Christianity by Non-Apostles

Obviously the apostles were the major instruments in the spread of the gospel and the creation of churches. I have argued elsewhere that initially there were two apostolates, led by Peter to Jews as from Pentecost and by Paul to Gentiles as from his conversion/call.[6] After *c.* AD 47, however, it appears there were also two other apostolates, James' and John's. After the private meeting in Jerusalem in that year it seems that Peter's and John's missions, though directed initially to Jews, increasingly came to be directed to Gentiles in the Diaspora when Jewish doors

---

4. By AD 50 there were Christians in Rome independently of the ministry of an apostle, so it appears. Most likely the gospel was planted through the work of converted Jews, whose work as traders or Roman officials brought them to the Eternal City. Paul's letter to the Romans is not addressed to 'the Church in Rome'. Rather Christianity in Rome consisted of a series of house churches as yet not united in the one fellowship.

5. Galatians 2:11; 1 Corinthians 9:5; *cf.,* 1:12.

6. Galatians 2:8. See P. W. Barnett, *Jesus and the Logic of History* (Leicester: InterVarsity Press, 1998).

everywhere slammed shut. The literature of the New Testament, for the most part, arises out of the four apostolates of James, Peter, John and Paul, often written by co-workers of the great leaders (*e.g.*, Matthew with James?, Mark with Peter and Luke with Paul). This literature is mission literature, written to convert outsiders or for the upbuilding of the nascent churches and their members.

Nonetheless, apostles were by no means the only instrument for evangelism. Within a year or so of the First Easter there were believers in Damascus, whom Saul was coming to root out but who ministered to him after Christ appeared to him on the way there.[7] These were Jewish believers, very probably converted through the ministry of disciples of the Lord from nearby Galilee. Philip, a non-apostle, evangelised the Samaritans, the Ethiopian treasurer and all the coastal towns from Azotus to Caesarea Maritima. This occurred after his expulsion from Jerusalem through Saul's persecutions. Appropriately he is called 'Philip the evangelist.'[8] The Judaean towns of Lydda and Joppa were probably evangelised by a non-apostle; there were already believers in those places when Peter visited them.[9] Unnamed Hellenist-Jewish disciples, scattered through Saul's attacks, created churches up the Mediterranean coast, eventually establishing a church in the great metropolis, Antioch, by the early forties. None of this was the work of the apostles, who remained in Jerusalem.[10] In other words, there had been significant gospel preaching in Judaea, Samaria, Galilee, Phoenicea and Syria in the decade after the First Easter, much of it done by non-apostles. For the most part, this work was done by unnamed evangelists, working by local extension.

The same is true of the spread of Christianity in the Lycus Valley in the fifties, a tributary of the great Maeander River and located one hundred or so miles from the eastern coast of the province of Roman Asia. The letter to the Colossians suggests that the evangelist was Epaphras who was from that region and who, upon his conversion by Paul, returned to evangelise his own people, establishing churches in Colossae, Hierapolis and Laodicea.[11] The Acts states that, in con-

---

7. Acts 9:1, 10, 19.
8. Acts 8:5-8, 26-40; 21:8.
9. Acts 9:32, 36.
10. Acts 8:1.
11. Colossians 1:7-8; 4:13.

sequence of Paul's two year ministry in Ephesus, 'all the residents of Asia heard the word of the Lord.'[12] Most probably this occurred by local extension through the ministry of men like Epaphras.

The famous letter of Pliny, governor of Bithynia, to the Emperor Trajan speaks of Christians in that province as from the nineties.[13] We know of no apostle having visited that region. Very probably the gospel was brought by evangelists from adjacent provinces.

The Christians addressed in 1 Peter had been preached to, though we do not know by whom. In our view it was most probably by an Epaphras-type evangelist from not too distant parts.

Whatever the case the New Testament makes quite clear that there was a ministry of someone called an 'evangelist.'[14] Philip the Hellenist Jew become Christian was called 'the evangelist.' Paul encourages Timothy to 'do the work of an evangelist.' The ascended Christ gave 'evangelists' to the church, along with apostles, prophets and pastor-teachers.[15] It appears that Euodia, Syntyche and Clement and others not named worked alongside Paul in the work of evangelism, very probably in Philippi. People like this went out from their churches to bring the gospel to the people of that locality.

2. An Implicit Mandate: Local Church Evangelism

Peter has no explicit mandate for members of churches to engage in local church evangelism. However, the impact of evangelism for good on these readers, so evident in this letter,[16] must surely support the proposition of an implied encouragement to them for this ministry. If the gospel came to them by local extension, this would imply that they, too, were to carry the torch on to the next towns and cities.

It is surely time that church leaders, denominational as well as local, began to encourage their members to do the work of local district evangelism, in the manner of Epaphras, Euodia, Syntyche and Clement. These were not apostles. Yet as much as the apostles, perhaps even

12. Acts 19:10.
13. Pliny *Epistle* x.96.6.
14. Acts 21:8; Ephesians 4:11; 2 Timothy 4:5.
15. Acts 21:8; 2 Timothy 4:5; Ephesians 4:11.
16. See, *e.g.*, 1:12; 1:14-18, 22; 2:1-3.

more, they were the instruments of God in apostolic times for the conversion of others and the establishing of churches.

Fortunately we are blessed at this time with a wealth of resources and training materials to place in the hands of those who would go forth to bring the message of Christ to others.

Distinctive Witness in the Wider Community

The apostolic writings call for a distinctively Christian interface with the wider communities. 'Conduct yourselves wisely with outsiders, making the most of the time,' writes Paul to the Colossians.[17] This he amplifies by, 'Let your speech always be gracious, seasoned with salt, so that you may know how to answer every one.' 'Pay all of them their dues,' he advises the Roman Christians,[18] 'taxes to whom taxes are due, revenue to whom revenue is due, respect to whom respect is due, honour to whom honour is due.'

This sense of moral distinctness from society, yet with a recognition that it is part of God's ordering of the world derives from Jesus himself. His people are, and are to be, the salt of the earth, the light of the world. Their 'good works' are to 'glorify' their heavenly father.[19] His people are to 'render to Caesar' — that is, the payment of taxes — 'the things that belong to Caesar'.[20]

Peter, too, makes this point very strongly with his readers, though with a particular twist. Not only are they to be subject to human government, whether imperial or gubernatorial, they must also submit in a distinctively Christ-like manner when treated unjustly. Apart from the more generally persecuted for Christ's sake,[21] Peter singles out two groups among his readers who were most vulnerable to injustice — the household slave with a cruel master and the wife of man who is an unbeliever. The response of those at such disadvantage is referred to by Peter as 'good behaviour . . . good works' and as 'doing good.'[22]

17. Colossians 4:5.
18. Romans 13:7.
19. Matthew 5:13-16.
20. Mark 12:17.
21. 1 Peter 4:12-19.
22. 1 Peter 2:12, 15.

Whereas, it may be thought that Peter has in mind practical assistance to widows and orphans spoken of elsewhere,[23] the unfolding of his letter shows that he was thinking along different lines. Peter is reflecting upon Jesus, whom he has seen, but whom his readers have not seen.[24] Peter, eye-witness of his master's sufferings in Jerusalem,[25] holds up before these distant readers the example of Jesus at Golgotha. At that time Jesus was (1) submissive to human authority,[26] unjust as it was in his case; (2) blameless and open in his behaviour; (3) trusting of God as the just judge; and (4) forgiving and non-vindictive towards his oppressors.[27] In all of this Jesus was the 'pattern' or template which they were to copy, footprints left for them to tread in.[28] It is this imitation of Christ as submissive, blameless, trusting, forgiving which Peter calls 'good behaviour . . . good works . . . doing good' by which they the persecuted sufferers glorify God before the eyes of those who vilify them.[29]

Slavery, though not expunged, is now an aberration, and thanks to more enlightened times in some parts of the world, there is protection for wives from their husbands. These beneficent social changes were not anticipated in the New Testament era. Moreover, they only apply in a small proportion of the world community. Whether in the 'liberated' west or in cultures more approximate to the milieu of the apostles, Christians often find themselves in situations of grave injustice and cruelty, sometimes precisely on account of their allegiance to the Lord Jesus Christ. Where justice and protection from abusive behaviour is to be found, the Christian should, of course, seek such respite. All too often, however, there is no relief from oppression. Either way, the witness of the Christian is informed by the manner of Jesus in the face of the injustice and cruelty which he suffered.

The potent witness of a life modelled upon Jesus, however, is generally not wordless.[30] When called by those in authority to give

---

23. *Cf.*, James 1:27; Acts 2:44-45; 4:32-37; 6:1; 1 Timothy 5:3-16.
24. 1 Peter 1:8.
25. 1 Peter 5:1.
26. It was 'for the Lord's sake' *(dia ton kurion)* that the readers were to be subject to human authority (1 Peter 2:13).
27. 1 Peter 2:21-23.
28. 1 Peter 2:21.
29. 1 Peter 2:12.
30. Except in the case of the wife of the unbeliever (1 Peter 3:1).

account of their loyalty to Christ these believers were to speak of their 'hope', that is, of their 'living hope' based on the resurrection of Jesus Christ from the dead.[31] Their Christlike lifestyle arises from redemption from a futile past by the death of Christ and from their hope for an endless future by his resurrection from the dead.[32] Yet this explanation of their behaviour is to be given with 'gentleness and reverence,' that is, in keeping with the 'gentleness and reverence' of the One in whose footsteps they tread.[33]

Two things are clear from these passages. One is that Christianity was chiefly about the people, not about the clergy. First Peter, in common with other apostolic writings, has little to say about presbyters, pastors, deacons and other 'official' church people. Clearly they are important, yet one can read whole documents from the apostles, Romans, 1 and 2 Corinthians, for example, and find not even one reference to such ministries. Rather, the apostles' interest is on the ordinary believer, what he believed and how he lived in fellowship with other believers and the face he showed to the watching world. Christianity according to the Bible is not a clerical religion. But under historical process it has become just that, whether 'catholic' or 'protestant'. The history of the church written by historians is the history of the clergy. The stories and photographs in church magazines are generally about bishops and priests. We Christians make saints and heroes out of priests and missionaries, not of the ordinary people. But the First Letter of Peter is all about the attitudes and actions of the people. They are the priesthood, whether in the church as gathered or out there in the world among the 'Gentiles.'

Second, it is evident that these attitudes and actions were to be crafted by a thought-out imitation of Christ in his unjust sufferings. The outsider, the 'Gentile,' is to meet Christ in the 'good behaviour' of the Christian, that is, in his *imitatio Christi*. The typical human reaction to injustice was and is 'pay-back,' vengeance; with the Christian there is something else. The Christian is to be blameless, upholding God-ordained structures of society, non-retaliating but rather commending his way to God who is the just judge.

31. 1 Peter 3:15; 1:3, 22.
32. 1 Peter 1:13-21.
33. 1 Peter 3:15.

The Beauty of the Church

First Peter is written out of the conviction that the church, that is the church as *community*, rather than institution, is and is to be a thing of great beauty. When Peter says that 'the end of all things is at hand,'[34] the word he uses for 'end' is *telos*, which in the context of 1 Peter means the 'perfection' of God's kingdom.[35] Now the point is that Peter goes on immediately to speak about church life in the here and now. 'The end of all things is at hand *therefore. . . .*' The *telos*/perfection of the end-times is to be anticipated *immediately* in the prayerfulness, love, forgiveness and mutual ministry in the church.

The beauty of the church is not aesthetic. Rather this beauty is seen in the love of God, the truth of God and the holiness of God incarnated in the lives and behaviour of the community of faith. This beauty is deeply attractive to hungry hearts seeking for God and for meaning for otherwise meaningless lives. Moreover, many people in the depersonalised world of mass communication, public transport, supermarket shopping and job-insecurity are searching for a sense of community, a place to belong. The church of God when it is true to its Lord's truth and love has magnetic power to draw outsiders into God's kingdom. In the experience of this writer, the church itself is God's greatest instrument of evangelism.

It is right that church members should take the word out to people who are on the outside of its life. But this must be done from a church which is healthy in love, truth and holiness. If the congregation's own house is not in order, obedient to God's word, various efforts at outreach are futile.

Peter has another piece of good advice about the church. It is that when its members meet they 'tell forth the praises of him who called [them] out of darkness into his wonderful light.'[36] Here is a clear reference to the life-changing impact of the preaching of the gospel upon them.[37]

---

34. 1 Peter 4:7.

35. *Telos* is used earlier in relationship with 'the salvation of your souls' (1:9) which will occur at 'the revelation of Jesus Christ' (1:7) when believers will enter into an 'inheritance which is imperishable, undefiled and unfading, kept in heaven for [them]' (1:4).

36. 1 Peter 2:9.

37. 1 Peter 1:12, 23, 25.

Beforehand, their lives were controlled by the passions of their former ignorance, the futile behaviour received from their parents.[38] This is the behaviour the 'Gentiles' continue to pursue, licentiousness, passions, drunkenness, revels, carousing, and lawless idolatry.[39] Having come to Christ, the living stone, and as living being built into a 'house,' as a 'holy priesthood' they offer spiritual sacrifices to God through Jesus Christ.[40] These 'sacrifices' are the declaration of God's actions calling them from their dark past into the light of their present redemption and hope.

How might they do this? Their declaration to one another will be by means of song, confession, testimony and preaching. But not *any* song, confession, testimony or preaching. The conversion of individuals and of families must be in view, not merely remote and removed doctrinal statements.

The congregation needs to be reminded that God is active in changing the life-direction of people. If he isn't then something is wrong. Is it because there is no evangelism to those outside? Is it because the members are unprepared and untrained to give an account of the hope that is in them? (All church members need to learn how to share their testimony and to give the main elements of the gospel). Is it because the church is not the place of beauty the apostles say it should be?

Where there is the telling forth of God's praiseworthy acts in liberating and giving hope then at least two things follow. One is that the members will be reinforced in their relationship with God in Jesus Christ. The other is that visitors and outsiders will hear the gospel in the normal course of events during the gathering of the people.

Finally, our churches need to give expression to the perfection of the last day. There is to be a reciprocal ministry of forgiveness, hospitality and care. The gatherings should echo with the praises of God for his mercy and deliverance of the people. Let the people know that their God reigns and is alive.

---

38. 1 Peter 1:14, 18.
39. 1 Peter 4:3.
40. 1 Peter 2:4-5.

Questions

1. While there are many obvious differences between our own times and those of the apostles, does this justify us in thinking that the teaching and practice of the early church is irrelevant to our mission today? Why are we often tempted to see our own age as so different? In addition to those listed above, are there any other ways in which history seems to be repeating itself?

2. Do our local churches believe in evangelism? If not, why not? If they do, do they have a 'working strategy to bring the gospel to the neighbourhood'?

3. Despite the threat of persecution Peter still urged the Christian believers to pay attention to holy living. What excuses do we make to avoid this challenge and what are the areas of modern life where there is the greatest need for this distinctive lifestyle to be seen?

4. Does the corporate life of our local church reflect God's future kingdom? Is it an effective 'instrument of evangelism'? Does the corporate life of our Anglican denomination help or hinder the task of witness in any way?

Lifestyle as Proclamation

BENJAMIN A. KWASHI

Summary

Actions speak louder than words. Jesus' proclamation of the Kingdom called for faith which proved itself in a changed way of life. Similarly, Paul's doctrine brings forth action and transformation. The gospel is not a static object; it is a catalyst. Evangelism is costly, demanding love, a changed lifestyle and a total obedience. It is an urgent task and we press on, rejoicing in the Lord, following in his footsteps, with our focus fixed on Christ alone.

'Actions speak louder than words' is a well-known saying. If we look back to the days of our primary and secondary school education we quickly realise that we have forgotten many of the facts that we were taught, but we remember the teachers: we still know who was kind and who was short tempered, who were the ones we trusted and who were those we tried to avoid! What a person is and what a person does make a far deeper impact than all the many words that he or she may say. The implications of this for the gospel, however, are not always realised; indeed they are often ignored.

The teaching of Jesus as recorded in the gospels is concerned with the Kingdom of Heaven and with how we are to live in the light of the coming of that Kingdom. The first two gospels introduce Jesus in this way: 'After John had been arrested, Jesus came into Galilee proclaiming the gospel of God: The time has arrived; the Kingdom of God is upon you. Repent and believe the gospel' (Mark 1:14-15; *cf.*, Matt. 4:17).

This is not a call to accept a new philosophy: it is a call to a new way of life. True repentance is a *metanoia,* a 'turning round', not just in intellectual matters, but in action, in behaviour, and in character. Faith which does not reveal itself in this manner is a sterile or purely intellectual belief: it is not true faith.

This is further amplified in Luke's introduction of Jesus — 'He stood up to read the lesson and was handed the scroll of the prophet Isaiah. He opened the scroll and found the passage which says, "The spirit of the Lord is upon me because he has anointed me; he has sent me to announce good news to the poor, to proclaim release for prisoners and recovery of sight for the blind; to let the broken victims go free, to proclaim the year of the Lord's favour." He began to address them: "Today" he said, "in your hearing this text has come true"' (Luke 4:16b-19, 21). The Old Testament prophecy is being fulfilled; dry bones have come to life. This is not an academic syllabus; it is a programme for that action which must necessarily spring out of a living faith.

In the fourth gospel Jesus first appears in the vicinity of John the Baptist and two of John's disciples follow Jesus. 'What are you looking for?' he asked. They said, 'Rabbi (which means teacher), where are you staying?' 'Come and see,' he replied (John 1:38-39).

They address Jesus as teacher, but they are not told to sit down and listen or even to take notes: they are commanded to come and to see. They will watch and they will take part. There will be teaching, but it will be teaching geared to action, to renewal, and to transformation. This is made clear from the outset, as Jesus heals the sick, drives out demons, feeds the hungry, and seeks the lost, until ultimately he gives up his life on the cross.

The long section of teaching put together at the beginning of Jesus' ministry in Matthew's gospel, and commonly referred to as the Sermon on the Mount, is itself about the character and manner of life expected of those who wish to enter the Kingdom of Heaven. The standards set are the opposite of the world's standards. Those who are blessed are the poor in spirit, the sorrowful, the gentle, those who hunger and thirst to see right prevail, the merciful, the pure in heart, the peacemakers, and those who are persecuted in the cause of the gospel. Those who follow these guidelines will not necessarily attain worldly status or possessions. They will face adversity and suffering in this life. Those who persevere will, however, enter the Kingdom of Heaven! On the way, the testing will be severe and those who survive will only be those whose life is built on the sound foundation of a firm faith. Faith there must be, but that faith must be proved by the fruit it yields.

In his epistles, Paul makes this same point very clearly. The opening chapters set out his doctrine; the final section translates this into action. In the epistle to the Romans, chapter twelve begins with a great 'Therefore': it is precisely because of the theology which he has been at such pains to expound in the preceding chapters that the Christians are to live in the manner which he now goes on to describe. Personal agendas, national traditions and also cultural issues must all come under the examining microscope of our faith. What God has done in Christ is of such primary importance that if men and women truly believe, their whole life must be changed: they are no longer to be conformed to the world around them; they are to be transformed. Then, as they begin to live this transformed life, they will more and more discern the will of God, and be able to know what is good, acceptable and perfect (Rom. 12:1-2). Faith brings about a transformed life which shows itself in action, and the living of this life in turn leads to a greater knowledge and a deeper faith. This cannot be attained all at once: perfection does not come instantly. Those who are 'born again' are at the beginning of a journey, not at their destination.

By the time Paul wrote his letter to the Philippians he had spent several years in the service of the gospel; his loyalty to Christ and the strength of his faith had been tested through hardships and sufferings of many kinds and of great severity. His life had been transformed by his encounter with the risen Christ on the Damascus road, but that transformation was not a completed operation, it was an ongoing process. His one desire was to know Christ and the power of his resurrection, to serve his master faithfully, to give himself totally to Christ, and finally to attain everlasting life. An onlooker might be tempted to think that surely Paul had done enough and that he had proved himself in every way. On the contrary, Paul said, 'It is not that I have already achieved this, I have not yet reached perfection, but I press on, hoping to take hold of that for which Christ once took hold of me. My friends, I do not claim to have hold of it yet. What I do say is this: forgetting what is behind and straining towards what is ahead, I press towards the finishing line, to win the heavenly prize to which God has called me in Christ Jesus' (Phil. 3:12-14).

As with Jesus, what Paul said, what he did and how he lived were all in perfect harmony. Had he said one thing and done another he would not have made an impact and he would not have been remembered in the same way. As it was, he proclaimed the gospel through his preaching and through his living. His lifestyle was what gave credibility to his words — indeed, his lifestyle was his ceaseless sermon, not spoken in ephemeral words, or written on paper and ink, but lived in flesh and blood.

A church which regards the gospel simply as a perfectly packaged parcel of belief to be handed on from generation to generation will not survive. Christ completed his work on the cross, but the effect of that has to be worked out in the lives of individuals and communities for as long as this world endures. The gospel is not an object which we can pick up, put down or hand on at will. For faith to be real, it must be lived. The gospel must so totally enter into the heart, mind and life of the believer, that he or she is completely taken over by it. The root meaning of the word 'baptise' is to be totally immersed or soaked. Those who are baptised are to be totally 'soaked' in the gospel with no area of life, no matter how small, omitted. When this happens, the life of the believer is transformed, and this has a contagious effect. Other people see the difference, and begin to ask questions. The gospel is not static; the gospel is a catalyst, and those who proclaim the gospel through their own lifestyle are catalysts for change in the lives of other individuals, of communities and of the world.

There are, however, many who actually believe that evangelism and mission can best be carried out only by specialists in that field. Others feel that the subject can only mean organising mass rallies and inviting prominent speakers to preach. Experience has shown that there are some committees on evangelism where all the members of that committee think that the best way to obey the command to evangelise is to seek to purchase a bus and equipment such as projector, generator, and loud-speaker systems. There has even been the case of a committee which put as its priority the organising of a fund-raising event to collect money in order to begin planning the task. Similarly, there are places where nothing has happened because no budget has been allocated to evangelism. No doubt money is useful in support of mission and missionaries, but there are no examples in Scripture of money being so important as to dictate whether or not the gospel can be preached. In fact if money were to become the ultimate determining factor, it would mean that the need for money has taken precedence over the command of Jesus, thus making money, and not Jesus, our God.

In contrast to this, Jesus emphasised the need for the life of the individual to become the evidence of the gospel. The good news must be proclaimed by our 'being': that is the meaning of Jesus' admonition that we are to be salt and light. Large gatherings and rallies no doubt have their place and their use, but they must focus on the 'becoming' and the change in life and character of the people. Then, and only then, is the gospel proclaimed. The approach which calls for people to receive Christ without emphasising the need for a corresponding change in character and lifestyle has no place in Scripture. Moreover, conversion is not a once and for all event: it is an ongoing lifelong process which requires continued nurturing and teaching.

Evangelism in this sense is indeed costly: it costs not less than everything. It cost Jesus his time, his resources, and most of all it cost him his life, in his obedience to the will of God. There is no substitute for the fact that, if we are to do the will of God and live as God requires, we must count the cost and bear the cost. That cost is the cost of love, which demands that we think thoughts of love, and constructively reach to all people, impelled by the power of that love. Our response therefore to the needs of people and of the world is not motivated by a mere concern for good works, but is a demonstration of the love of God. The demand and the price are high. No wonder that some denominations, some dioceses, some churches and some individuals will do everything to remove evangelism from the agenda of the church. In such cases, if evangelism is on the agenda at all, it is there just to satisfy the bishop or whoever is responsible for evangelism, but it will only be discussed as a subject and allowed to fizzle out, to be discussed again later; and so long as it is being discussed it remains just that — merely a subject for discussion.

We must accept that in doing evangelism we will bear the cost. It requires a lot of time in prayer, in preparation, in careful planning and training of individuals and of the church. It also takes a lot of effort to mobilise the people; it demands the total mobilisation of the church, not just of a few individuals, because the command is to the church. This takes time; it takes energy; it calls for a total dedication and commitment of one's life. Sometimes money is required, sometimes tools may be required, but most of the time it is people who are the number one prerequisite. To participate in this sacrificial service of love is to participate with God in saving the world. Not to participate in evangelism is to be opposed to God for God does not desire the death of a sinner; he does not wish the world to be condemned (John 3:16). Therefore he has saved us and called us and sent us to warn the world to turn to God through Jesus Christ. Whoever refuses to participate in evangelism is not only disobedient, but is actually guilty of wishing the world to be condemned. More than that, however, he is an enemy of the will of God. Evangelism is a whole lifestyle. It is not a once and for all event. It is an ongoing activity of the church in obedience to Christ to demonstrate his love to the world.

That obedience cannot be optional: discipleship without obedience is not Christian discipleship. Even in Old Testament times, God required obedience from his people; when they complied they prospered, and when they refused they suffered as individuals and as a people. Christ commands: we must obey. Obedience to Christ's commands is the key to mission, because only when we obey are we living according to the will of God. When the will of God is relegated to the background, other trivialities set themselves at the top. In fact, Satan is then able to set his agenda not from the outside but from within, because the doing of the will of God has become a lower priority for the children of God. This kind of situation is a direct consequence of the way in which we do, or do not, receive and act upon God's will. A church which does not hold evangelism as its top priority will find itself in a pool of turmoil of all sorts: everyone will seek his own interest; there will be hardly any united focus, voice or action of any kind; love of the brethren will be cold, selective and superficial — if indeed it exists at all. Everyone will be seeking his own interest and all for selfish gain. This kind of fellowship knows nothing about humility, service or compassion, or if it does, it will be a matter of theory only. Jesus, the Son of God, left his throne in heaven and came down for the salvation of mankind. Not only did this cost him his life, but it also demanded his time, energy and resources. This was the will of God for Jesus Christ in order that the world might hear and receive the good news of our salvation; the news that our sins have been forgiven; the news that we can now be called the children of God. Therefore we must demonstrate this to the world, following in the steps of Jesus Christ and following

145

his example in sacrificial living. As children of God we must obey God; as children of God we must do the will of God; as children of God we must live like children of God. That must be our lifestyle.

This means that at whatever point we are in evangelism there is always room to do more. There is a place for everyone in the mission of God, and we all must live for God as a demonstration of the grace of God upon our lives. Where we are coming from is not as important as where we are going to. The people in the street, the traders, the homeless children, the prostitutes, the poor, the sick, the rich, the rural people, the young people, the old: everybody must be told by word and deed about the good news, and they must be shown the direction in which we are heading. This means a radical change and transformation. This means that we must talk to the hearts of people in ways they will understand. This means that, in love and in the power of the Holy Spirit, God's word must be presented uncompromisingly through our words, our desires, our actions and our character.

This is an urgent task which cannot wait until tomorrow. In his teaching Jesus constantly emphasised that we must always be ready: we do not know when Christ will return; we do not know when we shall be called to account; our lives are not in our hands. Therefore, today and every day we must live lives which reflect Christ's love; we must be about our Master's business. If not, we shall be like the foolish virgins, the lazy steward and the goats (Matt. 25). They delayed; they did not live the gospel. To them was given the dreadful verdict, 'Depart from me' (Matt. 25:41). Let us so live today that at the end we hear the words, 'Come, you who are blessed by my Father' (Matt. 25:34).

We must know that the Kingdom of Heaven is our goal. This is the prize for which God has called us. Our prize is in heaven; it is not in New York; it is not in Geneva; it is not in Abuja; it is not even dollars; it is not gold, not silver; it is indescribable; it is in heaven. It is a prize that God gives. It is where God is, and it will be given to those who do the will of God. It has been prepared for all who are saved.

Therefore our sole focus is on Christ. Every talent and every gift; all money and energy; every person's effort and every person's life are all put together towards this one goal, this one task, of evangelism. There is no room for a competing goal of making money, or success, or prosperity, or of speculative and corrupt theologies. Indeed, any business, or learning, or contribution which does not further this one task of making Christ known and leading people to heaven has no value other than that which is temporal and ephemeral. The apostle Paul had only one task, one goal, and nothing could come between him and this one task. He presses on; his focus is right and he strains towards the prize. We must all sharpen our focus. We have only just started and, like Paul, we must forget what lies behind and focus on this one goal, the task of making Christ known, of getting people to live righteously, to live holy lives, and to put all their energies, all their money, all their efforts into the mission of God in evangelising the world. We must press on.

Later in his letter to the Philippians, Paul dares to say to them, 'Put into practice the lessons I taught you, the tradition I have passed on, all that you heard me say or do; and the peace of God will be with you' (Phil. 4:9).

In other words, he is saying to the church, 'Imitate me!' This is a great challenge to the church today, both to the leaders and to the members. Are our lives so transformed by the gospel, is our lifestyle such that we can say to others, 'Imitate me'? The fact is that we can never be 'off duty' as Christians. Whether we are at home or at work, in the market or on a bus, in church or out walking on our own, we are to live for Christ. God sees all. Other people too will see us, and will judge us and the gospel which we claim to profess. Time and again one hears testimonies of the impact made by a word or an action of which the speaker or the doer was completely unaware. The converse is of course also true. When people have deliberately turned away from God, their lifestyle speaks loud and clear saying, 'there is no God'.

The world would want us to believe that it is wealth, power, status and entertainment which have the pre-eminence. Unfortunately, some preachers and churches have been captured by the world's vision. Such religious leaders collect for themselves power and become wolves instead of shepherds. They cause much distress and hardship in an already difficult and strenuous situation, thereby making the people suffer and feel the effect of the bad situation twice over. For Paul, and indeed for every believer, it should be known and be made known that power belongs to God, and that therefore for those who believe in Jesus Christ, to live is Christ and to die is gain. This is a crucial fact and a comfort for the realisation of our joy in the gospel. The commercialisation of the Christian gospel has increased in our generation. Many have taken the world's system of entertainment into the church and have made a mockery of the cross of Christ. For them, Christ must be an entertainer, and Christianity must present itself in a way which will make them feel good in order for them to be satisfied. The first side effect of this is that they are unable to stand in the face of hardship. They know only a momentary happiness instead of true joy. Worse than that, their faith, if it is faith at all, is temporal and emotional. The joy that Christ gives is more than entertainment; it is not temporal; it is not controlled by circumstances and situations, it is real.

We are called to follow in the steps of Christ. Jesus himself calls us to follow him; the apostle Paul invites us to imitate Christ, and to imitate himself. The apostle admonishes the Christians to be careful; we should not live as enemies of the cross of Christ, for the end of that is destruction (Phil. 3:18-19). Those who remove the cross from the gospel have nothing to show in this life except their stomach, as their god and their glory is in their shameful actions. Those who live like this have their minds set on earthly things, but we are called to be citizens of Heaven, where Christ is. Therefore ours is to see what God is doing; to give him our absolute loyalty; to trust him; to listen to him; to follow him and to obey him. To turn aside from this is to turn away from real joy. We are called to rejoice only in the Lord. Outside the Lord there is no joy. In the Lord, however, our joy is full and overflowing, regardless of prevailing circumstances. 'Rejoice in the Lord always, and again I say, Rejoice!' (Phil. 4:4).

Moreover, we rejoice and we press on, because we know that our Lord is with us. When the risen Christ commanded his disciples to go to all nations, to preach, to teach and to baptise, he also promised to be with them, always. If, however, we refuse to obey, we lose his presence with us. Christ goes ahead of us, calling us to follow, but if we sit still where we are we are left further and further behind, until his presence is only a dim light on the horizon, a shadow of a fairy-tale once believed in. But to those who truly believe, who are transformed by the renewing power of the gospel, who live in the power of the Holy Spirit, who proclaim the Kingdom of God by all that they say, by all that they do, by their very lifestyle — to those, the living Christ continues to reveal himself as he leads them on, living in them, and through them continuing to call his people into his Kingdom.

Questions

1. The generally accepted idea in the world is that you should be yourself. How does this agree or conflict with proclaiming the gospel by your lifestyle?

2. Has the Christian gospel transformed your culture? If so, in what ways and in which forms?

3. What impact does the proclamation of the gospel have on lives and communities of the world? Give examples.

4. What are the negative results of our not proclaiming the gospel by our lifestyle today?

CALLED TO BE FAITHFUL IN A PLURALISTIC WORLD

Confessing Christ in a Pluralist Culture

CHRIS SINKINSON

Summary

In this chapter we consider the pressing need for Christians to evaluate the religious diversity of the age in which we belong. The term 'pluralism' is used here to identify one particular evaluation of that diversity. John Hick's radical example of this is considered to reflect the secularism of our age. Reasons for understanding his account to be secular are offered and certain alternative emphases that should mark a truly Christian engagement with religious diversity are outlined. It is noted that diversity is not something new but has often been the cultural background for Christian confession. Whatever steps we take in our response to current concerns, it is imperative that we continue to do so with Jesus Christ at the centre of our thinking and as the criteria for any legitimate developments to the tradition we might wish to make.

The Spirit of the Age

There is little doubt that our secular age retains a religious feel. Throughout the media there remains a continuing fascination with the spiritual, the paranormal and the inexplicable. From religious documentaries to popular science fiction series, the all-pervading thirst for something spiritual continues to find forms of expression in our otherwise secular society. For many years this religious feel has been most clearly exhibited in the rise of the new age movement and its offer of ancient syncretism dressed up in the marketing of modernity. Though this movement has proven somewhat less cohesive than had at first appeared to be the case, its central themes have a much deeper hold in our culture.

Two themes stand out as obvious hallmarks of modern culture. The first is that of tolerance. One of the great fruits of modernity, or so it is claimed, is the establishment of genuine principles for the toleration of diversity.[1] Tolerance here means more than resisting the impulse to do violence toward those with whom we may disagree. It implies disowning the very notion of absolute truth in favour of an attitude which concedes validity to every sincerely held belief. Thus a tolerant society will be one that not only permits diversity but values that diversity as a range of varyingly valid options for belief and behaviour.

Underlying tolerance is the theme of relativism. This provides the popular theory of truth and knowledge reigning in our society today. The reason why diversity of belief or behaviour should be tolerated is that no one claim to truth has an absolute status. Each claim is only relatively valid and thus its "rival" claims must be conceded to have some truth value. Relativism demands that we understand truth as a matter of degree rather than a matter of kind. This seems plausible as the relativist points out that all truth claims are only true to some degree and in the future various revisions will draw those claims closer to the truth itself. If that is so then why not admit that all such claims, whether made by any religion or none, offer some degree of truth and abandon the notion that any individual or tradition has an exclusive grasp of truth? However contrary they may seem we are urged to piece together beliefs and doctrines like small, obscure pieces of a great jig-saw the meaning of which will only become clear when every last element finds its place.[2]

1. I. Markham, *Plurality and Christian Ethics* (Cambridge: Cambridge University Press: 1994), pp. 23-25.
2. The hope of Keith Ward's 'convergent spirituality' in his *A Vision to Pursue* (London: SCM Press, 1991), pp. 159-61.

Christians and Diversity

A basic question to which Christians must address themselves is one of interpreting or explaining the fact of diversity. There are many diverse religious traditions each claiming the ultimate loyalties of their adherents. Perhaps in an earlier age Christians, at least in the West, lived largely in ignorance of the sheer scale of diversity, only dimly aware of the existence of Muslims, Jews and heretics as alternative options.[3] Popular explanations of diversity may then be quite simple. Non-Christian religions are seen as the result of sin, ignorance, mistake or the activity of demons. However, in keeping with the rise of a more global awareness the scale of diversity has demanded fresh explanations. In the light of such vast diversity the older more exclusivist options have seemed to some to be less plausible. Why are there so many dominant religious options around the world gaining such wholehearted and sincere devotion from their followers? The growing awareness of this fact has paralleled an increasing recognition of the plausibility of what is known as a pluralist explanation of diversity. In academic circles it is the philosopher John Hick who has perhaps been associated most with the articulation of the pluralist case. In his writing, lecturing and travelling he has not ceased from proclaiming the pluralist explanation of diversity and it is this explanation that resonates so well with themes in contemporary culture.

A New Revolution

During the seventies John Hick called for a revolution in Christian theology which was the culmination of both philosophical speculation and practical inter religious encounter. Since then the nature of the revolution has been further refined or perhaps, as some would claim, subjected to yet further revolutions.[4] However, the basic characteristic of Hick's pluralist theology has remained constant. Hick draws an

---

3. J. Sanders, *No Other Name* (Grand Rapids: Eerdmans, 1992).
4. Gavin D'Costa in Harold Hewitt (ed.), *Problems in the Philosophy of Religion* (London: Macmillan Press, 1991), pp. 3-18.

analogy with an epoch making discovery in astronomy in order to illustrate his idea.

According to the Ptolemaic astronomy dominant through the middle ages the earth is at the centre of God's created universe with the planets, stars and other cosmic objects revolving around it. The Church adopted this picture as consistent with the biblical world view and clearly the Ptolemaic outlook meshed well with the very human desire to be at the centre of things. Anomalies in the movements of the planets in their orbits around the earth were explained with reference to a pattern of epicycles in which they followed slightly different courses. Increasing knowledge of the movement of the lights in the heavens became increasingly difficult to explain and the Ptolemaic world view lost plausibility. In the sixteenth century the Polish astronomer Copernicus offered an entirely new paradigm in which to make sense of the place of the earth in the universe. He described the sun, and not the earth, as the central body in the movement of the spheres. Thus the Copernican revolution in astronomy had begun. Resisted by the Church but supported by the truth it was only a matter of time before the new astronomical picture was to be adopted as correct.[5]

Hick adopts the role of Copernicus in his description of the need for a theological revolution. Christians have assumed the validity of a Ptolemaic theology with regard to other religions. At the centre is the Church and Christ its head with all the other traditions and ideologies of the world revolving around it. Where these religions contain truth this is explained with reference to their connections with Christianity. Where they are in error this is explained with regard to their distance from this centre. However, more recent history with its growing awareness of the sheer scale of diversity and the apparent morality and wisdom of those alternative traditions has brought about the need for theological explanations of diversity reminiscent of those astronomical epicycles. Hence, Karl Rahner and other Roman Catholic thinkers of the second Vatican council era have attempted to explain those traditions in terms of an implicit connection to Christ and the

---

5. Diogenes Allen provides an alternative account of the dispute in *Christian Belief in a Postmodern World* (Louisville: Westminster/John Knox Press, 1989), pp. 27-49.

Church.[6] Continuities between religions and Christ have been emphasised instead of the discontinuities emphasised by the exclusivist world view. Hick rejects these laboured explanations as increasingly complex attempts to avoid the obvious need he feels to reposition the place of Christ and his Church away from the centre of the universe of faiths.

However, a difficulty arises in the attempt to state what, exactly, ought to stand in the centre of the universe of faiths. In his first expression of his Copernican revolution Hick argued that God is the sun around which the religions orbit.[7] This becomes problematic when some of the satellites have little or no place for God. One thinks of certain agnostic schools of Buddhism or Hindu movements where ultimate reality is non-personal. Hick's problems become more intense when he wishes to extend his generous interpretation even to some secular ideologies such as Marxism.[8] For this reason Hick's revolution has been subject to a continuing modification. At the centre of the universe of faiths lies the transcendent Real — above and beyond and utterly incommunicable. The Real may be described as He, She, It or, better still, as the Real. Debate and discussion over the personal or non-personal status of this Ultimate Reality is rather futile for such categories belong to a finite world and cannot apply directly to infinite reality.[9] In this way the Thing at the centre of the universe of faiths recedes from view, becoming less and less clear or connected to either our own tradition or to those of anyone else. As Keith Ward suggests of Hick it 'is not so much that all traditions are equally true as that they are all equally false'.[10] All religions revolve around something but they share a common ignorance regarding what that something is. Any claims they make to describe that something must be reinterpreted as the mythological speak of blind people attempting to refer to something they stumble across in ignorance. Diversity results from the attempts to explain and appropriate the Infinite in finite terms and all claims to exclusivity or absoluteness should be regarded with suspicion. What might compel a Christian to

6. G. D'Costa, *Theology and Religious Pluralism* (Oxford: Basil Blackwell, 1986).
7. J. Hick, *God and the Universe of Faiths* (London: Macmillan Press, 1988), pp. 120-32.
8. J. Hick, *An Interpretation of Religion* (London: Macmillan Press, 1989), pp. 308-9.
9. Hick, *An Interpretation*, p. 246.
10. Ward, *A Vision*, p. 174.

undergo this revolution and confess the pluralist account of diversity? We shall consider three reasons that have compelled Hick.

An Argument from Philosophy: How Do We Know?

Hick's first published work was a revision of his PhD thesis on Christian faith and the nature of knowledge.[11] His most recent major work includes a more developed statement of his theory.[12] Bringing this work together we might say that there are two strands to Hick's notion of how we know anything at all. These strands provide compelling reasons, if they are correct, to adopt the pluralist outlook.

The first strand is the role of interpretation in knowledge. Hick describes the situation of someone seeing a tree stump on a hill and mistakenly identifying it as a rabbit. He uses this situation to expose the human role of interpretation as we experience things according to very personal factors. Highly complex aspects of reality are highly ambiguous and thus demand an even greater degree of human interpretation to make sense of them. The religious claims and experience of individuals is understood in the light of this basic factor: human beings must employ interpretation in order to see reality the way they do. The important concession that this point demands regarding pluralism is that we acknowledge the fundamental ambiguity of spiritual reality. To some it seems silent and devoid of the divine while to others reality is charged with the presence of angelic beings, divine avatars or the personal-creator God. Hick would understand the Psalmist's claim that 'The heavens declare the glory of God' as one interpretation among many of what we might learn from the skies above us. The role of interpretation is important because it emphasises the central role of our human mind in encounter with reality. The second strand in Hick's thought develops this point further.

In more recent writing Hick has introduced a picture of knowledge that relies upon a basic insight from the work of Immanuel Kant. According to Kant human knowledge is structured and filtered by

11. J. Hick, *Faith and Knowledge* (Ithaca, New York: Cornell University Press, 1957).
12. Hick, *An Interpretation.*

aspects of the mind and never has direct awareness of the objects we claim to know about. In other words, there is a radical distinction between knowledge of things as they appear to us and things as they really are in themselves. We can never step outside of our minds and see things as they really are. Hick extends this analysis of knowledge to religious knowledge in particular. He claims that this insight must compel us to distinguish between knowledge of the Divine as it appears to us through the structures and filters of our own religious tradition and the Divine as it really is in itself. Such an analysis enables Hick to explain the major differences between religions. Religions provide a finite context for experiencing an aspect of the Divine. In this way, religions are compatible with one another. Instead of viewing our differences as contradictions we should view them as compatible, limited, insights into a Divine Reality that can never be fully described.

An Argument from Biblical Studies: Who Was Jesus?

Christians who confess Christ as Lord claim as central to their faith a doctrinal commitment which seems utterly incompatible with the pluralist case. If Jesus really is God incarnate then what he claimed about himself and what he demanded have a privileged status.[13] It is not so much the uniqueness of Christ as the status of Christ that undermines the pluralist account. However, Hick commends pluralism as compatible with Christian confession and he does so by offering a reappraisal of the identity of Jesus.

According to Hick the claims of the incarnation and the trinitarian nature of God are later, mythological, pictures used by the early Church to identify how much Jesus meant to them but not disclosing a literally true description of the identity of Jesus.[14] Borrowing from the insights of some radical New Testament writers, Hick claims that Jesus was a man like anyone else but with a great spiritual awareness of the Divine and its moral nature. True encounter with the Divine, according to Hick,

13. One might consider Matthew 28:18-20; Mark 2:8-10; Luke 9:21-26; John 14:6.

14. *I.e.,* J. Hick (ed.), *The Myth of God Incarnate* (London: SCM Press, 1977), pp. 175-78.

leads to a transformation away from self-centredness to other-centredness which includes putting other people and the Divine before ourselves. This is exactly what happened in the case of Jesus. So intense was his experience of the Divine that the sick and needy felt themselves healed and satisfied in his presence.[15] Jesus is a great (though not supreme) example to us of what the Divine is like and how we should live before it.

An Argument from Anthropology: Who Are Non-Christians?

Hick describes the development of religion as a universal phenomenon which leads him to relativise the significance of Christianity. Religion is found all over the world and, Hick claims, can be shown to have evolved and cross fertilised ideas among the various cultural forms in which it is found. Given this universal status Hick believes it is possible to establish certain common sense rules of morality such as the golden rule to treat others as we ourselves would wish to be treated. These rules provide standards by which we can both affirm the relative validity of all the major religious traditions but also identify human error and evil when expressed in spirituality. The world's religions are affirmed because Christians have no monopoly on good behaviour. Rather, goodness and selflessness mark the saints and devout of all the world religions. Non-Christians are not unredeemed pagans requiring the gospel but people of God expressing their spirituality in forms different from those of Christians. Error and evil can be identified particularly in some cults and ideologies. Hick is not committing himself to the idea that all religions are valid regardless of their moral fruits. On the contrary, by the common standard of moral goodness such evil forces as those behind Nazism or the suicidal pact surrounding the Jim Jones cult are found to be false expressions of spirituality.[16]

According to Hick there is no qualitative difference between a Christian and a non-Christian. The only distinction is a matter of degree

15. Hick (ed.), *The Myth of God*, p. 172.
16. See Hick, 'On Grading Religions', *Religious Studies* 17/4 (1981), pp. 451-67.

from those who are very unholy to those who are very holy whatever religion they belong to. Salvation, in this analysis, is a matter of following the pattern of goodness expressed by many great saints, including Jesus, in order to be transformed from self-centredness to Reality-centredness or centred on the interests of others and of the Ultimate Reality. If one concedes that just such a transformation is going on in the lives of so-called 'pagans' then this becomes an important foundation in establishing the pluralist case.

Secularism Has Many Names

In the outset of our discussion we considered themes of our secular age. It is clear that Hick's pluralist case meshes well with them. Concerning the need for tolerance this is almost a cardinal virtue in his account. Indeed, one thread of his argument for the plausibility of pluralism is that it permits what he considers to be true tolerance. This means more than mutual respect for those with whom we have disagreements but even the valuing of religious diversity as a good thing in itself. Hick's project both appeals to tolerance as an argument to support the need for his hypothesis and a fruit that develops where it is adopted. The relativist approach to truth is also embedded in Hick's account. According to the relativist outlook truth is a matter of degree not absolutes. Given a notion of truth as something far beyond our reach it is plausible to argue that descriptions of truth apparently at odds with one another are limited approximations not incompatible with one another. Is the Divine Reality personal or non-personal? Hick declares that It is beyond both categories though either category is useful as a means to help us think about it and orient ourselves towards it. There is no stopping this relativist strategy. Apparent contradictions can be reinterpreted as helpful mythologies designed to orient ourselves to something beyond our reach but never really accessible. Perhaps the only truth claims not so easily relativised in this way are those that concern everyday matters of fact or claims about history. What of the claim that Jesus died on the cross made by Christians and the Islamic counter claim that he did not? Hick shows little interest in such squabbles as, according to his definition of religion as moral change, historical events have only contingent significance. Whether something

161

did or did not happen in history is interesting speculation but could not possibly be relevant to the fundamental significance of religion. The only area where Hick will not tolerate relativism is in the area of basic moral requirements. The need to be good, in the general sense of the teachings of Jesus, the Buddha or Mohammed, is the basic absolute of Hick's system.

Hick's Copernican revolution has led to an increasingly unobtainable Real at the centre of religious reality. Given that it cannot be described in either personal or non-personal forms the actual character of the Real becomes harder and harder to conceive. Hick claims that this need not concern us for our worship need only be directed at the seven forms the Real takes for us and not the Real in itself. Hick's call amounts to the worship of an idol while the Real itself disappears from the focus of religious devotion. It is particularly important for Christians to note that if the Real is not personal then we must also reinterpret all those personal categories that we might apply to God as nothing more than descriptions of how something quite different appears to us. Revelation, the love of God, mercy, forgiveness and relationship have no place in discussion of a Real that is not personal. There is a form of agnosticism that results from this account. Hick's conception of religious knowledge is devoid of any notion of divine revelation. We fumble in the dark as blind men trying to describe and identify an elephant in our midst but mistakenly describing it as a tree, a snake or a spear. Hick follows the secularist methodology of denying revelation and permitting only speculation.

Consider further Hick's account of the identity of Jesus and the nature of humanity. In each case we can see examples of the application of a secular world view to religion. Concerning Jesus we are given to understand that the two natures doctrine is meaningless and that Jesus himself was a good man, like us, but with an intense awareness of the Real on a par with that of other great religious leaders around the globe. Regarding the nature of humanity it is important to note his basic description of salvation. Salvation is the human activity of giving up selfishness and becoming better people. It is not something God does for us but something we do for ourselves. In order for this view of salvation to be correct it must be the case that human beings have both the freedom and the natural inclination to do saving deeds. Given a long enough period of time, and Hick assumes further lives after this one, every human being will progress from self-centredness to Reality-centredness. Our goodness will one day save us. Such a view of human nature and salvation is devoid of any notion of divine grace. This optimism over the human spirit leaves little room for reference to the necessity of God's action whether in atonement, redemption, reconciliation or even revelation.[17] According to Hick, the most that we need are a few examples for us and we find these in Jesus and other religious gurus.

After Pluralism

The claim of this essay is that pluralism is another form of secularism. As such it is clearly wedded to the modernist project. This connection has been sharply drawn and incisively critiqued by many thinkers and particular attention may be drawn to the work of Lesslie Newbigin.[18] Though rapidly changing, our age is still held entranced by the achievements of the Enlightenment in the rise of liberal democracy and in dramatic scientific progress. Such gains are to be applauded but the false assumptions of modernism must also be identified and rejected. It is these assumptions that have led to the increasing secularity of our age and it is these assumptions that must be resisted by Christians who wish to account for diversity. Hick's account of diversity places a certain theory of knowledge as foundational to his project. That theory of knowledge is quite secular depending as it does upon the absence of revelation and the dualist distinction between human knower and the unknown reality. If this is the starting point for theology then it is not surprising that we are inexorably led to an agnostic position that must relativise the Christian account in favour of an approach that tolerates all sincere attempts to fumble in the dark and describe what is there. When the centre of religious knowledge is not the God revealed in Christ but the contemporary human knower it is quite natural that the result is a form of religious relativism. Hick has abandoned such a christological centre but only in order to enthrone the assumptions of

17. Such as in Romans 5:6-8.
18. Particularly in L. Newbigin, *The Gospel in a Pluralist Society* (London: SPCK, 1989).

secularism with its animosity towards the supernatural categories of a personal God, transforming grace and divine revelation.

In response to pluralism it is welcome that Christians are called to reappraise their account of diversity. Many evangelicals have taken up the challenge of outlining just such a reconsideration.[19] However, it is imperative that Christians remain true to their centre. Jesus Christ is Lord of all and therefore he must remain the central interpretative key to any assessment we may make. To replace Christ with any other norm, whether standards of religious studies or cultural moods, is to abandon historic Christian confession in favour of an idolatry. Christian confession has often taken place in pluralist societies and done so with Christ at the centre.[20] In the case of Hick's pluralism it is the secular world view and an attendant theory of knowledge that is given the final say. Yet surely any position that allows the God revealed through Christ in scripture to be relativised with respect to the centre of faith will quickly adopt the hallmarks of the culture in which it makes its confession. This is the danger that we must avoid for this is the risk of emptying Christian confession of its life giving content. Instead, it is the responsibility of the Christian to assess all claims to truth in the light of the person and work of Jesus Christ. It is not Christians or the Church who have the superior status to the world religions but it is Christ who is the telos of all truth seeking and so it is by him that all truth claims must be measured. This entails that certain particularities of history are not mere contingent events of no significance to human salvation but that within history there is the particular story of God in which his true nature and purposes are revealed. It is in this story that we must seek our account of diversity.[21]

19. With varying degrees of success one may note N. Anderson, *Christianity and World Religions* (Leicester: InterVarsity Press, 1984); P. Cotterell, *Mission and Meaninglessness* (London: SPCK, 1990); C. Pinnock, *A Wideness in God's Mercy* (Grand Rapids: Zondervan, 1992); V. Ramachandra, *The Recovery of Mission* (Carlisle: Paternoster Press, 1996).

20. As earliest examples one might consider Acts 4:12; Acts 17:31; Acts 19:26-27.

21. An example of which is found in D. Carson, *The Gagging of God* (Leicester: Apollos, 1996), pp. 193-345.

Questions

1. Consider forms, other than that of Hick, in which you have heard the pluralist type of argument presented. Why is it such a compelling and popular approach to the issues?

2. In what way should Christians be tolerant? Are there limits to tolerance and is there a distinction between being tolerant of positions we disagree with and being respectful?

3. Many people are relativists with regard to religious truth. In what ways do we see relativism in the world and in the church? What problems are there in adopting the relativist stance?

4. There is much debate today, even among evangelicals, over God's saving activity among unbelievers and the unevangelised. What are the basic biblical principles that we believe should guide any such discussion?

5. How should our interpretation of diversity help shape our approach to evangelism and Christian confession in a pluralist society?

Islam and Christ: Reflections on the Face of Islam — Signposts for Christians among Muslims in a Secular Age

VIVIENNE STACEY

Summary

Christ is a sign to both Muslims and Christians in different ways. Mutual understanding needs several key issues to be clarified. The complex nature of fundamentalism needs to be investigated in depth. The phenomenon of 'post modernity' needs to be acknowledged as a challenge for both Muslims and Christians; likewise the question of women's rights and feminism. The Islamic nature of mission should be compared and contrasted with that of Christianity. The increasing persecution of Christians is a growing problem demanding urgent consideration at the same time as closer relations between Christians and Muslims and organised interfaith interaction are developing. Clergy and laity need to listen, understand and interact with Muslims. Could this process bring fresh understanding, another epiphany, as Christ is revealed to the Muslims in a new way?

166

Introduction:
Christ, a Sign for both Muslims and Christians

In the Qur'an the frequently used Arabic word for 'sign' *(aya)* was probably taken from Syriac or Aramaic.[1] It was used of 'Isa, the Messiah, son of Mary. He was a sign not only to the Israelites but to the world as the following verses indicate. Q. 19:21 . . . and (We wish) to appoint him as a sign unto men and a mercy from us' (Yusuf Ali, *The Meaning of the Glorious Qur'an)*; Q. 21:91 '. . . and made her and her son a sign to the worlds' (Richard Bell, *The Qur'an Interpreted)*.

In the Bible at the presentation in the Temple of Jesus by Mary and Joseph, Simeon declared, 'My eyes have seen your salvation, which you have prepared in the sight of all people, a light for revelation to the Gentiles and for glory to your people Israel' (Luke 2:30-32, N.I.V.). After blessing the Holy Family he prophetically declared to Mary, 'This child is destined to cause the falling and rising of many in Israel, and to be a sign that will be spoken against, so that the thoughts of many hearts will be revealed. And a sword will pierce your own soul too' (Luke 2:34-35, N.I.V.).

The significant place given to Christ in the Qur'an and the uniqueness of Christ in the Bible present both bridges and barriers to Muslims and Christians studying each other's Scriptures. Over seventy verses of the Qur'an refer to the Christ or to Mary. He is *'Isa, Ibn Maryam, al-Masih* in the Qur'an — a servant or *'abd* of God, a prophet or *nabi* and a messenger or *rasul*, word or *kalima*, a witness or *shahid*, etc. These descriptions are all possible bridges. The main barrier is that while the Qur'an allows that the Jews intended to kill him and that he was willing to die, it denies the fact of the crucifixion. One day the Muslim view of Jesus will come in full focus and many will understand that he needs no protection from shame and that it was through the suffering of death that he was crowned with glory and honour (Hebrews 2:9). We maintain with Dr. John Stott that there are many Jesuses,[2] including the Jesus of popular Hinduism, the Jesus of Shi'a Islam and the Jesus of the Sunnis,

---

1. Geoffrey Parrinder, *Jesus in the Qur'an* (London: Sheldon Press, 1977) (reprinted), pp. 51-52.
2. J. R. W. Stott, *The Cross of Christ*, 2nd ed. (Leicester: InterVarsity Press, 1989), pp. 40-43.

but we are concerned with the Jesus of the Bible. If we compromise his uniqueness and undermine the inspired records we deny him.

Undoubtedly, Christians and Muslims have a considerable amount in common. It is part of Christian hospitality and obligation in love that we seek to understand and relate sensitively to the billion or more Muslims who form a fifth of mankind. Our common humanity is the greatest bridge but our two faiths provide many paths which can lead us to creative encounter and faithful salutation. We, therefore, now look for some of the signposts and seek to serve our generation according to the will of God.

The Complexity of Fundamentalism

Maha Azzam[3] in a recent article[4] has raised the question as to whether, in rejecting a definition of Islam that is monolithic, analysts have gone to the other extreme by substituting a set of rigid and compartmentalised notions. He sees a third possibility — 'It appears that the perceptions and practice of Islam are much more fluid and tend to overlap and that there is a common and integrated world-view amongst Muslims that can be delineated'. For Islamists God alone is sovereign, therefore *Shari'a* (the Qur'an and Sunna), not the sovereignty of an electorate, is the source of legislation and policy. Accountability and duty are more important than personal freedom. Here we have two views of democracy — this Islamic one and the Western secular humanist one. Helen Watson, a lecturer in social anthropology at the University of Cambridge, clarifies the issue with this statement, 'If debates about the institutions and structures of Muslim society are framed within Western notions of equality, individualism and freedom, the absence of equivalent concepts in Islam may lead to the misleading conclusion that "democracy and Islam" are incompatible . . .'.[5]

3. Associate Fellow at the Royal United Services Institute for Defence Studies (RUSI), Whitehall, London.
4. 'Islamist Attitudes to the Current World Order', *Islam and Christian Muslim Relations*, Vol. 4, No. 2 (Dec. 1993), p. 247.
5. Helen Watson, 'Women and the Veil: Personal Responses to Global Process', in Akbar S. Ahmed and Hastings Donnan (eds.), *Islam, Globalization and Postmodernity* (London: Routledge, 1984), p. 155.

Many see Islam as a 'threat', forgetting that many Muslims feel threatened by the attitudes and policies of Western powers in the Middle East, particularly in relation to the Palestinian question and the continuing presence of American troops on the holy soil of Saudi Arabia. These problems, as well as the treatment of Muslim minorities in some parts of the world (for example in Bosnia and Kashmir), emphasise the need to understand the Muslim world view and why and how politics and religion fit together. One can see Islamism with its infinite variety as not so much a rigidly defined system as a multitude of efforts to create bases from which to come to terms with the economic, social and political realities of the modern world without being Westernised, secularised and unfaithful to Islam.

The Western media often gives a very negative press to Muslims, even when the item under discussion may represent a small and extremist grouping. Dislike of the system quickly becomes dislike of the people. In the midst of much exaggerated reporting the church has a responsibility to be fair in its assessments of Islam. There are thousands of varieties of Islam. There is no monolithic system; the different parties and groupings can be described today but they may have changed by tomorrow. There is a fluidity and a movement like that of the clouds in the sky. Even fanatics can change. The apostle Paul probably qualified as a fundamentalist Pharisee and persecutor of the church before his vision of Christ on the Damascus road. Some modern day terrorists become humble followers of Christ. I have personally met one such who was trained for terrorism from the age of nine. He now works to help others come to know his Saviour, the Lord Jesus Christ.

Even the concept of Holy War or *jihad* is not always about military action. It is more often about striving in the way of God in the political, economic or social arena, or about the struggle against evil in the heart of man in the way that John Bunyan experienced it and then described it in his book *Holy War.* Likewise, fundamentalism is not always about terrorism, more often it is about going back to the fundamentals. Even the militant Muslim fundamentalist may feel on the defensive and be reacting to the modern scene at one extreme, engaging with the secular, pluralist, disintegrating Western world and seeking answers.

Post-modernity —
A Challenge for Both Muslims and Christians

The post-modern relativistic 'religion of tolerance' challenges Muslims as much as Christians. Professor Akbar S. Ahmed, one of Britain's leading Muslim academics, concludes the preface of his fascinating book *Postmodernism and Islam: Predicament and Promise*[6] by thus referring to his two year old daughter, 'Nafees will live, as a Muslim, in the post-modern world which is just beginning to shape our lives; therein lies the Muslim predicament: that of living by Islam in an age which is increasingly secular, cynical, irreverent, fragmented, materialistic and, therefore, for a Muslim, often hostile. In an age of cynicism and disintegration Islam has much to offer. I, therefore, pray she finds inspiration in her faith and culture, to assist her in making sense of, and resolving, the predicament of living as a good, caring and decent human being in the post-modernist world'.

The devout Muslim lives in the knowledge that Islam covers every aspect of life and that truth and morality are not relative but absolute. The Christian position is parallel to this, although through the influence of secular humanism many Christians have privatised their religion and forgotten the world view of the Bible and its absolute standards. Post-modernism in the prevailing intellectual climate of the West today means we have moved from an era of rationalism and materialism to a kind of unreason, where there is no absolute truth or ethical standard. Many people believe anything that seems to offer to fill the spiritual void. The post-modern mind seems to be marked by gullibility bringing in a new paganism. This is of great concern to the practising Muslim as well as to the committed Christian.

Women's Rights and Feminism in Islam

Nearly all Muslim countries have signed the United Nations Universal Declaration of Human Rights. However, to ensure full rights for women means that all women know their rights and how to proceed if their

6. Akbar S. Ahmed, *Postmodernism and Islam: Predicament and Promise* (London and New York: Routledge, 1992).

rights are violated. In some countries the low level of literacy means that women are in ignorance of their rights. The law may say that a man should only have one wife but if there is no means of enforcing the law he may choose to have two or more wives. There may be a minimum age for marriage but where records are not properly maintained and where again there is no punishment for breaking the law women are at a disadvantage.

Most well-known Muslim civil rights campaigners and feminist leaders come from urban middle-class, professional backgrounds, but they have a following among the poor and oppressed. Professor Fatima Mernissi, a distinguished Moroccan sociologist and writer born in 1940, is a noted feminist and equal rights campaigner. In her book *Forgotten Sultanas, Women Heads of State in Islam*, she chronicles and analyses the histories of remarkable women rulers. Then she reflects on politics in the modern Islamic world in which even well-educated women are often excluded.[7] Professor Mernissi has boldly reconciled feminism with the Prophet's teachings. She describes how he discussed politics with his wives who even went to war with him. In another of her books she shows how Muhammad, far from being an oppressor of women, upheld the spiritual equality of all in Islam[8] (Q. 16:97). She points out that while the Qur'an teaches that men and women have different but complementary roles in society, the *Hadith* or Traditions of Islam sometimes give a very different picture. In her writings Mernissi stresses that often women have had a bad press because so many of the writers have been male.

Riffat Hassan,[9] Pakistani lecturer and writer, now teaching in the USA, has long been engaged in Quranic exegesis. She claims that some of the *Hadith* or Traditions distort the Quranic teaching on the equality and mutuality between women and men. She especially focuses on the creation of man and woman in the Qur'an and exposes three faulty theological assumptions which are based more on the Traditions than

7. Fatima Mernissi, *The Forgotten Queens of Islam* (Cambridge: Polity Press, 1993), a translation from the French, *Sultanes Oubliées, Chefs d'Etat en Islam* (Paris, 1990).

8. Fatima Mernissi, *Women and Islam: An Historical and Theological Enquiry* (Oxford: Blackwell, 1991).

9. Catherine Jones, 'Women in Muslim-Christian Dialogue', *Encounter*, Nos. 207-8 (July 1994), Rome, p. 13.

on the Quranic text. Besides being a prolific writer on these matters, Riffat Hassan has also been active in the promotion of human rights. She maintains that 'the distinction between "private space" of the home and family reserved to women, and "public space" as the prerogative of men, is a false dichotomy, diminishing the potential of both women and men, to the impoverishment of all'.

The obituary of the Iranian writer Qazaleh Alizadeh, born in 1948, appeared in *The Guardian* on 21 June, 1996. After studying in Paris she returned to Iran but eventually became disillusioned with the political regime. She committed suicide. She was one of Iran's best-known authors. 'She carved a space for the voice of women in a society experiencing a harsh imposition of male theocratic values.'

The importance of the 'voices' of the feminists and human rights campaigners has a significant place in the long struggle for the proper recognition of the dignity of human beings whether male or female. Christians, recognising in each person the image of God, can ally themselves with those seeking to implement the U.N. Universal Declaration of Human Rights. The incarnation of the Lord Jesus Christ speaks of humanity and not of gender.

Winning the World: Two Different Agendas

1. 'Lord of the Worlds', Q. 1:1 — The Muslim Agenda: World Mission

For Muslims the world is divided into *dar al-islam* or the House of Islam and *dar al-harb* or the House of War. The former consists of those parts of the world ruled by Muslims and under *Shari'a* or Islamic law, thereby submitting to God. The latter has yet to be brought into submission to God, thereby joining *dar al-islam*. Ideally there is one God, one community and one *Shari'a*. It is incumbent on Muslims to work for this one world as there is, in their world view, no division between religion and politics nor between sacred and secular. The mission of Islam is called *da'wah*. Basically this Arabic word means 'call' (a call to Muslims to be truly muslim) or 'invitation' (an invitation to those outside the community of Islam to embrace Islam). In specialised usage *da'wah* means 'missionary activity'. It is not surprising that Muslim leaders have a concerted strategy to make each continent Muslim. For example, the Headquarters of the Islamic Council of Europe, based in London, co-ordinates all Islamic centres and organisations in Europe, working in close co-operation with international Islamic organisations and the governments of all Muslim states.

Saudi Arabia, the religious centre of Islam, possesses a quarter of the known oil resources of the world and generously finances the Voice of Islam, the world's most powerful radio transmitter. Also in Saudi Arabia, the world's largest printing works produces over twenty-eight million copies of the Qur'an every year. Now the Internet is becoming another way of strengthening and spreading Islam. Project Café Medina is a scheme to link all mosques and Islamic schools in the U.K. to each other and to the Internet. Dr. Ghayasuddin commented on it, 'The Muslim community must be at the cutting edge of technology, not on the back seat. I want to see our children become at one with the Internet and all the tools that are necessary to comprehend this new massively expanding medium of communication'.[10] A similar project has begun in Singapore. In Iran one computer firm has an annual output capacity for six million audio and video CDs as well as CD ROMs for computers and hopes to double this soon. It is reported that orders to produce 600,000 audio discs with verses of the Qur'an for both the domestic and export markets have already been received. In Egypt, the intellectual centre of the Muslim world, the al-Azhar University continues to train Muslim missionaries from most Muslim countries for all the lands of the world. For the whole world to be Muslim would be the Muslim view of success.

2. 'The Lord of Heaven and Earth', Acts 17:24 — The Christian Agenda: World Mission

Although the Muslim and Christian views of world mission superficially look the same, they are actually very different. The agent of world mission in the Bible is the suffering servant, the Messiah, the Lord Jesus Christ, who came from God and having accomplished his mission on earth and entrusted it to his disciples and his church, returned to heaven from whence he came. The will of God is to be done on earth as it is in heaven, not through political rule but through the offer to all of God's

10. Islamic Parliament Web Site (May, 1996).

love in Christ and through those who respond willingly. In Isaiah 52:13-15 we see a completely different kind of success than that valued by Islam. What seemed utter failure in the life of the suffering servant was the very reason for his exaltation. The cross was followed by the resurrection and exaltation of Jesus. His disciples and his church are to follow his way until the earth is full of the glory of God as the waters cover the sea. Now, his success is not apparent but it will be when he comes again in great glory (Phil. 2:5-11).

Increasing Persecution of Christians

Persecution of Christians has been, and is increasingly, a stern reality in the twentieth century. More believers have been martyred for their faith in Jesus Christ as Lord and Saviour in this century than in all the previous nineteen centuries combined. Much of this persecution has taken place under Islamic rule. Generally, Muslims have perceived religious freedom as freedom to become Muslim, not as freedom to leave Islam. It is difficult for them to conceive of anyone wanting to leave the Household of Islam. So it is that Muslims who have sought to confess faith in Jesus as Lord have faced persecution and sometimes death. There are several present-day examples — Indonesia, Pakistan, Egypt and Sudan.

In Sudan, a nation of twenty-eight million people, seventy per cent are Muslim. Most of the Christian minority is either from the South or from the Nuba mountain area. The United Nations reports that the militant Islamic government of Sudan has declared a systematic campaign against Christians. At least 300,000 Sudanese Christians have been killed since 1982. The situation had changed little when the Archbishop of Canterbury visited in 1994. Sudanese Christian leaders urge believers around the world to pray. 'We need your prayer support so that we might be able to love those who cause our sufferings and show them that the love of Christ is a stronger weapon than those used against us.' We are, indeed, constrained to pray for the church in the Islamic world (primarily in the Middle East, North Africa, Central Africa, Western and Central Asia), that the laws of apostasy which forbid the renunciation of Islam will be abolished and that new converts can give testimony to their faith without fear of repercussions. Let us pray also for new and creative ways of sharing the gospel in countries where persecution is occurring.

Closer Relations between Christians and Muslims, and Organised Interfaith Interaction

In recent years interfaith networking has prospered. In 1988 the Interfaith Network (U.K.) was officially formed. On 29th November, 1990 Dr. Robert Runcie, then Archbishop of Canterbury, addressed the Interfaith network. We see further developments in networking in the links being formed between institutions committed to inter-faith dialogue. For example, there are now links between the Centre for the Study of Islam and Christianity (C.S.I.C.) at Selly Oak Colleges, Birmingham, U.K., and the Royal Institute for Inter-Faith Studies in Amman, Jordan.

Other links are through exchange of lecturers and students. In 1996, Dr. Anara Tabshalieva, lecturer in History at Kyrgyz National University, was the Dorothy Cadbury Fellow at the Selly Oak Colleges. She is Director of the Kyrgyz Peace Research Centre in Byshkek, Kyrgyzstan. She has a particular interest in Christian-Muslim relations and spent considerable time at the Centre for the Study of Islam and Christianity. She wrote in the Centre's newsletter,[11] 'Since the fall of the Soviet Union in August 1991, life in Kyrgyzstan has greatly changed. The declaration of freedom of religions for all people has laid the groundwork for a religious renaissance, mainly Islamic and Christian. Kyrgyzstan has only just entered into the world community as a free and independent country. The need to promote democracy as well as peaceful resolutions within the area is of utmost importance. It would be far more costly in terms of energy and material means to compensate for the consequences of a conflict, than to prevent it. . . . The Kyrgyz Peace Research Center . . . intends to create a model which will provide recommendations for the prevention of religious and ethnic tensions, helping to maintain multi-faith peace within Kyrgyzstan. This N.G.O. has two main programs, one on research on ethno-religious development and another on civic education'.

11. June, 1996.

The visit of the Archbishop of Canterbury, Dr. George Carey, to the al-Azhar University in Cairo on 4th October, 1995 was widely reported in both the Egyptian and British press. It was remarkable that the Archbishop of Canterbury was invited to give a lecture at the al-Azhar University. The full text is published in the journal of the Centre for the Study of Islam and Christian-Muslim Relations.[12] Dr. Carey listed some attitude-transforming statements which are a challenge to us all. He counselled friendship not hostility; understanding not ignorance, reciprocity not exclusivism, and co-operation not confrontation, in all our relationships. In speaking about co-operation he noted that Muslims and Christians share in a common witness against secularism as a system which defines life, knowledge and culture without any reference to what lies beyond this life. He advocated co-operation in fighting poverty and human misery and in promoting peace and harmony among peoples with tolerance and understanding.

Clergy and Laity:
Listening, Understanding and Interacting with Muslims

A new situation calls for a fresh look at how the church prepares for its ministry. I hope it will become a matter of further discussion in the church wherever it is found. These few recommendations have arisen from discussions with Asians, Africans and Europeans.

1. That Islamics be taught in Christian Seminaries and Bible Colleges around the world. Arabic could also be offered, at least on an optional basis.
2. That suitable people should be encouraged and enabled to study and do research on Islam and related subjects for doctorates.
3. That in the U.K. more Christians should try to learn one of the languages used by the minority ethnic groups.
4. That more Christians should be made aware of the value of video, satellite television and the Internet in listening to, and communicating with, Muslims. It has been recently observed that Islamic groups have been quick to exploit the potential of news groups

12. *Islam and Christian-Muslim Relations,* Vol. 7, No. 1 (1996), pp. 95-101.

(on the Internet), and in doing so have given Christians an excellent resource — the chance to 'watch them in action' and learn first hand what they really think and feel, not what we think they think and feel! Dr. Ida Glaser in a note about her new course on Islam at Northumbria Bible College stated that the first term is on 'Islam and the Muslim'. The idea is to try to listen to what Muslims say about Islam, and to understand how Islam affects their lives. It is interesting that both Dr. Glaser and the other Christian observer emphasise the importance of listening to Muslims.

5. That more churches plan and train laity to welcome, understand and interact creatively with those from Muslim backgrounds who link in any way with Christian churches and fellowships. A report of June, 1996 from an Asian country in which Muslims are a 12% minority and the Christians an even smaller minority states, 'One miserable problem we Muslim converts face here is non-acceptance in the churches. Muslims mostly live in a close-knit society, very dependent upon one another. After conversion we experience loneliness as our society totally rejects us while, on the other hand, we are always treated with passiveness and indifference by the majority of Christians when we try to share with them'. It took an Ananias for the apostle Paul to be accepted in Jerusalem and a Barnabas and a Lydia to encourage him in his ministry. Things have not changed that much.

Another Epiphany? The Revealing of Christ to the Muslims: The Harvest to Come

The revealing of Christ to the Gentiles was unexpected, far more widespread and extensive than anyone foresaw. It was mind-boggling and changed the face of the Hebrew church. The difficulties in accepting it and the contextualisation called for resulted in the Council of Jerusalem. God's preparation for the coming in of the Gentiles involved elements which can be paralleled today.

1. The inter-testamental Jewish Dispersion can be compared with modern dispersions in the Middle East resulting from the discovery of oil. Because of these dispersions more Christians are

177

living in the Arabian peninsula than at any time in the history of the church. Whatever the restrictions, where God's people are, his Spirit is active through them. Economic and political factors have also contributed to larger dispersions of Muslims in Western countries. Muslims and Christians have more opportunity to 'greet' each other than ever before.

2. Greek was the universal language at the time of Christ. Compare this with the increasing use of the English language and with the widespread use of modern media as ways of communicating the gospel.

3. Sovereign acts of God, for example, miracles, visions and dreams of Christ, feed a hunger and increasing demand for the Bible as in Acts 2:17-21.

Conclusion

We live in a very exciting time in the history of the world. The great opportunity of the church in our time is to be what it is called to be, especially in regard to Muslims. Let one of the martyrs have the last word. Such a spirit cannot be defeated. Wherever the grain of wheat falls into the ground and dies it brings forth much fruit (John 12:24). Father Christian de Chergé was one of seven Trappist monks killed by Algerian terrorists in May, 1996. In the translation from the French of his last testament 'to be opened in the event of my death' he wrote:

> . . . I could not desire such a death . . .
> I do not see, in fact, how I could rejoice if this people I love were
>   to be accused indiscriminately of my murder.
> It would be to pay too dearly for what will, perhaps, be called
>   'the grace of martyrdom',
> to owe it to an Algerian, whoever he may be, especially if he says
>   he is acting in fidelity to what he believes to be Islam.
> I know the scorn with which Algerians as a whole can be regarded.
> I know also the caricature of Islam which a certain kind of
>   idealism encourages.
> It is too easy to give oneself a good conscience by identifying this
>   religious way with the fundamentalist ideologies of the extremists.

For me, Algeria and Islam are something different: they are a body
and a soul. . . .

And you also, the friend of my final moment, who would not be
aware of what you were doing.

. . . I wish . . . to commend you to the God whose face I see in
yours.

And may we find each other, happy 'good thieves', in Paradise,
if it pleases God, the Father of us both. *Amen.*[13]

Questions

1. In what ways could Christians and Muslims co-operate in social
and economic projects in your country?

2. How can your church better prepare its members to be responsible and sensitive witnesses to Muslims?

3. How would your church express its welcome for new believers
from Muslim background into its fellowship? (Rom. 15:7).

4. How could you, personally and in groups, increase informed
prayer for Muslims, regularly and at certain special times of the year,
i.e., during the Muslim month of fasting or during Lent? .

5. What steps can now be taken to implement one or more of the
above recommendations in section 7?

6. What other suggestions would you like to add to section 7?

13. *The Tablet,* 8 June, 1996.

Unity, Diversity and the Virginia Report

TIMOTHY BRADSHAW

Summary

The *Virginia Report* has been produced for consideration at the Lambeth Conference 1998. It considers the nature of the church and its structures, especially because of intensifying disagreements between Anglican provinces over ordination and consecration of women and people whose lifestyle incorporates homosexual practice. The report draws on the earlier Eames Commission which laid down a principle that provinces should accept each other's practice over women's ordination and not split over the issue. This principle is argued as the way forward over homosexuality. In order to hold the communion together the report recommends giving legislative power to a central world-wide institution. But is this reaction to a crisis merely a bureaucratic one which might make the situation worse?

Disagreement among Anglican Provinces

How does the Anglican communion hold together world-wide? That is the basic question taken up by the *Virginia Report*.[1] Archbishop Robert Eames of Armagh, in an introductory essay, says, 'As Anglicans we accept the concept of unity in diversity. It lies at the centre of the *raison*

1. J. Rosenthal and N. Currie (eds.), *Being Anglican in the Third Millennium* (Harrisville, PA: Moorehouse Publishing, 1997).

d'être of Anglicanism. The *Virginia Report* attempts to relate our understanding of that principle in the light of theological and practical experience to the Instruments of Unity'.[2] In short, how can different parts of the Anglican communion which may disagree strongly over important issues maintain fellowship?

The obvious recent example was over the ordination of women to the presbyterate, and indeed today the communion is split over the consecration of women bishops which some provinces do and others do not. Of particular potential for strong disagreement is the area of sexual ethics, since some American and Canadian bishops are openly ordaining practising homosexuals, and some of their seminaries are facilitating accommodation for cohabiting homosexual couples preparing for ordination.[3] Such developments have, as is now well known, caused moral indignation among many Anglican provinces and have led to powerful reaffirmations of traditional biblical ethics gathering widespread support.[4] Such intense disagreements have prompted thought about the future of world-wide Anglican relationships, decision-making and enforcement.

The Eames Principle

It may be as well to take the concrete example described and analysed by the report as our starting point for discussion, that of the disagreement in the Anglican communion over ordaining women. The bishop of Hong Kong ordained women in the 1960's, and in 1971 the Anglican Consultative Council informed the bishop that his ordinations would be acceptable to the Council, which would urge other provinces to maintain communion. Likewise, resolution 1 of Lambeth Conference 1988 told ECUSA, which was ordaining and consecrating women, 'that

2. Rosenthal and Currie, *Being Anglican*, p. 79.

3. Most recently Virginia Seminary, formerly known for its relatively orthodox ethical stance.

4. The Kuala Lumpur Statement, most notably (see Appendix I). See also the account of pressure to 'disinvite' ECUSA from the Lambeth Conference given by Bishop Mark Dyer, professor of theology at Virginia Seminary, in *United Voice Digest* (unitedvoice@episcopalian.org) 'Bishop Dyer at Yale' (14 Oct. 1997) by Douglas L. LeBlanc.

each province should respect the decision and attitudes of other provinces . . . without such respect necessarily indicating acceptance of the principles involved, maintaining the highest degree of communion with the provinces that differ'.[5]

The Eames Commission was set up to seek to hold together provinces in their disagreement. Meanwhile, ordinations and consecrations of women proceeded, and according to this Eames principle, provinces agreed to differ. Whether or not an issue might have arisen to provoke a legitimate disruption or expulsion is not clear. It would seem that the ordination and consecration of women was being regarded as what was called a matter 'adiaphoron' in Reformation terms, that is a matter of second order importance on which legitimate disagreement was possible. Some Lutherans held such practices as the veneration of the saints to be 'adiaphora', for example, but the obvious difficulty lies in the contesting of what constitutes such a matter. Is the Eames principle claiming that there are no issues which should not be defended absolutely, and that therefore all issues are adiaphora? Nothing should override the imperative for Anglican unity?

On the face of it, changes to the ordained ministry and especially the episcopate are not second order issues for Anglican polity, notably because the Lambeth Quadrilateral of 1888 claimed to state the essentials for a reunited Christian church as including the scriptures, the Apostles and Nicene Creeds, the two sacraments, and the historic episcopate. Likewise the structure of ordained ministry inherited from before the Reformation has been jealously guarded as a part of the means of enacting continuity with the early church. Hence changes to the ordained ministry and episcopate hardly seem to qualify for the category of second order or 'adiaphora', and indeed the very careful theological work resulting in the Porvoo agreement with the Nordic Baltic churches demonstrates this.

The Eames principle of fellowship despite severe disagreement therefore does not rest on a doctrine of adiaphoron, that is 'we can agree to differ over issues which we regard as less than crucial'. On the contrary, the issue of women's ordination and consecration was indeed regarded as a critical matter, and still provokes large scale dissent among Anglicans, sufficient even to have warranted the legally struc-

5. Rosenthal and Currie, *Being Anglican*, p. 261.

tured provision of 'flying bishops' to minister to those English clergy and parishes unable conscientiously to agree to the change. The principle then appears to be that no doctrinal, ethical or ecclesial disagreements should provoke excommunication or disruption; at least there seem to be no theoretical criteria laid down at present by which one might define a 'communion breaking' belief or practice.

The Process of 'Reception'

The *Virginia Report* cites the Eames Commission in terms of principle and practice, charting the progress of the introduction of the ordination and consecration of women in the Anglican communion: from one Asian province, to the wave of change in ECUSA, with the response of the Anglican Consultative Council and Lambeth 1988. The Eames Commission held together provinces which disagreed, while the practice of change went ahead, and gained increasing acceptance in other provinces.

In the Church of England the vote to ordain women to the presbyterate was accompanied by provision for dissenting traditionalists. In Canada and America the reverse path is being followed after Eames. General Convention has voted not to ordain men who disagree with the changes, thus *de facto* excluding one large constituency from the ordained ministry. Canadians disagreeing are excluded from ordination already.

The principle of reception, however, is very much part of the Eames and Virginia ethos. The *Virginia Report* speaks of reception being an important part of the process of any change.[6] That is to say, reception of changes by the church as a whole must have significance in assessing the development. In the Roman Catholic Church, for example, the almost total refusal of the ban on artificial birth control by the faithful means a lack of 'reception', which in turn might give pause to the church authorities in evaluating the policy. Time would seem to be an important element in the process of 'reception', so that the people can experience and evaluate what is happening and whether it feels right.

In turn, the power structure of the churches will be significant in

6. Rosenthal and Currie, *Being Anglican*, p. 261.

commending change or even enforcing it on possibly reluctant congregations, hoping that it will eventually become popular if at first regarded suspiciously. Churches with a congregational polity, such as the British Baptists, do not have such a factor at work in the same way as do episcopal and hierarchical polities.[7] The Eames principle appears to appeal to a pluralist way of holding together, a genuinely 'liberal' ethos. Action after a decision has been taken in favour of change to suppress dissent often of a large minority, will either drive that minority out of communion or cause a profound pathology in the church, with accusations of illiberality on the part of those claiming to be tolerant, liberal and pluralist beforehand. The Canadian Anglicans now refuse to ordain any men who disagree with the ordination or consecration of women, and their American cousins likewise, despite a vociferous dissenting minority and even a large petition of ordained women against such an exclusion. What was a matter of free discussion has become a test of faith.

This might lead one to ask whether the Eames notion of a process of reception is a somewhat empty piece of rhetoric. The Eames principle clearly favours revisionist pressure, since it prevents any genuine sanctions being taken against provinces in breach of the current rules, making space for 'modernist' campaigns to run, free of any fear of discipline or accountability from the provinces holding the majority conservative view. When change is won, however, this spirit of tolerance is no longer employed: the dissenting conservatives are excluded from ordination. That seems to be the case over the ordination of women as priests, and now the consecration of women as bishops. The minority of provinces are consecrating women bishops, the majority simply accepts this, and if the same trend persists, the conservatives will suffer exclusion from the episcopate if they disagree with the change, should it become law across the whole communion. 'Reception', sometimes adduced as a mitigating factor to revision, looks to be a rather thin mask: changes are quickly enforced, certainly by some

7. For example, Baptists in England and Wales have been permitted to ordain women since the early part of this century, but it is known that women often find it difficult in being called by local congregations. The Roman Catholic change to the vernacular for liturgical language, after Vatican II, however, was a 'top down' change, and was accepted by the vast majority of Roman Catholics quickly.

provinces, with little concession to any 'test of time' or developing 'sense of the faithful'.

In his address to General Synod of the Church of England at York in July 1997, the Archbishop of Canterbury said, 'When the Primates met in March this year, it is true that a number of differing views about homosexual practice were expressed vigorously, and it was suggested that a number of Provinces might feel so strongly about the issue that they would find it difficult to remain in communion with Provinces that decided to ordain practising homosexuals or welcome "same sex" marriages'.[8] But the situation is that some provinces are openly pursuing this policy. The Archbishop stated his own view unequivocally in his speech: 'I do not find any justification, from the Bible or the entire Christian tradition, for sexual activity outside marriage. . . . I do not believe any major change is likely in the foreseeable future and I do not myself share the assumption that it is only a matter of time before the Church will change its mind.'[9]

He also said that the 1998 Lambeth Conference would engage in some consideration of this issue, and will ask whether an International Commission should be set up to examine the matter, along the lines of the Eames Commission. If the above analysis of how the Eames principle works out in practice is accurate, then this is bad news for the orthodox provinces, because it will merely give permission for the revisionist provinces to continue 'doing their own thing', pending increased pressure for change. If this parallels the Eames process on women's ordination and consecration, then it may not be long before some dioceses are refusing to ordain men, and women, who regard homosexual practice as wrong. Lambeth 1998 may be best advised to 'draw a line in the sand', rather than adopt the Eames technique again. If this is not done, then it must be open to question whether the Anglican communion can ever be said to have binding 'communion-wide' law: it will always be open to be breached, with no disciplinary sanction feared, by a confident and assertive province, convinced of its own case and, in imperialistic fashion, merely waiting for others to catch up with its modernity.

8. Archdeacon of Wandsworth's Private Member's Motion, speech by the Archbishop of Canterbury (14 July, 1997), General Synod, York.
9. Archdeacon of Wandsworth's Private Member's Motion, speech by the Archbishop of Canterbury (14 July, 1997), General Synod, York.

In truth, the 'reception process', according to the Eames principle, happens during the time when the conservative provinces agree to forgo their right to protest and act against what they regard as the integration of wrong into the fabric of the body of Christ. To use the language of 'inclusivity', which is deployed so much in favour of permitting homosexual conduct, what eventually happens is the exclusion of the conservatives. An Eames-type commission on this question would inevitably contain a number of theologians arguing for change disproportionately large in relation to opinion in the worldwide Anglican communion. Likewise, in terms of power deployed by management of language and sharpened ideological skill, a weight of advantage accrues to the revisionist cause.[10] Again, the issue becomes neutral once such a commission is set up: whereas the tradition is clear, and the burden of proof to change it should lie on the side of 'modernisers'.

Philosophically such a process has roots in the philosophical movement associated with Dewey and Pierce, American Pragmatism, according to which the truth is known as we move into the future, not from a past orientation. 'The principle of pragmatism, according to [William] James was first enunciated by C. S. Pierce, who maintained that, in order to attain clearness in our thoughts of an object, we need only to consider what conceivable effects of a practical kind the object may involve. . . . In this way theories become instruments, not answers to enigmas.'[11] There is no 'truth' against which to test a novel idea; rather we incarnate that innovation and see if it makes sense to our experience. As William James put it, 'The true is only the expedient in our way of thinking . . . our obligation to seek truth is part of our general obligation to do what pays'.[12] ECUSA's 'Righter principle', that it has no core ethical doctrine, exemplifies the American pragmatist philosophical tradition perfectly.

10. Bishop Stephen Sykes makes the point that theological expertise carries with it power over others in the church. *The Identity of Anglicanism* (London: SPCK, 1984), pp. 54ff.

11. As explained by Bertrand Russell, *History of Western Philosophy* (London: George Allen & Unwin, 1946), p. 844.

12. Russell, *History of Western Philosophy*, p. 844.

Ecumenical Catholicity and Apostolicity

There is no doubt that following the 1988 Lambeth Conference the Orthodox hoped that, as serious ecumenical partners in dialogue, they were to be consulted and engaged in high level work on the issue of the ordination of women, before any major changes were implemented. They were disappointed in this, as the Anglican communion went ahead, and the Church of England soon afterwards. The Anglican communion makes no claim to be the church catholic world-wide, but to be part of that. This immediately raises the question of the legitimacy of the Eames principle, unless other major world churches are drawn into the theological process. World-wide Anglicanism may agree to consecrating women as bishops and that would take it further away from Rome and Constantinople, not to mention the most sizeable Protestant churches around the globe. Can the Anglican communion claim an inner 'catholicity', say on approving homosexual practice within church life if that were to happen, when this breaks with the established pattern of the rest of the catholic church?

Further, if an Eames-type commission were set up with an ecumenical dimension to take account of the above problem, could it possibly be right for the novel ethical practices to continue, if the discussion were in good faith rather than a cloak of words covering what was actually happening? If Lambeth 1998 does decide to set up an Eames Commission to examine the issue of homosexuality, there is every reason to insist on ecumenical partners' participation beyond merely the politesse of observer status, and on the implementation of the current status quo of traditional teaching, which has not been changed by most provinces. Those who have acted autonomously can hardly claim, afterwards, the benefits of being part of the greater family unless they conform to that family's understanding. There is even a case for not allowing their participation in such a commission, on the grounds of their decision to break with the family's ethos unilaterally and irresponsibly. Some degree of repentance for this could reasonably be looked for. The ecumenical dimension raises the issue of catholicity and the dubiousness of some intra-Anglican notion of this as the Eames doctrine of staying in communion at any price — as if being in communion were the supreme end in itself. Being in communion with provinces in breach of communion with the vast majority of Christians in the world in terms of ethics, may seem a less than supreme goal, and one designed to protect revision and novelty. In short, the Eames principle is less than catholic, although it is operating some version of catholicity as unbreakable fellowship. But beyond this problem of an insulated catholicity, we might also ask whether Eames exalts the principle of catholicity over apostolicity. Is communion at any price ignoring the vast weight of the tradition, almost choosing to bracket that out and to live in a fantasy world where the ethical apostolic tradition is absent, rather as if in a space capsule where suddenly there is no law of gravity? Again, it would be much harder to sustain this artificial state of weightlessness if a serious ecumenical dimension were part of any discussions.

The *Virginia Report* seeks to build a concept of *koinonia* (communion) on a trinitarian theology, and this is to be applauded. The type of trinitarian emphasis developed is that of divine communion, with no mention of the complementary divine order of Father, Son and Spirit. This is a view that privileges mutuality over order, and portrays a free-wheeling trinitarian life as the basis for human communion.[13] Unity and diversity are modelled in the doctrine of the Trinity. This principle of mutuality and interplay also dictates the attitude of the report towards Scripture, which is presented as one equal factor along with reason — equated with 'common sense' (3.9) and tradition. The principle of ongoing interplay and discovery is rooted in this reading of trinitarian doctrine.

This life of God conditions our life, since 'The Holy Spirit lifted up the community into the very life of God' (2.11). This unusual description of Pentecost illustrates the same tendency set to work in interpreting history. History is open and constantly bringing forth new discoveries, so the report can say 'The Church is the icon of the future' (2.14), looking backwards to the Christ event which broke down barriers and opened people up to each other. The trinitarian life of love in its unity and diversity is worked out in the life of the church. But is this a sufficient basis for ethics? Are there any guide posts, beyond that

13. The doctrine of the Trinity can be used as a basis for all manner of unlikely causes. See, *e.g.*, A. Thatcher, *Liberating Sex: A Christian Sexual Theology* (London: SPCK, 1993), and the fine review by Francis Bridger in *Anvil*, Vol. 11, No. 3 (1994), pp. 253ff. Thatcher reconstructs orthodox sexual ethics arguing that the Trinity, a freely-flowing, interdependent loving communion, warrants a freer sexual ethic.

of 'love'? At this point we need to look to the historical Jesus and his whole Hebraic ethical tradition to give us some orientation: Jesus, the true Israelite and the new Adam, sums up the law and the prophets. We find an order in creation which the resurrection of Jesus renews and confirms. The apostolicity of the church of Christ is accountable to this doctrinal and ethical tradition — departure from that means departure from real catholicity, and no amount of mutual reaffirmation can gainsay that.

The picture of the church constantly moving from the past into the future, making new syntheses as she progresses, may fail to give sufficient weight to the normative phase of the apostolic tradition. So the report can say: 'no one period of history has a monopoly of insight into the truth of the Gospel' (3.11). Clearly this statement is true, but also misleading, since the apostolic era and the product of its witness as the New Testament and the patristic theological developments do have a greater weight of authority than any subsequent era. This is the Anglican position for all strands of opinion in the church. The idea that the Anglican church teaches a freely evolving form of faith, whose main feature is a mutual commitment, irrespective of apostolic teaching, cannot be sustained.

Indeed it is evident that no communion could retain its identity without some fundamental doctrines and ethical norms which are not hostages to the future or to contemporary secular culture. The report acknowledges the danger of 'the corrosive effects of particular environments' which are often not perceptible to those who are immersed in them (4.14); but the antidote suggested for this cultural blindness is — other provinces in the Anglican communion, rather than the apostolic tradition. The underlying theme stresses interplaying ideas and authorities leading to new syntheses, new insights.

More Centralised Power

The fact of disagreements between provinces, and indeed within them, gives rise to a treatment of communion rooted in trinitarian unity with diversity to consider the structures of the church, and it considers primarily the structures of ministry, which are to serve the personal and relational life of the church. Without sufficient structures the personal aspect cannot flourish. This is so at all levels of church life in the Anglican communion.

At present, however, provinces govern themselves, in communion with Canterbury, but there is no internationally binding law from a central body. The Anglican communion rests on consultation and moral respect. The report asks whether the time has now come for central legislation and oversight across the world-wide Anglican communion (5.20). This would mean a more powerful Anglican Consultative Council, a more powerful Primates Meeting, and a more papal Archbishop of Canterbury, operating in collegial unity with the other Primates and provincial churches. In short, this would herald a very different Anglican communion, one moving from the moral authority of the centre, towards a legislative centre. The report also encourages the internationalisation of the post of Archbishop of Canterbury, envisaging the possibility that a bishop from ECUSA, for example, might well occupy the throne of Augustine in future years.

These are major structural changes, conveying a radical shift. It would essentially mean a move from world communion held together by an authority accepted by all, formerly that of Scripture, tradition, the sacraments and the episcopate as interpreted through the classical Anglican liturgy and articles. But that glue is felt to be ceasing to hold, and the report sees a move to central, legislative power, rather than the old theological authority, as the answer to the disagreements breaking out.

There is a major difference between power and authority, and a move from the latter to the former indicates a bureaucratic response to the perceived crisis of disagreement, a trust in central instruments to enforce positions. Orthodox provinces will regard such a move with suspicion, since it looks like a mechanism designed to enforce changes on a reluctant communion, rather than one designed to uphold the classical Anglican faith in the matrix of Scripture and tradition. The only reason for any such precipitate change is the crisis over sexual ethics and the consecration of women bishops: if those two items were not troubling the Anglican communion, no such pressure for a radical change in the world-wide Anglican communion would be called for. In essence, such a reversion to a power in the centre emanates from the revisionist minority of the communion.

The obvious question arising is why legislative compulsion would help matters in resolving disagreements? The threat of force to gain acquiescence to ministerial and ethical guidelines felt to be opposed to the apostolic tradition would be resisted by any conscientious province or diocese, or indeed parish — as is being experienced now in ECUSA, for example. Nervously implementing a more centralised system of power in order to counter perceived disintegration[14] may in fact make matters worse, encouraging parties to gain control of the structures to implement their programmes, rather than be patient and allow the Spirit to work over time to achieve greater harmony.

Ecumenically, this would be to move away from our existing parallel with the Eastern Orthodox and towards a Roman model. At present, 'like the ecumenical Patriarch, the Archbishop of Canterbury makes no claim to a primacy of universal jurisdiction . . . the Anglican communion has developed on the Orthodox rather than the Roman Catholic pattern'.[15] Alexander Schmemann articulates the Orthodox fear of Western church polities by arguing that Roman Catholic 'authority' means external and repressive authority and that this inevitably bred a reaction in the name of 'freedom', hence the splitting of the church in the West and its continuing oscillation between claims for powerful authority and for freedom. Schmemann rejects external authority and false freedom in favour of the church's spiritual and personal nature.[16] The bishop is the central focus of the unity of the church, and leading the people in worship is his primary ministry.

The Eastern tradition similarly fears Western 'technique' as well as Western ecclesiastical autocracy and reactive voluntarism. Managerial techniques have become part of the way church bureaucracies conduct things. Standardisation and centralisation, exemplified by episcopal erosion of the freehold in the English context and the recent American decision of General Convention to exclude traditionalist clergy, may in fact only increase the crises they intend to control or manage.

The level for discipline to be exercised is that of province or

14. I owe this insight, that organisations classically respond to crises by centralisation, to David Mills.

15. *The Dublin Agreed Statement, Anglican-Orthodox Dialogue* (London: SPCK, 1984), p. 18.

16. A. Schmemann, *Church, World, Mission* (New York: St. Vladimir's Seminary Press, 1979), p. 184.

diocese. It is a matter of ordinary episcopal oversight to uphold the doctrinal and ethical teaching and practice of the church, and to prevent collusion with what is wrong through individual concession and exceptions. The bishops are charged with upholding the tradition; they are primarily trustees of the faith rather than exploratory innovators seeking new insights. No strengthening of power at the centre of the Anglican communion can affect this episcopal responsibility, and the evidence of the Eames process is that determined revisionists will simply continue with their innovations locally despite central admonitions. It is to be hoped that discussion of the trustee role of the bishop will take place.

The essence of the Anglican communion's problem is that of Western cultural adoption of moral relativism, narcissistic hedonism, scientific reductionism, and autonomous individualism, to use Oden's pithy summary.[17] The churches living in this cultural climate are suddenly faced with moving into a more counter-cultural mode and facing many claims for lifestyles to be accepted which are rejected by the Judaeo-Christian tradition. The language of 'rights' is deployed in this regard,[18] to describe not fundamental human rights but the rights of sub-groups to publicly validated institutions. This language is deployed against the church especially over 'rights' to be ordained and consecrated to the ministry. The phenomenon is especially strong in the 'White Anglo-Saxon Protestant' cultures, where post-colonial, post-patriarchal 'white middle class guilt' is now part of the social psyche, a dynamic bitterly self-critical of its cultural and religious past traditions. Until the extent of the fever gripping Western culture is fully diagnosed, the world-wide Anglican communion might be well advised to let the patient sweat the high temperature out rather than pay too much attention to its delirium. Pressure long term and short term, for change, from provinces rooted in such cultural crisis will be advisedly treated for what it is, the product of a distorted social context.

In conclusion, the proposal of the *Virginia Report* to deal with the crisis of ethical disagreement by means of developing centralised

---

17. T. C. Oden, *Agenda for Theology: After Modernity, What?* (Grand Rapids: Zondervan, 1990).

18. See O. O'Donovan, *The Desire of the Nations* (Cambridge: Cambridge University Press, 1996), pp. 247-49.

powerful bureaucracy is a chimera, and wishful thinking again of a Western type. Advisory boards and committees, in Western fashion, are made up of 'experts' in all manner of academic disciplines, rather than pastors and evangelists. To such will a centralised board give power. The *Virginia Report* leads us to a world-wide communion with greatly increased structures of power, but greatly reduced doctrinal and ethical content. The unity proposed comes through such structures; the diversity envisaged will always favour revisionism. What is really needed is for the Anglican communion to retrieve its true identity, which is much more like that of the Orthodox, centred on the apostolic tradition and worship, but with a greater degree of mission and evangelism than is generally associated with the East: Anglican Christians world-wide are looking for this kind of renewal, rather than to Western bureaucratic re-structuring, to take them into the next millennium.

Questions

1. Is the church in need of leaders with qualities of spirituality before managerial expertise? How are such people to be identified, given their refusal to advertise themselves?

2. Are your church structures 'democratic' in any real sense? Should they be? Can they be?

3. How can we tell 'what the Spirit says to the churches'? How does this relate to Scripture and to tradition?

4. Is the church wasting its energies on internal campaigns and arguments?

5. Consider Revelation 1–3, the word of the Lord to the seven churches; Ezekiel 34, judgement upon the shepherds of Israel; Acts 15 with Galatians 2:1-10, the conference at Jerusalem.

Reverencing Truth

CHRISTOPHER D. HANCOCK

Lie not; but let thy heart be true to God,
Thy mouth to it, thy actions to them both.
George Herbert, 'The Church Porch'[1]

Summary

The theme of this essay is the Anglican communion's obligation to reverence truth in word and deed; that is, to be, and be seen to be, an agent of truth and a bastion of truthfulness. The 1998 Lambeth Conference has set itself to consider 'what it means to be truly human, as individuals and in community'. It's right that truth and truthfulness be addressed. Both are integral to a Christian doctrine of humanity. Humans are made by Truth for truth. As Jesus promised, 'the truth will set you free' (John 8:32).[2]

Truth is a tough theme and truthfulness a weighty calling. Pilate's cynical question 'What is truth?' is loudly echoed by our post-modern world. On every side truth and truthfulness are questioned or corrupted. Karl Rahner noted some years ago that a less-than-serious attitude towards truth is a by-product of societies that are schooled in

---

1. George Herbert, 'The Church Porch', in F. E. Hutchinson (ed.), *The Works of George Herbert* (Oxford: Clarendon Press, 1972), p. 9.
2. Biblical quotations are from the New International Version.

relativism and constantly subjected to seductive advertising, mass media, and political propaganda.[3] As he pointed out, truth suffers alike from consumerism (generating false needs) and from politicisation (propagating false views). As Allan Bloom's subsequent study *The Closing of the American Mind*[4] has confirmed, Rahner's interpretation of the impact of modernity on western culture is correct. Truth has been subjected to extreme social, educational and political pressure both in society and, alas, in the church. It is time for Anglican Christians to work to liberate truth from the shackles of ideology and to venerate veracity for the sake of the gospel.

In keeping with an historic passion for truth, Anglicans world-wide should, I believe, take a lead in reverencing truth and resisting its distortion or neglect. But how? The Swiss-American scholar Francis Schaeffer claimed in *The God Who Is There* that *truthfulness* is the place to start. As he states, 'In an age of relativity the *practice* of truth is the only way to cause the world to take seriously our protestations of truth'.[5] This is sound biblical wisdom for today's church. In the Judeo-Christian tradition, as Anthony Thiselton's article in the *New International Dictionary of the New Testament* makes clear, truth is an existential reality, 'The God of Israel reveals his truth not only in words but in deeds, and this truth is proved in practice in the experience of his people. Similarly, men express their respect for truth not in abstract theory, but in their daily witness to their neighbour and their verbal and commercial transactions'.[6]

The particular thrust of this essay is, then, that the complex issue of truth, as it pertains to human identity and conduct, may be made both more accessible and more immediate by recognition of the holistic, existential manner in which it is presented in scripture. The effect of this upon the world-wide Anglican communion could be decisive. For

3. Karl Rahner, 'On Truthfulness', *Theological Investigations VII*, translated by David Bourke (London: Darton, Longman and Todd, 1971), pp. 220-33. An excellent study of the relationship between truth and truthfulness.

4. Allan Bloom, *The Closing of the American Mind* (New York: Simon and Schuster, 1987).

5. Francis Schaeffer, *The God Who Is There: Speaking Historic Christianity into the Twentieth Century* (Chicago: InterVarsity Press, 1968), p. 169.

6. A. Thiselton, 'Truth', *New International Dictionary of the New Testament*, Volume 3 (Exeter: Paternoster Press, 1978), p. 881.

truth and truthfulness are inseparable. Both shape Christian identity and integrity. They are the ground of the church and the basis of its character. They inspire its fellowship, unity, mission, and worship. In short, they are 'good news' for humanity today.

Truth Defiled

No serious consideration of truth and truthfulness today can ignore the pressures brought to bear upon them by society on the eve of the third millennium. It is worth briefly considering some of these to set the later discussion in a realistic context. But first an important disclaimer. This essay is not based on the conviction that Anglicans are, like the proverbial Cretans in Titus 1:12, 'always liars, evil brutes and lazy gluttons'. No, Anglicans are not that unique! But, as George Herbert's 'The Church Porch'[7] reminds Anglicans, they are subject to the same pressures on truth as others. The world Isaiah envisioned is not so different from our own: 'truth has stumbled in the streets, honesty cannot enter. Truth is nowhere to be found, and whoever shuns evil becomes a prey' (Isa. 59:14b-15a). Perhaps a renewed Anglicanism can prove the wisdom of Czech President Vaclav Havel's claim that people 'living in the truth' enlighten others.[8]

The most general pressure exerted on truth and truthfulness today is *social*. This takes many forms, ranging from a carelessness about words to a deliberate denial of truth *per se*. In many respects this is not new. As long as there have been humans there have been liars, cheats and sceptics. As the Psalmist says of his enemies, 'Not a word from their mouth can be trusted' (Psalm 5:9). Hilaire Belloc's 'Matilda', who 'told such Dreadful lies,/it made one Gasp and Stretch one's Eyes',[9] is one of literature's more memorable liars. The Devil, the 'father of lies' (John 8:44), is to some the most obvious cause of such behaviour. So, Hotspur in Shakespeare's *Henry IV, Part I* bursts out, 'O! while you live,

---

7. Herbert, 'The Church Porch', p. 9.

8. *Cf.*, Vaclav Havel, 'The Power of the Powerless', J. Vladislav (ed.), *Living in the Truth* (London: Faber and Faber, 1990), pp. 36-122.

9. Hilaire Belloc, 'Matilda', *Puffin Book of Verse*, compiled by Eleanor Graham (London: Puffin Books, 1988), p. 152.

tell truth, and shame the devil!'[10] To others the causes of social pressure on truth are as varied as humanity itself. To one it's character that prefers evasion to honesty, to another ambition that prefers accommodation to confrontation, to another insecurity that leads to deception or envy that leads to misrepresentation. The causes are myriad, the results consistent; as the Victorian Josh Billings quipped, 'As scarce as truth is, the supply has always been in excess of the demand'. The crucial thing for the church to recognise is that cavalier attitudes towards truth and truthfulness render their meanings empty and their significance void.

The second related pressure on truth and truthfulness today is *political*. This is again a generic term to encompass a range of responses to truth, from a canny eye to political advantage, to a bold statement of an ideological commitment, to firm acceptance of 'political correctness'. In each case truth is more than correspondence to fact and is subject to advantage, feeling, or rights. The pressure upon truth in the realm of national politics was noted recently by a newly-elected member of the British Parliament, who commented, 'It will be interesting to see whether you can be a practising MP and continue to tell the truth. I am about to find out'.[11] He perhaps feels as Emily Dickinson did, writing in a letter in 1870, 'Truth is such a rare thing, it is delightful to tell it'.[12] That truth and truthfulness are manipulable is almost a truism of politics: it becomes more worrying when the same tendency appears in the church. As to the effects of ideology upon truth, a recent article by Lynn Cheney, the wife of a recent US Defence Secretary, shows how education has become the play-thing of ideology (as C. S. Lewis frighteningly anticipated in the *The Abolition of Man*[13]). She writes, 'A growing number of educators simply dismiss notions of objectivity and evidence. They teach that "what's fact" depends solely upon our point of view. . . . All the things we think are true, they say, are merely inventions'.[14] Of such is the rewriting of history, the manipulation of reason, and the relativising of truth. When truth deserts (or is driven from) 'the public square' it is soon repossessed by occupying powers. The effects

10. William Shakespeare, *Henry IV, Part I*, Act III, Scene 1.

11. Martin Bell MP, quoted in *Third Way*, Vol. 20, No. 4 (May 1997), p. 5.

12. Emily Dickinson, quoted in *The Oxford Book of Aphorisms*, p. 223.

13. C. S. Lewis, *The Abolition of Man* (London: Collins, Fount Paperbacks, 1990).

14. Lynn Cheney, 'The Truth Is Never Out of Date', *Reader's Digest* (Jan. 1996).

of this 'political' process on human identity and integrity are devastating. As the nefarious actions of Nehemiah's enemies Sanballat and Geshem reveal, those denying truth in the 'political' realm become play-things of power and emotion (Neh. 6:1-14). It is time for the church to lay claim to 'public truth' once again, as Lesslie Newbigin has argued.[15]

The third cause of pressure on truth today is *intellectual*. Again, many aspects of this are neither new nor overt. The history of intellectual debate from Aristotle to Gadamer, and from Plato to Kant, affects the way truth and truthfulness are perceived today. Much recent debate need not detain us, thankfully; for, as Thiselton has noted, 'Discussions about truth in modern philosophy are extremely complex'.[16] As his article makes clear a number of discernible factors have combined to produce what he calls 'a measure of scepticism about truth in our day'.[17] He writes, 'Our own age often feels obliged to rest content with a kind of relativism which reveals extreme pessimism about questions of truth'.[18] He cites, first, a shift from Cartesian confidence in truth *per se* (grounded in the fact and truth of God) to 'an entirely secular climate of thought' in which 'an inevitable tendency towards greater scepticism and relativism' prevails.[19] Second, he identifies the Kantian bifurcation of unknowable *noumena* and intelligible *phenomena* as the start of a basic fragmentation of truth traceable through Bultmann's dialectic between history, faith and romantic 'feeling' *(das Gefühl)* to later denials of objective knowledge and definitive (scientific) data. The third factor to erode the status of truth and truthfulness today is, as we saw earlier, the influence of politics, the media and advertising on the moral climate and intellectual ethos of society. For a variety of reasons, many would, as a result, echo Kierkegaard's complaint in *The Concept of Dread*, 'there has been talk enough about truth'.[20] Here's surely something of the ennui evident in Pilate's cynical question, 'What is truth?' (John 18:38).

---

15. *Cf.*, L. Newbigin, *The Gospel as Public Truth: Applying the Gospel in the Modern World* (London: CEN Books, 1992).

16. Thiselton, 'Truth', p. 894.

17. Thiselton, 'Truth', p. 899.

18. Thiselton, 'Truth', p. 899.

19. Thiselton, 'Truth', p. 899.

20. Søren A. Kierkegaard, *The Concept of Dread*, translated with an introduction and notes by Walter Lowrie (Princeton: Princeton University Press, 1973), p. 123.

The fourth pressure brought to bear upon truth today is *psychological*. This is present in each of the above, but deserves brief elucidation. Various issues may again be placed under this heading. It encompasses a pathological aversion to the constraints of 'absolute truth' or the obligation not to lie, the most general intimations of alternate priorities to those dictated by honesty or veracity (like the golfer who shifts his ball, the bishop who acts out of pique, or the treasurer who tweaks the figures!), and even the cryptic deconstructionists' reconfigurement of reality.

Psychological pressure on truth involves recognition of its potential for manipulation not now by political power or human reason, but by subjective (or selective) feeling and pre-cognitive or pre-conceptual energy within the human psyche. Christian thinkers in the existentialist or phenomenological tradition from Kierkegaard to Heidegger, Fuchs, Gadamer and Ebeling, have variously owned the impact of subjectivity on truth. As Thiselton points out, according to this perspective 'truth is not primarily a property which resides in propositions at all'. Rather, 'It relates first and foremost to the human subject, who alone can appropriate and live out the truth'.[21] Søren Kierkegaard, for example, emphasised the need for a passionate, personal engagement with truth in order to find truth, leading to his famous dictum 'truth is subjectivity'.[22] Likewise, Bultmann's existentialist critique of New Testament faith stressed the place of 'decision' *(krisis)* in grasping the truth. Martin Heidegger, however, saw truth as first 'openness to being' or 'behaving' (his *Offenstandigkeit des Verhaltens*) then reality 'unveiled' by 'letting-be' (his *Gelassenheit der Milde*), whereas Gadamer interpreted truth as experienced, not reasoned, by encounter at a deep level with another 'world' (as in 'art' or a 'game'). Applying this to the gospel, Fuchs and Ebeling speak of a 'prehensive' grasp of the truth of the gospel (in parables, for example), and of its power to lead a listener to engage with the truth of their life before God. In short, philosophy has engaged with human psychology in its response to the problem of truth. If the church isn't careful it can be paralysed by this reflection and forget its

21. Thiselton, 'Truth', pp. 897-98.
22. Søren A. Kierkegaard, *Concluding Unscientific Postscript to the 'Philosophical Fragments'*, translated by David F. Swenson (Princeton: Princeton University Press, 1941), p. 169.

199

own existential duty before God 'to speak the truth from the heart' and instead, as Paul warns in Romans 1:25, 'exchange the truth about God for a lie'.

The fifth pressure on truth today is *spiritual;* that is, truth is subject to the vicissitudes of the soul, the work of spiritual 'powers' and the tensions of pluralism. Truth, like human life, is subject to pressure from 'the world, the flesh, and the devil'. Inconsistency, conflict and diversity are not new phenomena: they are facts of the spiritual life. Ephesians not only speaks of cosmic conflict (6:12), it also contrasts mature 'speaking the truth in love' (4:15) with an 'infant' spirit that is 'tossed back and forth by the waves, and blown here and there by every wind of teaching and by the cunning and craftiness of men' (4:14). Likewise, Timothy is warned of a time when 'people will not put up with sound doctrine' but will prefer to listen 'to what their itching ears want to hear' (2 Tim. 4:3). Spiritual pressure on truth is both internal (from a struggling soul and a dangerous tongue, *cf.,* Romans 7; James 3:1-12) and *external* (from a plethora of religions, a plague of sects, and 'the spiritual forces of evil in the heavenly realm', Eph. 6:12).[23] Spiritual truth is always being clothed in fine new clothes and Christians respond to it in various ways. Some reflect an *inclusive* attitude (Cervantes' 'Where truth is, there is God'), others an *imperial* stance (Justin Martyr's 'All truth, wherever it is found, belongs to us as Christians'), others, again, an *institutional* bias (Pascal's 'The history of the church ought properly to be called the history of truth'), others, lastly, an *intellectual* suspicion (Oscar Wilde's 'A thing is not necessarily true because a man dies for it'). Anglicanism's proclivity for diversity and inclusivity (under the banner of 'comprehensiveness') renders it susceptible to considerable ambiguity when deciding which of these responses it owns. Indeed, its indecision risks the immaturity of Ephesians 4:14 and the inanity of 2 Timothy 4:3. Yes, there may be spiritual pressure on truth today (what's new?!): Christian faith still believes and lives.

Truth has, then, in various ways been 'defiled' both conceptually and experientially. This is not the only data with which a Christian has to engage. It's important for the Anglican communion to be clear about

23. For a valuable interpretation of the language and imagery of 'the spiritual powers', see Walter Wink's trilogy, *Naming the Powers* (1984), *Unmasking the Powers* (1986), *Engaging the Powers* (1992).

the Bible's position on truth, as 'Truth Revealed'. This is essential to classical Christian teaching on 'what it means to be truly human, as an individual and in community'. To this we therefore now turn.

Truth Revealed

This section is built on the assumption that Anglicans are, or should be, interested in what the Bible says about 'truth'. Frankly, if they are not, they are guilty either of cultural barbarism (ignoring the historic wisdom of their primary spiritual text) or spiritual suicide (preferring the sea of secular doubt to the rock of Christian faith). Neither seem to the present writer to commend themselves. Though to many Anglicans the Bible has shifted its status from regulator of doctrine to resource for reflection, it possesses wisdom we ignore at our peril. But let the wisdom of scripture be its own defender. The church has too often done the Bible's work for it.

The first point to make is that truth in the Bible is both *theological* (expressing the character of God) and *existential* (involving a particular mode of behaviour). As Thiselton argues, it is rarely 'a merely abstract theoretical concept' and 'never located, as in Plato, in some timeless extra-historical realm'.[24] The root of the Hebrew word for truth, *'emet*, is 'stability' or 'support' and means also 'faithfulness' or 'reliability'. In this sense God is 'true' in the Old Testament, and his word 'reliable'. As we find in Jeremiah 10:10, 'the Lord is the true God'; that is, he does and says what he is — both to comfort and disturb faithless Israel! Nehemiah admits, 'you have acted faithfully, while we did wrong' (9:33), but Psalm 132:11 remembers, 'The Lord swore an oath to David, a sure oath that he will not revoke'. God's faithfulness becomes a criterion of human conduct. As we saw in Psalm 145:18, 'The Lord is near . . . to all whom call on him in truth' (*viz.* with integrity). Integrity in word and deed is measured by a divine standard; and, just as God's words conform to his character, so they conform to reality. Hence *'emet* also means true (as in not false), real (as in not fictitious), and straightforward (as in not crooked or deceitful). So, the Psalms pray 'guide me in your truth' (25:5), commend 'speaking the truth', and condemn

24. Thiselton, 'Truth', p. 881.

truth's corruption in every place and form (*cf.*, Psalms 5:6; 15:2, 3; 101:7; 119:69; and *cf.*, Prov. 6:17; 12:19, 22; Isa. 59:3). As Proverbs 12:22 concludes, 'The Lord detests lying lips, but he delights in men who are truthful'. In other words, the God who is true and truthful seeks such from his people; for the Old Testament sees no gulf either between truth and truthfulness or between divine and human action. So the Psalmist prays, 'Surely, you desire truth in the inner parts' (Psalm 51:6). If Anglicans are to be faithful to biblical wisdom they will seek this truth and image the 'true' God in word and deed. Theirs will be a vision of reality and humanity in which truth informs the structure of experience and creates the epistemological ground of the Christian moral life.

The second point to be made is that truth in the Bible is both *christological* (pertaining to Jesus Christ) and *evangelical* (pertaining to the gospel). For, though there is much continuity between what is said about truth and truthfulness in the Old and New Testaments new light is shed in the advent of Jesus. In the New Testament God is again described as the 'true' God (*i.e.*, genuine: unlike Satan, idols and false gods, *cf.*, John 17:3; 1 Thess. 1:9; 1 John 5:20) and 'truthful' (*i.e.*, veracious and worthy of confidence, *cf.*, John 3:33; Rom. 3:4; Rev. 6:10). The truth is still 'God's truth' (Rom. 1:25; 3:7; 15:8), his word is reliable because it is 'the truth' (John 17:17; 2 Tim. 2:15; James 1:18), and first the 'Law' and then the 'gospel' are embodiments of truth essential for salvation (Rom. 2:20; Gal. 2:14; Eph. 1:13; Col. 1:5). But if God is related to truth so is his divine-human Son. In the New Testament *aletheia* (truth: lit. 'unhidden' or 'noticed') has both a *christological* and an *anthropological* application. For Jesus is both the bearer of divine truth and the perfection of true humanity. His word and works are the 'truth' that will set humanity 'free' (John 8:32). Jesus is both the *indicative* of God's truth and the *imperative* of humanity's life. He is 'what God has to say to us' and the perfection of authentic humanity. He says, 'I tell you the truth' (Luke 4:25; 9:27; 12:44), and even enemies acknowledge his truthfulness (Matt. 22:15). He challenges Pharisaic hypocrisy which wants to 'preach but not practice' (Matt. 23:2ff), and tells people 'the whole truth' about themselves (Mark 5:33). In other words, Jesus lives and dies the messianic message he bears; as Thiselton stresses, 'Jesus' own words always accord with his deeds and with actuality'.[25]

25. Thiselton, 'Truth', p. 883.

In John's Gospel particular stress is placed on Jesus as 'the truth'. He is 'the way and the truth and the life' (14:6), who comes to 'witness' to the truth (5:33; 18:37), 'full of grace and truth' (1:14), to bring 'grace and truth' to humanity (1:17). He calls for worship of 'the Father' 'in spirit and in truth' (4:24) and promises his Spirit to lead his disciples 'into all truth' (14:17; 16:13). In John 'truth' means both *factual* truth (*viz.* conformed to reality and opposed to falsehood) and *substantial* truth (*viz.* defining reality and fulfilling expectations[26]). John is not unique. Throughout the New Testament truth is the reality embodied in and imparted by God in Jesus Christ, and is the heart of the church's 'gospel' witness in word and deed. Biblical Anglicans will always permit this *christological* and *evangelical* perspective on truth to interpret their account of humanity. It is 'good news'. As seen in Jesus, it means an end to human fragmentation and an ideal integration of thought, word and deed.

Thirdly, truth is in the Bible both *pneumatological* (relating to the person and power of the Holy Spirit) and *ethical* (understood as an obligation to speak and act in conformity to God's will). The strength of the Old Testament's affirmation of God's truthfulness, and its repudiation of lying and deceit, is substantially reinforced in the light of the New Testament doctrine of the Holy Spirit. God's Spirit, as 'the Spirit of truth' (John 14:17; 15:26; 16:13; and *cf.*, 1 John 4:6; 5:6), is in John the dynamic agent who 'exposes' *(elenchein)* the facts of a situation, 'prosecuting'[27] the world proleptically (and prophetically) in relation to its response to the One to whom the Spirit as 'paraclete' bears faithful, continuing, eschatological witness. As we have seen, this same Spirit leads God's people into all truth — understood as the truth about God, themselves, 'true' worship and 'the world'. This is in contrast to the work of the devil who 'has nothing to do with the truth, because there is no truth in him' (John 8:44, 45). In John, then, it is the Spirit who imparts God's life by 'new birth' (3:6f.), interprets God's truth to the believer (16:15), and convicts the world of 'sin, righteousness and judgement' (16:8). So Jesus prays 'sanctify them by the truth' (17:17f.) and encourages his disciples to 'do' (*viz.* live) the truth (3:21; *cf.*, 1 John 1:6).

---

26. *I.e.*, John's use of the epithet 'true' of Jesus: *viz.* the true light (1:9), true bread (6:32), true vine (15:1), etc.

27. C. K. Barrett, *The Gospel according to St. John* (London: SPCK, 1976), p. 76.

For just as 'true worship' accords with God's nature, so 'true disciple-ship' accords with God's truth. To settle for less is to 'walk in the darkness' (1 John 1:6f.) and to call God a liar (1 John 1:10).

The explicit connection between the Spirit and truth in John is implicit in much of the rest of the New Testament. In Ephesians, for example, truth is part of the corporate life and spiritual armour of a Christian (6:14; *cf.*, also 2 Cor. 4:2). A life 'worthy of the Lord', that does not 'grieve the Holy Spirit', rejects falsehood and 'speaks the truth in love' (Eph. 4:1, 3, 15, 25, 30). In 2 Corinthians, Paul likewise appeals to his renunciation of 'deception' and 'distortion of God's word', and his use of 'truthful speech' (4:2; 6:7; *cf.*, also Rom. 9:1; 2 Cor. 7:14), which he parallels with the power of God and weapons of righteousness, in defence of his ministry. It is clear that he sees God's truth as mediated in and through a Christian's spiritual and practical integrity. And, as we see in Galatians and elsewhere, he is more than ready to speak and suffer for this truth (Gal. 4:16) for love 'rejoices at the truth' (1 Cor. 13:6) and gladly suffers for it.

Throughout the New Testament, then, truth, as the fruit of the work of God's Spirit in the life of the individual and the community, involves a direct correspondence between word and deed, between gospel and life. As in the Old Testament, Christian truth is a spiritual, ethical and existential reality. It is this truth which forms humanity as a 'new creation' (2 Cor. 5:17). It shapes 'what it means to be truly human'.

The fourth point to be made about truth in the Bible is that it is both *communal* (as a corporate virtue and creative vocation) and *critical* (as a foe to sin and foil to error).[28] In both the Old and New Testaments truth and truthfulness are appealed to as necessary elements in the formation and maintenance of a godly community. Those who fail to seek or speak the truth deny to themselves and to their community the fruit of truth in patterned behaviour, mutual trust, personal respect, and social harmony. In the Old Testament a leader with integrity 'judges fairly' (*viz.* truthfully; Ezek. 18:8-9, and *cf.*, 1 Kings 2:3, 4; 3:6; 2 Kings 20:3; 2 Chron. 31:20; 32:1; Isa. 38:3; 59:14, 15), and God's people are

---

28. As Article VIII of the *Thirty Nine Articles of the Church of England* makes clear, the Creeds are to be believed, 'for they may be proved by most certain warrants of Holy Scriptures.'

called to 'speak the truth to each other', and to 'render true and sound judgement' (Zech. 8:16). 'Truthful lips' (Prov. 12:19), a 'truthful witness' (Prov. 14:25), 'true instruction' (Mal. 2:6, 7; NB the expectation on 'priests'), and 'true justice' (Zech. 7:9) are expressions of conscious obedience to the revealed truth of God's law, precepts, commands and ordinances, in the life of the community. The liar, deceiver, cheat and disobedient break faith with God's law and his people. Perjurers, false witnesses, and blasphemers (*cf.,* Ps. 5:6; 101:7; Prov. 6:17; 12:19, 22; Isa. 59:3) corrupt community and are uniformly condemned. As quoted earlier, in the Old Testament, 'men express their respect for truth not in abstract theory, but in their daily witness to their neighbour and their verbal and commercial transactions'.[29]

In the New Testament a similar picture emerges. Though *pistos* (*viz.* faithful, reliable, trustworthy) takes on some meanings of the word *'emet* noted above, *aletheia* and its cognates are used to refer not only to 'the truth of the gospel' but also to veracity and integrity, virtues which are commended as warmly as their opposites are condemned (*cf.,* John 7:18; Rom. 3:7; 2 Cor. 6:7, 8; Eph. 4:25; James 3:14; 1 John 1:6; 2:4; 2:21, 27; 4:6). In John 1:5-10 we see clearly that living obediently the revealed truth of God is, for John, the basis of a loving Christian community. It is a wayward Christian who 'disobeys' the truth (Rom. 2:8) or 'wanders from the truth' (James 5:19; cf. 2 Peter 2:2; 2 John 4; 3 John 3, 4). The gathered people of God are to be distinguished by their common commitment both to the revealed truth of God in Christ and to their gospel obligation to speak and live truthfully in accord with that truth. It is truth and truthfulness in the New Testament that define 'what it means to be fully human as an individual and in community'. Just as Jesus' life establishes the standard for the community's integrity, so his death in love for truth provides the model for sacrificial witness to the truth of the gospel. It is against this background that Paul declares, 'I am speaking the truth in Christ — I am not lying' (Rom. 9:1), and 'Everything we said to you was true' (2 Cor. 7:14). To the willing reader the Bible provides an inspiring vision of community indwelt and transformed by the living truth of God.

In summary, the Bible provides a remarkably consistent account of 'Truth Revealed' in and to the glory of God, through Jesus Christ,

29. Thiselton, 'Truth', p. 881.

by the power of the Spirit, among the people of God. At every point the existential integrity of truth and truthfulness is apparent. A church committed to knowing and living God's truth will be committed to God's standard of truthfulness in its public and private life — for, to a Christian, that is 'what it means to be truly human'.

Truth Applied

As we have begun to see, an historic biblical perspective on truth and truthfulness is relevant to the life and witness of the church in the world today. This section considers briefly four applications of this discussion to contemporary Anglican thinking.

In the first place, as intimated already, biblical teaching on truth and truthfulness is readily applied to *Christian understanding of personhood*. Alas, too often, humanity reflects the paradox expressed in Alexander Pope's *Essay on Man:*

> Created half to rise, and half to fall
> Great lord of all, yet a prey to all;
> Sole judge of truth, in endless error hurled;
> The glory, jest and riddle of the world.[30]

As was said of Mark Twain's Huckleberry Finn, 'There were things which he stretched, but mainly he told the truth'.[31] To a biblical Christian, as we have seen, God's truth and the practice of truthfulness are fundamental to human self-understanding. They are the ground of human identity and Christian virtue. As John Macquarrie's existentialist classic *Principles of Christian Theology* puts it, 'The fundamental truth with which we have to do . . . brings to light what humanity really is'.[32] In the post-modern world, outlined in Section 1, God's truth affords the possibility of human identity and personal integration in a world

---

30. Alexander Pope, *An Essay on Man*, Maynard Mack (ed.) (London: Methuen, 1950), pp. 55-56.
31. Mark Twain, *The Adventures of Huckleberry Finn* (London: Penguin Books, 1994), p. 11.
32. John Macquarrie, *Principles of Christian Theology* (London: SCM Press, 1977), p. 146.

of radical flux and ideological fragmentation. If the so-called enlightenment 'turn to the self' has in the end led to cynical disillusionment and progressive despair, the 'truth' of the gospel is still the gift of 'new life' in Christ both for an individual and for the world.

Interestingly, the role of truth and truthfulness in human liberation and self-understanding is a recurrent theme in the mid-century writings of the Russian dissident Alexandr Solzhenitsyn. There the human soul is found coming alive in individuals liberated by and for truth. It is not always an easy process, though it constitutes for Solzhenitsyn the only means to discovery of a full, free humanity. As Gleb Nerzhin, his *alter ego* in *The First Circle*, declares, 'Everyone forges his inner self year after year. One must try to temper, to cut, to polish one's soul so as to become a human being'.[33] Force and ideology cannot accomplish this, only truth can — when diligently pursued. As Solzhenitsyn's writings warn, truth eludes us as soon as our concentration begins to flag, all the while leaving the illusion that we are continuing to pursue it. To Solzhenitsyn and other dissident writers, the Christian appeal to truth and truthfulness is 'good news' in an unjust, violent, corrupt, oppressive world. For Jesus' promise 'the truth shall set you free' is proven again and again in lives freed from self-deception and corruption for godly character and Christian service. But Solzhenitsyn warns the individual Christian and the church never to give up the watchful pursuit of truth and the disciplined practice of truthfulness. As he stated in his Nobel Speech on Literature '*One word of truth . . .*,' 'And the simple step of a simple, courageous man is not to take part in the lie, not to support deceit. Let the lie come into the world, even dominate the world, but not through me'.[34]

Truth and truthfulness, as seen above, are also applicable to *the formation of human community*. Indeed, but for a common hermeneutic

---

33. Alexandr Solzhenitsyn, *The First Circle* (London: Collins, 1968), pp. 451-52. For a useful introduction to Solzhenitsyn's thought, see Edward E. Ericson, *Solzhenitsyn and the Modern World* (Washington, DC: Regnery Gateway, 1993).

34. Alexandr Solzhenitsyn, '*One word of truth. . . .*' The Nobel Speech on Literature 1970 (London: Bodley Head, 1972), p. 27. Karl Rahner's essay 'On Truthfulness' similarly stresses the importance of truth known and lived by an individual: 'Now one who loses his own truth is lost indeed, because one who has lost himself cannot possess God either. But he who finds this truth, he who accepts it in an attitude of truthfulness, lives it and makes it manifest, has God, who is *the* Truth, and this truth is freedom and eternal life' (p. 259).

CHRISTOPHER D. HANCOCK

of truth and a shared commitment to truthfulness social coherence is virtually inconceivable. In their absence discord, deceit and suspicion prevail. The value of a direct appeal to truth and truthfulness rests today in its power to free an individual or society from the constraints of an oppressive, totalitarian ideology; for it provides in both a foil to manipulation of data and criteria for evaluation of them. The key is an individual's sense of accountability to truth and truthfulness for the sake of her 'soul' and community. An illuminating perspective on this emerges again from the writings of Alexandr Solzhenitsyn. Ed Ericson points out in his book *Solzhenitsyn and the Modern World*, that Solzhenitsyn was a fierce critic of 'ideology' (understood, *pace* Kenneth Minogue, as 'the propensity to construct structural explanations of the human world' and to present 'the hidden and saving truth about the evils of the world in the form of social analysis').[35] According to this critique of ideology, truth is merely a matter of human analysis premised on the perfectibility of human society and the perspicuity of human insight. To Solzhenitsyn this will not do. For him, humans are sinful, historical creatures, limited both in power and perspective, who need to discover objective truth, goodness and beauty in life through a relationship with God. Apart from this discovery, ideology merely inspires a blinkered determination to construe data in a particular way to the benefit or detriment of a predetermined agenda, which (as Solzhenitsyn's novels reveal) leads to social coercion and ideological manipulation. Godly truth and the practice of truthfulness are, though, the basis of a 'free' society, for they provide the possibility of constructing and preserving a coherent community. As we find in John 8:36, 'If the Son sets you (plural) free, you (plural) will be free indeed'. It is always God's truth not human invention that makes this corporate freedom possible.

Third, as indicated earlier, a biblical perspective on truth and truthfulness is directly applicable to *the life and identity of the Christian church*. They are about both the *esse* and the *bene esse* of the church. This is evident in two crucial respects. First, the church as 'the Body of Christ', gathered to honour and scattered to worship the One who is 'the way, the truth, and the life', is constituted and commissioned by his word of truth. Jesus is the church's truth and life. His word of truth

35. Kenneth A. Minogue, *Alien Powers: The Pure Theory of Ideology* (New York: St. Martin's Press, 1985), p. 2.

208

is the church's message of hope. At the deepest level truth and truth-fulness are a matter of ecclesial ontology. For, if Jesus Christ does *not* inhabit the words and works of the church it builds on a liar (who promised in Matthew 28:20 to 'be with us always') and it lives by deceit (having no divine 'truth' to proclaim). The faith and hope of the Christian church is, however, that God's truth does indeed inhabit the church and holds the church accountable to both seeking and speaking the truth, and to offering 'true worship' to God day-by-day.

Truthfulness is, though, second, the existential behaviour of a community constituted by and committed to God's word of truth in Jesus. It, too, is part of both the *esse* and the *bene esse* of the church. It is because the church is inhabited by Christ 'the truth', that truthfulness is a possibility. Truthfulness in the church is a matter of christology not just veracity. But it is not sufficient for the church to assume it always speaks truthfully. A lecturer in a Baptist seminary, writing after his dismissal, articulates what many fear: 'The fact is that the majority of the clergy have long ago surrendered the intangibles of the gospel for the sake of a secure career. . . . If this sounds harsh, it is a judgement on myself as well as my colleagues. I have participated in the gentle distortion of the truth for the sake of the expediency. I have been the silent witness to the scapegoating of dissidents and prophets'.[36] How many church leaders suffer like one bishop who in depression admitted, 'I have known what I ought to say but have not said it'. Truth today, as ever, suffers alike from negligence, corruption and passion. Consistent appeals in the Bible for God's people to 'speak truthfully' and reject lying and deception, are a sombre reminder of humanity's proclivity towards falsehood. As John Henry Newman warned in one of his *Parochial and Plain Sermons*, 'It is not in human nature to deceive others, for any long time, without, in a measure, deceiving ourselves'.[37] The corporate character of the Christian church is fostered and maintained by a disciplined pursuit (*pace* Solzhenitsyn) of the practice of truthfulness. Apart from this the uniqueness of the church is lost. Hence, John's description of Christians as 'fellow workers in the truth' (3 John

36. Mike Riddell, 'The Bestiary in the Belfry', *Third Way*, Vol. 20, No. 4 (May 1997), p. 31.
37. John Henry Newman, 'Profession without Practice', *Parochial and Plain Sermons*, Volume I (London, Oxford and Cambridge: Rivingtons, 1869), p. 125.

8), Paul's charge to Timothy to 'rightly handle the word of truth' (2 Tim. 2:15) and Ephesians' challenge to 'speak the truth in love' (Eph. 4:15).

Fourth, a biblical account of 'truth' and 'truthfulness' is significant for discussion of *Anglican integrity*. All that has been said of individual Christians and the church so far applies, of course, to Anglican Christians. That goes without saying. But Anglicans are uniquely reminded of this biblical tradition in their liturgical prayers. This deserves brief comment. John Chrysostom's collect in Morning Prayer in *The Book of Common Prayer (1662)* requests, for example, 'grant us in this world knowledge of thy truth, and in the world to come life everlasting', and the 'Collect for the First Sunday after Easter' specifically asks, 'Grant us so to put away the leaven of malice and wickedness, that we may alway serve thee in pureness of living and truth'. The effect of these and other references to God's truth and godly truthfulness in Anglican liturgy,[38] is that they keep before Anglicans the ultimate source, authority, and spiritual fruit of the truth that is at the heart of their life and worship. However, added significance may be drawn from these as a clear reminder that Anglican integrity is preferably interpreted *not* as the dispersed structural consequence of Anglican liturgical praxis (*pace* Sykes),[39] but as the distinctive spiritual character of a worshipping Christian community (*pace* Scripture). Understood in this way, Anglican unity (and authority) is built not on the shaky foundation of human behaviour but on the sure foundation of divine truth. What's more, as we have seen above, preservation of Anglican coherence becomes a possibility because of spiritual *not* liturgical praxis. Built on biblical (and, as we have seen above, liturgical) truth and truthfulness, discussion of Anglican integrity (*viz.*, moral propriety) becomes a question of both the *esse* and the *bene esse* of the church — so buttressing the definition of Anglicanism *per se* by a firm ecclesiology (which it needs!).

Applied in this way to the discussion of human personhood, the formation of community, the identity of the church, and the integrity of Anglicanism, truth and truthfulness are vital elements in the discussion of 'what it means to be truly human as an individual and in

38. The Collects for Purity, and for the Feasts of Saints John, Peter, Matthias, Mark, Philip & James, and John the Baptist (among others) deserve careful consideration as reinforcing this point.

39. *Cf.*, S. W. Sykes, *The Integrity of Anglicanism* (London & Oxford: Mowbrays, 1978).

community'. In the last section of this essay, I consider three final reasons for reverencing truth and, in conclusion, propose two practical steps the Anglican communion might take to implement a conscious recommitment to truth and truthfulness in its common life.

Truth Reverenced

Why should the church reverence truth? Why should it be, and be seen to be, an agent of truth and truthfulness? In many ways these questions have already been answered, albeit implicitly. In this final section I want to draw together what has been said and focus the rationale behind explicitly naming truth and truthfulness on three fundamental principles, as matters of primary concern to the Anglican communion, as it considers 'what it means to be truly human'.

In the first place truth and truthfulness should be reverenced in the church *for the sake of God's glory and name.* As we saw earlier, the Bible sees no possible bifurcation between the 'true God' and a truth-speaking community. To worship God as 'truth' is to be committed to the practice of truthfulness; indeed, as we have said, only faith in a God of truth makes truth a possibility in the church and truthfulness an obligation. Those who seek truth must speak truth. It's a matter of personal integrity. So the Psalmist prays, 'Send forth your light and your truth, let them guide me; let them bring me to your holy mountain' (Psalm 43:3). Without God's presence and help truth is an impossibility. Again the Psalmist asks, 'Lord, who may dwell in your sanctuary? Who may live on your holy hill?' And the answer comes, 'He whose walk is blameless and who does what is righteous, who speaks truth from his heart and has no slander on his tongue' (15:1, 2). Entry into God's presence is conditional: truth and truthfulness are necessary criteria. This isn't an arbitrary judgement. It is consistent with the biblical call to worship the 'true God' 'in spirit and in truth'. Those who reverence truth and practice truthfulness honour God's glory and name. However tempting it may be today to dismiss a discussion of truth as impossible (given its status in society) and an expectation of truthfulness as un-workable (given its voluntary nature), a biblical Christian can accept neither. Truth and truthfulness *are* on the church's agenda as the people of this God.

211

It is important for the church to recognise one serious implication of accommodation to cultural relativism (that is, when complexity and controversy in discussion of truth lead to acceptance of a conditional or relative status for 'truth' by the church). Put simply, if truth is relative, relative truthfulness is sufficient. Why be absolutely truthful, if there is no such thing as truth? Indeed, is truthfulness a possibility without truth itself? The Bible's holistic, existential account of truth and truthfulness avoids this confusion. The God of truth is honoured by his truth-speaking people. When the church succumbs to the social, political, intellectual, psychological and spiritual pressure on truth today, and permits its expectation of truthfulness in public and in private to be compromised, it loses touch with the God of truth it seeks to serve.

As a consequence of this, the second reason for reverencing truth is *for the sake of God's church*. We saw earlier the importance ascribed to truthfulness in the Bible. This biblical wisdom needs to be taken seriously. Communities are built on truth and trust, and truthfulness is essential to trust. The biblical appeal to 'speak truth to one's neighbour' is not only to honour God, it is also to honour one's neighbour and build community. It makes good sense. It points Anglicans to theological and spiritual foundations of their faith and common life. It's a matter of community morality. But it raises two practical problems.

First, those who claim to 'speak the truth' have an alarming reputation for destroying communities! They are so clear about the truth that their honourable conviction lapses into disruptive bigotry. Church history is littered with their victims. Theirs is not the 'wisdom from above' commended by James, which is 'peace-loving, considerate, submissive, full of mercy and good fruit, impartial and sincere' (3:17). But let's be clear, a church without a sense of public truth and conviction is a weak, reprehensible thing. For what does it exist? Surely, not for 'the truth of the gospel'. Indeed, how can its apathy honour the God of truth? The key issue before many mainline churches today is not simply 'How does one "speak the truth in love" to build up the church?', but 'Is our commitment to truth matched by a commitment to truthfulness?' The force of the latter question in a politicised or divided church is that it holds the myopic ideologue and fiery bigot accountable to something beyond their passion and perspective. They are still accountable to veracity, so there is still a basis for community. Too often it seems, truthfulness is victim to pressure on truth *per se*. A sense of accountability to truthfulness provides an inductive basis for constructing a renewed foundation for truth in the church, which avoids the pitfalls of apathy and bigotry. It is a biblical basis, too.

Second, there is the problem of simply telling the truth. Church leaders and pastors face daily the problems of speaking truth (within parameters) and speaking truthfully (without pain). 'How much should I say?' and 'How can I say this?' are frequent questions for a Christian leader. Wisdom rightly dictates restricting information (when confidences must be kept) and respecting feelings (when the whole truth may hurt). But wisdom also surely warns that the habit of partial disclosure is as corrosive as it is constructive. The very best reasons for exercising discretion in one sphere can too easily become the very worst reasons for misleading information in another. Though truth is rugged (and may be severely cross-examined), it is also elusive (and must be carefully safe-guarded). In personal relations and the dissemination of information, truth is an associate of truthfulness and truthfulness a client of truth. For truthfulness is the primary moral sphere in which the individual Christian and church community 'reverences truth'. A wise leader may walk the shady street called 'Partial Truth', but should not plan to live there. It houses too many souls without much light and with compromised convictions.

The third reason for reverencing truth in the church is *for the sake of God's world*. As Brunner memorably held, 'The church is the only organisation that exists exclusively for the benefit of non-members'. Though exaggerated, his words keep before the church its missionary vocation and vicarious responsibility for the well-being of the world. Its calling to reverence truth and truthfulness is not for its own sake alone. As Vaclav Havel has stressed, when an individual or community begin to 'live in the truth' the consequences are considerable.[40] Truth and truthfulness are powerful commodities with prophetic potential in the public domain. For what does the prophet do but speak God's true word to the world God has made? A church without truth is like salt without taste; a church that 'walks in the light' of God's truth and will is like a city on a hill or a lamp on a stand (Matt. 5:13, 14). Truth and truthfulness create a basis for the church to confront society (exposing falsehood and deceit), to convert society (overturning idolatry by the

40. *Cf.*, Havel, *Living in the Truth,* passim.

gospel), and to console society (bringing God's true word of unity, worth and hope). The very best reasons for the Anglican communion to recommit itself to truth and truthfulness today lie in the plight of the world all around us. 'What does it mean to be truly human as an individual and as community?' Surely this: to live God's truth for God's world.

Conclusion

In conclusion, I want to propose two practical steps the Anglican communion might take to turn theorising about a doctrine of humanity into sound Christian practice. Who will take seriously the church's professed interest in 'what it means to be truly human as an individual and in community' if its words are not accompanied by action? In relation to truth and truthfulness two possible steps might be taken.

First, that the church offer itself locally and nationally as a 'truth-supporting' agency: that is, as a body that will take up the cause of those who believe truth and justice have not been done. They have been the victim of untruth and injustice. They have no one who will believe them. If the church is committed to truth then let it be committed to them. In many parts of the world this is already the church's informal role. My new proposal is that this vocation be (somehow) institution-alised and its intention (somehow) advertised. What hope this would bring to the powerless and ignored. What credibility to the church's appeal to truth. What a challenge to the church itself to be worthy of this calling. It is, of course, none other than a recovery of the Old Testament role of the godly 'seer' as arbiter and judge, as the one who 'judges fairly' (Ezek. 18:8, 9) and 'renders true and sound judgement' (Zech. 8:16) — though in this instance, of course, the church is a supplement to and not a replacement for civil courts of justice. If the church is to take seriously the holistic, existential account of truth and truthfulness in the Bible it must seek some way to turn faith into action for the sake of society. The church as a 'truth-supporting' agency, is one way this might be done.

My second proposal is that the Anglican communion form a 'truth-tracking' body: not, I hasten to add, a secret force that monitors doctrine or behaviour (!), but a public forum where open discussion of truth and truthfulness takes place. The 'Truth and Justice Commission' in South Africa provides a fascinating example of the therapeutic power of truth and the urgent need for truthfulness. Here was a forum where the pain of lying and deception was voiced and the possibility of truth restored. The Anglican communion needs such a place. Not because it has suffered the horrors of apartheid (though some have surely felt marginalised and oppressed), but because it has suffered the traumas of truth's defilement at the end of the second millennium, and needs a forum for its healing. A 'truth-tracking body' might do much to stir Anglicans to reverence truth as we enter the third millennium.

Questions

1. Why does the quest for, and question of, truth still matter today?

2. What event(s) in Jesus' life best illustrate his commitment to be and speak the truth?

3. What are the implications for a community, such as the Anglican communion, if truthfulness is not upheld as a norm?

4. Is it possible for the Anglican church to function with integrity as a 'truth-tracking' body in a multi-cultural world?

CALLED TO BE ONE

Called to Be One:
Worshipping the Triune God Together

EDITH HUMPHREY

Summary

Our consideration of unity best begins with a focus on God, rather than with ourselves and our salvation. While the biblical story of salvation by God is our basis, it points beyond itself to the triune God who shares life with us. John's Gospel shows the link between love and unity, between Father and Son, in a way which involves both submission and mutuality. Today much theology challenges the aspect of submission and favours freedom or independence. New metaphors are proposed to displace the biblical and patristic trinitarian names. The Bible never implies God is male, but uses masculine imagery, and in ways which stress self-giving and generosity. To part company with this triune name is no mere formal break with the historic church, with catholicity. If we cease using the names of Father, Son and Spirit we can hardly be said to be formed, informed and conformed to them. The gradual erosion of the virtue of humility shows a drift from recognition of the Son, who is our way of reconciliation with the Father.

Reversing the Proposition

Nourished by the sacraments and formed by the prayer and teaching of the church, we need seek nothing but the particular place willed for us by God within the church. When we find that place, our life and our prayer both at once become extremely simple.[1]

Thoughts in Solitude seems an odd point to begin a discussion of unity, worship and the Trinity. This particular thought of Merton may seem an even stranger place to begin, given our late twentieth century context, and its inhospitable attitude towards obedience and 'place'. Yet, it is probably wise, in the midst of baffling complexity, to return to simplicity. 'Alone' with God, Merton speaks of the 'we' and the church, of what (or Who) nourishes and forms us, of praying and living with singleness of heart. To read Merton beyond this brief quotation is to discover that the quest for our particular place in the church comes not through a popularly-styled 'search for the self' but through a focus upon, and adoration of, the One who is 'the Center to which all things tend, and to Whom all our actions must be directed'.[2]

So it is in our 'quest' for unity in the church. If we are truly 'called to be one' and this is not a humanly-directed or corporately conceived project of unification, then our unity must spring from our steady gaze upon the One who 'gives life to the dead and calls those "not being" as "being"' (Rom. 4:17). Indeed, our unity springs not from our efforts (not even the effort of worship), but from that very One himself, as we gaze upon his Image and are transfigured from glory to glory through the Lord (who is the Spirit.) Our talk about the vocation of the church to worship as one is bound up with our corporate invocation of the One Who Is and who first called us. In making sense of our unity, we are thrust back to the source and foundation of unity; in making sense of our diversity, we must go first to the triune One in whom and from whom diversity generously springs. To truly begin, it seems that we must reverse the proposition, 'Called to be One' and begin with the caller, rather than with our calling.

I am well aware that in doing this reversal, I am rejecting the advice of numerous theologians who argue that it is a counter-intuitive move. Many have argued that to begin thinking about our salvation and about our humanity (or even talk about the Trinity itself) with talk of the triune God *in se* is not only counter-intuitive, but arbitrary. So,

---

1. Thomas Merton, *Thoughts in Solitude* (New York: Farrar, Straus and Giroux, 1958), p. 52.
2. Merton, *Thoughts*, p. 52.

in a particularly coherent but simple statement of the problem, Migliore warns, 'If talk of the triune God is not to be wild speculation, it will always find its basis and its limit in the biblical narration of the love of God for the world.'[3] It is quite clear that Migliore and others of his mind are intent to avoid a myriad of evils attendant upon arid speculation; we may also be sympathetic to their departure point, that is, the biblical narrative. However, while it is evident that the *basis* of our thinking about the triune God is to be the biblical story of God's love for us, we need not follow in Migliore's plea that this is to be our limit. For it seems that part of Jesus' calling of his followers as 'no longer servants, but friends' involved (and involves) the disclosure of mysteries beyond our own situation. Trustworthy knowledge about God does indeed come through the salvation narrative, which offers a picture or icon of God's incarnate Word; yet we may not limit what it is that Jesus intended (and intends) to teach to his new community. There are several points in Scripture where the apostles, and through them, we ourselves, are invited *beyond* the immediate realm of instruction in our salvation to think about the mystery of the relationship between the Father and the Son — one thinks immediately about the Johannine Last Supper discourse.

John 13:31-38, 14–17, in fact, provides an excellent *locus* for a discussion of worship, unity and the mysterious nature of God. In beginning here, we will be following in the footsteps of many church fathers who meditated upon this passage in order to understand and illuminate the mysteries of the Trinity and the church. Moreover, we will be, in a parallel way, exploring the ongoing basis for hope, as expressed by our Roman brothers and sisters, *ut unum sint* (John 17:21). In beginning with the gospel, and in the knowledge of traditional interpretation, we can hope to shed light on problems of worship and language which are confronting us today, and make godly decisions that will confirm us in the first and fourth 'marks' of the church: our unity and our catholicity.

3. Daniel L. Migliore, *Faith Seeking Understanding* (Grand Rapids: Eerdmans, 1991), p. 61.

EDITH HUMPHREY

Beginning at the Beginning: The Triune God

We must begin by acknowledging that there is no fully-developed doctrine of the Trinity outlined even in these chapters of the 'theological' Gospel. If this were the case, the church would not have laboured under the difficult discussions that preceded Nicaea and Chalcedon, nor would some sects or individuals which divorce the Scriptures from their traditional interpretation continue to express quasi-Arian theologies. Nevertheless, this passage, among others, was essential in the later articulation of the trinitarian mystery. Our purpose here is not to inquire into the understanding of the first-century Christian communities, nor to exegete the original 'intent' of the writer of the fourth Gospel; rather, it is to see our place within the entire tradition of the church, including the credal formulations to which we lay claim, and by which we are informed. With a full awareness that other types of questions may be asked of this passage, we fruitfully read it for an intimation of the trinitarian faith which we embrace.

Jesus begins, after announcing his impending departure, by calling his disciples to the new rule of love (13:34); he closes his teaching by praying for their unity (17:21-26). The vision of true love and unity therefore envelopes this passage, and characterises or names the community for which Jesus is praying — both the immediate historical community of the disciples, and those who will 'believe because of their word'. The basis of this love is made clear both within the intricacies of the teaching (chs. 14–17), and in the final summary, 'I made your name known to them, and I will make it known, so that the love with which you have loved me may be in them, and I in them' (17:26). Many studies have been written, of course, on the significance of the 'name' in the fourth Gospel and in the ancient biblical world in general. We do well to remember that the Gospel begins by speaking of those who, 'received him/believed in his name' (1:12) and so are made children of God: the parallelism here, plus the high importance of the 'name' and 'naming' in Hebrew and ancient Christian culture, demonstrate that the word 'name' refers to the whole person, to the nature of the one so evoked. It is not that Jesus had divulged to his disciples a secret or code name for God, so that they could live as an esoteric community, although this is the spin that Gnostic writers in the past, and present-day witnesses have put on 17:26. This manipulative, literalist or magical

222

view of the name's invocation is far from the text. Rather, Jesus has revealed God's nature, and the person of God, and promises that this revelation will be made even more full. In so knowing God (which includes knowing about him but extends beyond this to a growing knowledge of God himself), divine love will be created within his followers.

When we ask what it is that has been shown, and what promises to be shown by Jesus so that this love may be created, we begin, however, with the 'names' of Father, Son and Spirit that are given and explained in this discourse. Jesus speaks continually here of 'my Father' but implies throughout that the link between the Father and him will be extended to include others. This, of course, becomes explicit in the resurrection appearance to Magdalene: 'Go to my brothers[4] and say to them, "I am ascending to my Father and your Father, to my God and your God"' (20:17). The message is clear: it is on the basis of Jesus' right to call God Father that believers are given this name, for they have become God's children. Moreover, in thinking about this mystery we are pushed back beyond the 'human' experience of Jesus (if it is even sane to make such distinctions!); the bond between Father and Son and their relationship one with the other is no mere temporal condition. As Jesus suggests in his 'high-priestly' prayer, his glory, which he is about to fully receive, and pass on to the disciples, is a glory that he had in the presence with the Father before the world existed (17:5). The Father *is* in the Son, and the Son in the Father; the Son glorifies the Father, and the Father will glorify the Son; even left 'alone,' the Son is in the company of the Father; the Son comes from the Father and the Son goes to the Father; the Son does as the Father commands, to demonstrate his love for the Father; the Father and the Son will come to those who love the Son, and make their home with them. These are only a few of the chords sounded in Jesus' words. Our filial bond to the Father springs from the ineffable, eternal and fruitful bond of identity and relationship

---

4. It is essential to note here that although Jesus is sending a message first to the apostles, whom he terms 'his brethren', this is a message that is first heard and mediated by the female disciple given the title 'Equal-to-the-Apostles'. Moreover, the word about 'your Father' is an inclusive one that is passed on by the apostles to the church, including males and females. Jesus is not calling the apostles *alone* his brethren, but implying that all believers now have this new standing with God. This is consonant with the assurance and promise made in 14:7, 16:15 and 17:20.

between Father and Son. 'In' Christ, and not destined to be orphans, we are adopted by God as true children. Out of that status, brothers and sisters together, we forge true love, or indeed, have forged within us the love that comes from the inner being of God.

The creation of this love between us moves us directly to the third 'name' disclosed by Jesus. Jesus speaks, in personal terms (contrary to the grammatic neutral gender demanded by *to pneuma*) of the 'other Advocate' or 'Spirit of Truth' or 'Holy Spirit' *who* proceeds from the Father and *whom* the Father will send in the Son's name. In concert with the Father, the Spirit will glorify the Son; in concert with the Son, he will 'not speak on his own' but will witness to the divine will. Through his coming, what is the Father's, and therefore the Son's, will be given to the disciples (16:14-15). We are to share in the nature of God! Bound up with the gift of the Spirit is the keeping of the commandment of love, the ability to abide in God, the teaching of greater mysteries, the ability to do great things, the remembrance of the Son's words, and the imparting of divine peace. As the Fathers were later to describe this, it is out of the inner 'dance' *(perichoresis)* of the Father, Son, and Spirit (who share glory one with the other) that our glory as children of God springs.

One of the greatest mysteries to note here is that the 'dance' and mutuality do not exclude the notions of obedience and self-effacement. The Son goes to the Father who is, in one sense, 'greater' than he (14:28),[5] and demonstrates his love through obedience (14:31). Some commentators, in fear of losing the divinity of the Son, have softened the implica-

---

5. It does not seem adequate here to explain this away in terms of Jesus' 'human' subordination to the Father, since the Johannine thought speaks in the present tense of the ongoing relationship between Father and Son. While this verse is challenging to trinitarian thought, it is not idiosyncratic in the Scriptures. See also the eschatological ordering of 1 Cor. 15:24-28, where Paul explains the Son's glory in terms of the Father's super-order. Paul and John seem to hold to the equality of Father with Son alongside a certain subordination. If the former (the equality) is doubted, see the reconstrual of the divine 'name' of Isaiah 45:23 in Phil. 2:5-11, or the reconfiguration of the Shema in 1 Cor. 8:6. I owe this insight of Paul's implicit 'binitarianism' to the teaching of N. T. Wright. Typically commentators have noticed the subordination, without heeding the exaltation of the Son; inversely, 'conservative' theologians have highlighted the exaltation, without knowing what to do about the ordering. The patristic view, continued in the Eastern tradition, and now reclaimed by the ecumenical removal of the *filioque*, holds both together, in that it speaks of *perichoresis* alongside filiation and procession. There is a true triangle, but it may not be inverted.

tions of this passage by reference to *economia* and the filial subjection of the 'human' Jesus. Such an interpretation does not seem, however, to do justice to the ongoing and assertive present tense of the passage. Moreover, it is not only here in the New Testament that we are troubled by an enigmatic reference to an extra-temporal ordering of the Father and Son. Equally problematic are Paul's words about the *eschaton*. 'Then comes the end, when he hands over the kingdom to God the Father, after he has destroyed every ruler and every authority and power. . . . When all things are subjected to him, then the Son himself will also be in subjection under him, so that God may be all in all' (1 Cor. 15:24-28).

Alongside assertions of a high christology (a christology which would issue in the full-blown doctrines of the Trinity and the two natures of Christ) both the fourth evangelist and Paul assert an order. Adrienne von Speyer, in commenting upon the Johannine passage, does not skirt the 'subordinist' problem, but explores its meaning within an unmitigated trinitarianism:[6]

> Here the immense mystery begins. He, a man, goes as God to God. . . .
> [P]rofound depths of truth lie in this word of the Son: *The Father is greater than I*. No human person says this or could say it, nor is it a word of the Father, who would not say it; rather, it is a word that only the Son's love and humility can utter.[7]

---

6. The balance between high christology and ordering in the Johannine and Pauline passages would seem to affirm the kind of monarchianism *within* trinitarian thought displayed by the Cappadocians, rather than either Marcionite or dynamic monarchianism which were excluded from orthodox thinking. Monarchianism *within* trinitarianism sees the Father as eternally the font of the other persons (filiation and procession) while affirming the equal divinity and power of the entire Godhead. It is of course true that some Western theologians continue to affirm double procession while consenting to the removal of the *filioque* as a charitable strategy. There is, unfortunately, no time here to debate the difficulties cited by Moltmann *et al.* (in defence of double procession), where they reclaim the Anselmian principle of a necessary consonance between the inner relation of the Trinity and divine self-disclosure. Nor is there space to present (as a counter argument) Lossky's compelling restatement of the Palamite distinction between the essence and energies of God. On all accounting, we are on mysterious ground at this point; sooner or later analysis must cease, as we simply stand in awe, watching the unconsumed bush burn.

7. Adrienne von Speyer, *The Farewell Discourses; Meditations on John 13–17*, tr. E. A. Nelson (San Francisco: Ignatius Press, 1987), pp. 152, 155.

The Son demonstrates his obedience to the Father; similarly, the Spirit proceeds from the Father, and does not bear witness alone. Nevertheless, Father, Son and Spirit are duly given glory and worship. This tension between order and mutuality, while difficult to grasp, may be helpful in understanding the complex roles which we fulfil in our human but divinely conceived community: mirroring the Godhead (or better, sharing in its nature) our family will include both order, and equal glory or honour. As St John Chrysostom puts it, 'if you love, you ought to submit to the one you love'.[8]

The Problem of Language: Our Corporate Worship

So, then, when we begin with the story of the Gospels, we find that our names of Father and Son (together with the more shadowy person of the Spirit) come from Jesus' own way of referring to himself, and the language used by the Gospels and letters in referring to God. While the Old Testament uses metaphor to speak of God *as* a father, it is not until the New Testament that we find the word used consistently as a kind of name, a name that goes beyond a mere picture. Jesus, the Son of God, taking up in himself the role of Israel as God's Son, but also transcending it because he is the 'uniquely begotten Son,' addresses his Father personally. 'Abba, Father,' he says. As Pannenberg notices, 'On the lips of Jesus, "Father" became a proper name for God. It thus ceased to be simply one designation among others.'[9] Until recently, there was no question about this characteristic and family manner of thinking about and referring to God. Of course, other titles and names were used to speak of the one who is not to be contained. Yet, those who were in Christ considered it a privilege and a glory to call upon the Father in God-given boldness, *parresia*, and considered that this particular invocation rested upon the revealed character of the Father. This was no Johannine aberration, but a name and relationship found generally enough in the New Testament to inform later thinkers on trinitarian

8. Chrysostom, *Commentary on St. John the Apostle and Evangelist, Homilies 48-88*, in *The Fathers of the Church, A New Translation*, tr. Goggin (New York: Fathers of the Church Inc., 1960), p. 283.

9. Wolfhart Pannenberg, *Systematic Theology*, I, tr. G. W. Bromiley (Grand Rapids: Eerdmans, 1991), p. 262.

theology: 'No one knows the Son except the Father, and no one knows the Father except the Son and those to whom the Son . . . reveals Him.' (Matt. 11:27) Let us leave, for a moment, the rich implications of such language, and turn to the challenge that has been directed towards this peculiarly Christian way of naming God, based on the link between Father and Son.

In fact, a very different story of origins has now been urged in the church and academy, and accepted by many. 'Role-model theology'[10] has convinced not a few that every religion projects social values onto the figure of god to construct a picture of a god[11] after which we can confidently pattern ourselves. Since hierarchy and patriarchalism are in the late twentieth century undesirable, our picture of God should avoid gender terms, or use both equally. Metaphor, then, is seen as our way of seeking to name the unnameable, and good theology should use appropriate and (enlightened) pictures, or society and the church will suffer. A creative and vocal spokesperson for this view is the hymn-writer and thinker Brian Wren, who is well known for encapsulating the 'patriarchalist' view of God (enshrined in the culture-bound Scriptures, and from which he hopes the church will be liberated) in the acronym KINGAFAP ('King and Father All-Powerful').[12] Here the orig-

10. Here I adopt the terminology of Garrett Green, in his interaction with Sallie McFague. See 'The Gender of God and the Theology of Metaphor', in Alvin F. Kimel, Jr. (ed.), *Speaking the Christian God: The Holy Trinity and the Challenge of Feminism* (Grand Rapids: Eerdmans, 1992), pp. 44-64.

11. See, for example, the argument that 'Father', etc. are 'our images, not pictures of God in the reality and fullness of the divine being', *Commentary on Prayer Book Studies 30* (New York: The Church Hymnal Corporation, 1989). This view is actually taught in one of the hymns of the proposed Canadian Hymnbook, where role-model theology is ascribed to Jesus himself. In Hymn 283, option for March 19, St. Joseph's day, the relationship of Joseph and Jesus is described in this manner:

All praise, O God, for Joseph
the guardian of your Son,
who saved him from King Herod,
when safety there was none
He taught the trade of builder,
when they to Nazareth came,
and Joseph's love made 'Father'
to be, for Christ, God's name.

12. Brian Wren, *What Language Shall I Borrow? God-Talk in Worship: A Male Response to Feminist Theology* (New York: Crossroad, 1990). See especially p. 196.

inal metaphors are seen within their (inadequate) biblical narrative and traced throughout several theological moments in church history. For Wren, even the distinction between double and single procession is incidental, although he is taken with the Augustinian depiction of the Holy Spirit as the 'love-link' (*De Trinitate*, 7:3-6, 8:10-14, 5:19-37) without realising the difficulties which this picture (compounded by the *filioque*) may have caused or may cause in our full acceptance of the Spirit as a person.[13] Though he makes use of the Augustinian view,[14] his major point is that Eastern and Western theologians alike accepted and continue in the twentieth century to accept 'the sequence given in the KINGAFAP system'.[15]

Wren's experimental renaming and creative re-narrativisation of the Christian story is, interestingly, often right in what it affirms, but wrong in what it denies. The same may be said, it seems, of more nuanced and 'traditional-friendly' deliberations, such as those of Jane Williams.[16] Williams is content to retain the names of Father and Son; Wren seeks 'more adequate' terms. On one major point, however, both are in agreement. So Williams: 'to call God "father" is not to evoke the "patriarch" . . . "authority" and "headship" are not characteristic of God's fatherhood, in the biblical tradition;'[17] so Wren: 'In keeping with the biblical record, "Father" is Abba, and the "kingdom" of God is marked not by hierarchy, but by freedom.'[18] While Wren revises, and Williams qualifies, both see mutuality and freedom as incompatible with headship and obedience. Thus, Wren faults Moltmann for his depiction of the Son as responding in submission (although this is in

13. It is interesting to note that while the Eastern tradition did not use this language to refer to the *hypostasis* of the Spirit, there is to be found in Palamas, for example, an analogy of love directed towards describing energy of love *common* to the three persons of the Godhead.

14. The Spirit becomes, in his reformulation, 'The Mutual Friend', p. 210, a rather dependent, or relative, role!

15. 'A KINGAFAP sequence with the King-Father giving orders to his Son and the spirit being sent by the Father alone or Father and Son together,' 'The Mutual Friend', p. 198.

16. J. Williams, 'The Fatherhood of God', in *The Forgotten Trinity; A Selection of Papers presented to the BCC Study Commission on Trinitarian Doctrine Today* (London: BCC/CCBI Interchurch House, 1991), pp. 91-101.

17. Williams, 'The Fatherhood of God', p. 96.

18. Wren, *What Language Shall I Borrow?* p. 198.

concert, as we have seen, with both the fourth gospel and Paul). Again, he cites with approval the dancing metaphor of C. S. Lewis's *Perelandra*, while totally missing Lewis' own emphasis on subordination as inherent in the dance![19] Wren rightly characterises the dance as 'not a solo performance, but a communal enterprise, like an eightsome reel, a square dance, or barn dance'.[20] Lewis would, while agreeing with the 'communal' aspect, also point out that the dance is courtly, with a leader, and key players, not a free-for-all or a mere 'line-dance'. The drama is not to be tamed by the conflation of leader and follower: yet there is freedom and mutuality!

With other trinitarians, Wren, in hymn, celebrates 'every kind of unity . . . [which] begins with God, forever One,/whose nature is Community'.[21] This 'Community' is, however, re-formed along contemporary egalitarian lines, in agreement with other theological and exegetical moves that are being made today, such as 'the brokerless Kingdom,' the egalitarian 'Q community' or the picture of 'God as Friend'. At this point several questions demand a hearing: What is at stake in 'correcting' the root biblical metaphors and story? What is lost in reducing the tension between the liberty offered, and the submission required, by the rule of God? The new vision, and new dance affirm the first (liberty), while denying the second (submission). This is no mere squabble about arbitrary metaphors or appealing names. Rather, we are in the realm of root issues: metaphorical theology urges us to 'try out new pictures'[22] more suited to the *Zeitgeist* of the day; traditional theology continues to cry out 'Abba, Father!' because it sees itself in solidarity with Jesus, the humble one who has made the Father known.

We do not need to remain naive or rigid at this point in order to remain faithful. The apophatic tradition of the church rightly reminds us that no name comprehends the living God, and that we must also

---

19. Lewis' protagonist Ransom describes the great dance thus: 'yet the former pattern not thereby dispossessed by finding in its new subordination a significance greater than that which it had abdicated'. See Wren, *What Language Shall I Borrow?* p. 213.

20. Wren, *What Language Shall I Borrow?* p. 212.

21. Wren, *What Language Shall I Borrow?* p. 212.

22. Sallie McFague, *Models of God: Theology for an Ecological, Nuclear Age* (Philadelphia: Fortress Press, 1987), xii.

murmur, 'Neither is this thou'. However, to speak of the limitation of human words, images and concepts is not an open door to the complete relativisation of all words, images and concepts. To recognise that we do not fully comprehend God, even in the pictures and ideas that he has given us, is not the same as saying that we can substitute more palatable images or terms. There is the initial difficulty in knowing what constitutes the essence and what the separable vehicle in a theological symbol: no human mind can be entirely sure, when naming a mystery, about what is 'like' and what is totally 'other' in contrasting the symbol with its referent. We would have to be outside of our own world, and able to compare this (independently) with the greater reality, in order to be certain.

Careful thinking about the ways in which the names are used will nonetheless free us from the inevitable imprisonment suspected in the complaint 'If God is male, then the male is God'.[23] It is helpful here to contemplate the *shape* of the biblical story. When the story speaks about a Father and Son, how does it use these pictures? We do well to remember that the Bible (and subsequent Jewish as well as Christian thought) never speaks of God as *male,* although it does picture God in masculine terms. The Anglican Thirty-nine Articles declare 'there is but one living and true God, everlasting, without body, parts or passions'.[24] Second, the Christian story presents us with a very unusual turn of events. In the words of Garrett Green, 'This God does not jealously hoard his power. As a husband he does not beat his unfaithful wife but cries out with the pain of a jilted lover and redoubles his efforts to win her back (Hos. 2) As Father he "did not spare his own Son but gave him up for us all" (Rom. 8:32). As Son he did not claim the prerogatives of power and lord it over his subjects but "emptied himself, taking the form of a servant.... He humbled himself and became obedient unto death, even death on a cross" (Phil. 2:7-8). As Spirit he incorporates us into the mystical body of Christ, in whom "there is neither slave nor free, there is neither male

23. Mary Daly authored this phrase, since become a motto, in *Beyond the Father: Toward a Philosophy of Women's Liberation* (Boston: Beacon Press, 1973), p. 19.

24. We may, of course, want to question the totalising concept of an impassive God, in the light of the drama of the incarnation, and in the knowledge that such language owes much to classical philosophy as absorbed by church tradition. Nevertheless, the citation demonstrates the intent of Anglican (and Christian) theology to eschew the notion of a male god.

nor female" (Gal. 3:28). As king he does not isolate himself in heavenly splendor but wills to dwell with his people, to "wipe away every tear from their eyes" and to deliver them from all that oppresses them, even from death itself (Rev. 21:4)'.[25]

Here is a poignant reversal of the All-powerful One who yields all, even dying for those whom he loves. This masculinely-pictured God is neither male nor oppressive, but overturns our presuppositions. The historical Christian faith, then, is a revealed religion, which uses masculine imagery for God in a very surprising way. God, if you like, takes up our human metaphors, but uses them in a way we never could have expected. The names of Father and Son function iconically, but also iconoclastically, affirming order, but also disrupting our fond ideas of what that order might mean. We might venture to say that hierarchy, which includes both grandeur and tenderness, is affirmed, but hierarchial*ism* is squarely judged.

Our First and Fourth Mark: One and Catholic

This affirming and disorienting vision of Father, Son and Holy Spirit must be faithfully and reverently maintained if we hope, as a communion, to retain our God-given birthright of unity, and if we hope, along with our sister communions, to express ever more fully our catholicity. We need the name of Father, Son and Holy Spirit, to safeguard the characteristic idea of our faith, the idea of 'otherness in relation'. To put this less functionally, it is by mirroring the ordered and communicative reality of the Trinity, as revealed to us in Scripture, and expounded to us in the church, that we find our own life. This does not mean that other names may not be used in reference to the One we adore — many names and even the action of not-naming have been faithfully employed within our Christian family as a reminder that our God may not be contained. Nevertheless, many of the new projects of renaming seem, at root, to spring from the assumption that we *know better*[26] than

25. Green, 'The Gender of God and the Theology of Metaphor', p. 60.
26. See, for example, the self-congratulatory mood of Wren's conclusion to 'Naming Anew', p. 214, where he shows the advantages of 'Beloved, Lover and Mutual Friend' over the traditional triad.

our forbears (even the witnesses in Scripture!). Where renaming is conceived as a substitutionary endeavour, or as a way of marginalising the normative trinitarian name, there is inevitable fallout. Loss of particularity, functionalism, depersonalisation, panentheistic interconnection with the creation and sexualisation are some of the vicious possibilities encountered in the well-meaning attempts at revision.[27] Even those who work diligently to avoid such problems fall prey: Wren, for example, is concerned to give the Holy Spirit a *more* descriptive definition than he perceives in the traditional name, but in adopting the term 'Mutual Friend' makes the Spirit's role wholly determined by her *(sic)*[28] relation to the first and second persons.

A better route would be to affirm the scriptural and apostolic witnesses, alongside careful teaching about the key Player(s): the interrelationship of the persons of the Godhead, and God's unfathomable love for humankind. The problem is not with the story. The problem is not with the pictures or the name. The problem is in not hearing the story, in not explaining the name well enough. God is self-revealed to us in history and in the name of Father, Son and Holy Spirit. To hastily alter that name is to abandon the truth to ideology and political correctness, is to risk a subtle or even decisive change in our story and our knowledge of God, and to endanger our catholicism. If we follow the course of one of our sister communions in Canada (which has allowed, in some jurisdictions, baptism into the 'name' of 'Creator, Redeemer and Sustainer') we not only risk serious rupture with present apostolic communions, but we effectively cease integral connection with the historic church. There is no way that the 'intent' of the officiant to

27. Particularly strong is the plea to picture God as Mother. However, this may well suggest a religion in which God is not personal and transcendent, that is, separate from the creation, but inter-connected with the creation which has proceeded from the womb of the Goddess. The implication is particularly strong when God is invoked as Mother, but not usually when a simile is used, disclosing the mother-like characteristics of God. Such similes, but never a maternal name, are also used in Scripture.

28. Wren uses the feminine pronoun as a 'move away from hierarchy . . . recognising that both *she* and *he* are inadequate', p. 210. He also attaches *sic* to those who refer to the Spirit as 'he'. The question inevitably arises: 'inadequate' to what? For while 'he' may be problematic to some revisionists, it is the surprising pronoun used in the fourth Gospel. Wren and others find themselves *sic*ing not only the traditionalists, but the evangelist!

232

baptise into the name of the Christian Trinity can be assumed if such a reformulation is used.[29] Such distancing from the church might even be accomplished were the traditional formula to be made simply *pro forma* at "high occasions" such as baptism, without reflecting the normal and natural use of our community. (We may, in fact, be on the way to this divorce, with the growing preference for substitutions at the prayer before the homily or at the dismissing benediction.) Nor would such suspicions about catholicity be arising simply on a formal or technical basis. For it is reasonable to suppose that where other considerations relegate the traditional trinitarian name to the antiquarian past, that that community will eventually no longer be formed by the Father, informed by the Son and conformed by the Spirit,[30] the triune source of perichoretic unity. Already, a primary mark of the Son, his humility, is finding little room in our communities, even as a desired virtue: independence has supplanted it. Together, we learn a different way of being from the Trinity. For the one upon whom we call is the one who calls us into being. Let us therefore cleave to Father, Son and Holy Spirit in our adoration, but explain the drama of the salvation story, as well as the free and humble 'dance' which that name enacts, evokes, engenders and brings to birth.

All language is, of course, insufficient to comprehend the living God. Yet, paradoxically, God has made himself known in the one whom we call the Word, and who spoke to us about himself as Son, as well as about the Father and the Spirit of Truth. What we can know, as yet by far, of our triune God, is truly if not exhaustively represented in the names of Father, Son and Holy Spirit. These names speak first of all about God's own nature, and second, of God's intimate relationship to us. In times of controversy and struggle, even over principal issues such as our mode of worship, and the names that we use, we can take

29. Interestingly, 'Creator, Redeemer and Sustainer' found approval from a Jewish friend outside of the Christian communion who did not, obviously, accept the doctrine of the Trinity: his God was equally a creator, redeemer, and sustainer. Paul Minear offers this anecdote in 'The Bible and the Book of Worship', *Prism* 3 (1988), pp. 52-53.

30. I adopt these terms as an extension and reformulation of 'institution' and 'constitution' suggested by Karl Rahner, *The Trinity* (1970) *passim* as cited by John Zizioulas, 'The Doctrine of God the Trinity Today: Suggestions for an Ecumenical Study', in *The Forgotten Trinity*, p. 28.

courage from the church's past and remember that it is out of such difficult times that rich theology may come to light. Remembering that we do not ask alone, but with the whole of the church, and in concert with the Spirit, who prays in us, let us pray that these names will not become a barrier in our communion, but that they will continue to be the effective token of our reconciliation. For the Son is our peace, and through him we have access to the Father by one Spirit.

Questions

1. Are we grateful for the privilege of the revelation of God as Father, Son and Spirit, or worried and resentful at the divine self-disclosure?

2. Do you agree that gradual displacing of the trinitarian language is a risk for the church's life and communion with God?

3. How can we learn to live out the way of the Son's self-giving in our lives?

Unity and Truth: The Anglican Agony

J. I. PACKER

Summary

The older Anglican churches of the Western world are deeply divided and starting to split over questions of truth raised by the policies and pressures that flow from their mainly liberal leadership. The historic concept of Anglican comprehensiveness as liberty of opinion on secondary matters within a stable framework of worship, discipline, and agreement on fundamentals has ceased to apply. The New Testament ascribes to the church a given unity in Christ that is bounded by Christ-centred truth, but within Anglicanism this is being eroded. The only hope for recovery lies in a moratorium on hasty constitutional changes where consensus is lacking, sustained adherence to the historic orthodoxy that centres on the Trinity and the incarnation, and co-operative labour in spreading the gospel of Jesus Christ.

Crisis

In this age of media hype, crisis language gets overworked, and it usually proves wise to take scare-mongering talk with a pinch of salt. Knowing this, the last thing I want to do is to line up with those who, as it seems, are endlessly auditioning for the part of the boy who cried wolf. Nonetheless, the news I bring in this essay is that we currently face a genuine crisis that truly threatens the continuance of Anglicanism as we know it. Driven unwillingly as I am to this conclusion, I think it

235

would be irresponsible not to express it, and I do so now in the hope that Lambeth 1998 will come up with something that defuses the crisis rather than escalates it. The situation I shall explore is one in which unity within Anglicanism is everyone's goal, and truth within Anglicanism is everyone's problem. While African and South American Anglicanism grows and prospers, what I shall call Anglo-Anglicanism — the Anglicanism, that is, of Britain, Canada, Australasia and the United States — shrinks and stumbles; and while African and South American Anglicanism stands solidly for biblical truth in its evangelical and catholic mutations, Anglo-Anglicanism is increasingly over a barrel with regard to basic questions of truth, as the communal structures that have hitherto preserved at least the form of truth are increasingly shaken loose. Surely the Anglican communion cannot long continue like this: the centre, it seems, cannot hold, and if things go on as they are going Anglicanism must find itself flying apart. The current crop of 'continuing' Anglican churches, splintered off from what is seen as the derailed Anglican communion, may thus (though I hope not) be an ominous harbinger of things to come.

To set the stage, now, for our discussion, I make three preliminary observations, as follows.

First, let us remember that world Anglicanism is itself *accidental*, in the sense of being a hybrid product of various historical contingencies. We may agree that the accident was a happy and indeed providential one, and others beside myself may want to claim that the Anglican heritage as we have received it from the past is the richest and wisest in all Christendom, but that does not alter the fact that empirical Anglicanism is a growth and development that could not at any stage have been predicted, and that is my point at present. If the house of Tudor had not come out on top in the Wars of the Roses; if Henry VIII had not had a succession problem; if Thomas Cranmer had not been a devotee of Reformational theology, as well as a liturgical genius; if the evangelical and catholic revivals, with their respective Puritan and Caroline antecedents, had not taken place; and if the church had not followed the flag in the Victorian era when the Union Jack flew over colonies covering a quarter of the earth's surface, then Anglicanism in its present form would never have existed.

Anglicanism, then, like other Christian traditions, is a historical accident, and as a type of Christianity it appears as a more delicate hybrid that most. It can certainly be argued — and I would argue myself — that its ecumenical significance is out of all proportion to its numbers (it is about one per cent of the world church, not more). But the point I would make now is that as there was nothing inevitable about its growth, so there is nothing inevitable about its survival. Delicate hybrids tend to be unstable and very vulnerable to outside influences, and as we shall see current Anglican trends are making Anglican continuance in line with Anglicanism's own heritage less and less certain. If we are to think realistically about the Anglican future, we must recognise that Anglicanism, like the rest of the Christian church, is, as the Archbishop of Canterbury periodically says, just one generation from extinction;[1] and with that we must recognise that any disregard for the essentials of God's truth, no less than any neglect of evangelism and nurture based on those essentials, would have a directly extinguishing effect.

Ambiguity

Second, let us note that world Anglicanism has become *ambiguous*, in the sense that some of its current practices are undermining its own principles. Let me spell out what I mean.

Genetically and generically, Anglicanism can be defined as a form of church life that links congregations in geographical dioceses under bishops in the historic succession, and that uses a Prayer Book derived in some way from the English Books of Common Prayer of 1549 and 1552. It has no papacy, nor anything like one. Historically, when each new extension became an independent province it affirmed solidarity with the Church of England and the rest of the Anglican world, and entrenched that solidarity in constitutional, pastoral, and liturgical form.[2] Lambeth conferences identified the integral elements in Anglican

1. For instance, in George Egerton (ed.), *Anglican Essentials: Reclaiming Faith Within the Anglican Church of Canada* (Toronto: Anglican Book Centre, 1995), p. 306.
2. The Solemn Declaration of the Anglican Church of Canada (1893), for instance, impressively states: 'We declare this Church to be, and desire that it shall continue, in full communion with the Church of England throughout the world as an integral portion of the One Body of Christ composed of Churches which . . . hold the One Faith revealed in Holy Writ, and defined in the Creeds . . . receive the same

solidarity as, first, the Bible, viewed as the rule and standard of Christian faith; second, the Apostles' and Nicene creeds, as sufficiently stating that faith; third, the two dominical sacraments, dominically administered, as necessities of church life; fourth, some form of the historic episcopate as heading up pastoral care. All branches of the Anglican family have at some point endorsed this Lambeth Quadrilateral, and with it the Elizabethan Thirty Nine Articles and the Prayer Book pattern of worship.

Now, within this frame three types of theology, calling themselves respectively, evangelical, catholic and (in this century) liberal or modernist or radical, have long coexisted, with a measure of convictional tension: a state of affairs often described by officialdom as a comprehensiveness that maintains unity on primary things but tolerates divergences on secondary matters. From all three theological perspectives this description is factually inaccurate, since each view claims to hold essentials that the other two negate; rarely, however, has the description been challenged, because it projects the idea that there is an Anglican unity of faith, devotion, and life that goes beyond externals and transcends all the disputes that Anglicans have with each other. It is clear that until recently this was what Anglicans everywhere believed, and hence the disputes were conducted with a restraint that showed respect for the present conscientious convictions of the conversation partners, and a hope of seeing a change in those convictions through continued persuasion. But Anglo-Anglicanism has recently altered its attitude at this point.

What has happened? Generalisations, like comparisons, are odious, and what I am about to say will not please everyone. The short answer to the question is that Anglo-Anglicanism has been politicised, not only in its agenda but in its style: that is, it has been conditioned no longer to think in terms of a stable frame of corporate life holding the ring, as it were, for questions of truth and wisdom to be thrashed

---

Canonical Scriptures . . . teach the same Word of God; partake of the same Divinely ordained Sacraments . . . and worship One God and Father through the same Lord Jesus Christ, by the same Holy and Divine Spirit. . . . And we are determined by the help of God to hold and maintain the Doctrine, Sacraments, and Discipline of Christ as the Lord hath commanded in his Holy Word, and as the Church of England hath received and set forth the same . . . and to transmit the same unimpaired to our posterity'.

out within the family by debate, but to embrace instead the pattern of power blocs imposing their will by legislative and administrative changes, never mind who gets over-ridden, jettisoned, and sent to the wall in the process. From one standpoint, this is a return to the pre-toleration ecclesiastical power plays of sixteenth- and seventeenth-century England, which we used to think we had left behind us; from another standpoint, it is an imitation of the executive ruthlessness that has come to mark civil government and business management everywhere in the Western world; from a third standpoint, it is an attempt to invigorate the church by attuning it to the world's beliefs and ways generally, which is rather like enlivening your voyage by knocking a hole in the bottom of your boat as you go along. This politicising, which happened quite quickly in all the Anglo-Anglican churches, came about through an executive-level landslide into liberalism — at least, into liberal ways of constructing the church's public policy. Liberals, with perfect good faith, are unable to make sense of either historic Christian supernaturalism or the historic belief in unchanging revealed truth, and the account of the liberal mindset that C. S. Lewis wrote at the end of his last book seems still on target. I quote —

> [Liberal Christians] find it impossible to accept most of the articles of the 'faith once given to the saints.' They are nevertheless extremely anxious that some vestigial religion which they (not we) can describe as 'Christianity' should continue to exist and make numerous converts. . . .
>
> It follows that, to them, the most mischievous people in the world are those who, like myself, proclaim that Christianity essentially involves the super-natural. They are quite sure that belief in the super-natural never will, nor should be revived, and that if we convince the world that it must choose between accepting the super-natural and abandoning all pretence of Christianity, the world will undoubtedly choose the second alternative. It will thus be we, not the liberals, who have really sold the pass. . . . Liberal Christianity can only supply an ineffectual echo to the massive chorus of agreed and admitted unbelief. Don't be deceived by the fact that this echo so often 'hits the headlines'. That is because attacks on Christian doctrine that would pass unnoticed if they were launched . . . by anyone else, become News when the attacker is a clergyman; just as a . . . protest against make-up would be News if it came from a film-star. . . . The

liberals are honest men and preach their version of Christianity, as we preach ours, because they believe it to be true.[3]

Since liberal ways of thinking gained effective control of policy, agendas, and public discussion in Anglo-Anglicanism, the churches have been under pressure from within to embrace, among other things, relativism in theology, syncretism in religion, naturalism in liturgy, a unisex or feminist approach to women's ministry, a positive evaluation of homosexual behaviour, and a socio-political view of the church's world mission. Perhaps these phrases are too terse to convey their full significance as they stand, so let it be said explicitly: relativism in theology means denying that any biblical or Christian utterance may be seen as a standard of orthodoxy, for there is no such thing as orthodoxy; syncretism in religion means that multi-faith worship and blending selected features of all faiths is the way ahead; naturalism in liturgy means highlighting the glories of creation, and blurring the realities of sin and salvation, whenever we celebrate God together; the unisex approach to women's ministry means offering women the presbyteral role, which in Scripture and history appears as a man's job; approving homosexual activity means putting gay partnerships on a par with marriage and treating them as no barrier to ordination and to the role-model vocation of the Anglican Priest; and the socio-political concept of the Christian mission means that church-planting evangelism should cease to be a priority concern.

It can be said without fear of contradiction that all evangelical and catholic churchpeople are unhappy with some of these causes, and some of both sorts are unhappy with all of them, for they seem so clearly to fly in the face of biblical emphases, ideals, and mandates. But political initiative these days does not lie with evangelicals and catholics, and all they can do is play black, so to speak, to these proposals for mental and managerial movement whenever they come up: as nowadays they regularly do, for the liberal leadership is far from passive. All Anglo-Anglican provinces have undergone some pressure, and some movement, along some at least of these lines, and as a result they are now to some extent internally split and out of step, both substantively and methodologically, with the mainstream Anglican heritage, as well as

---

3. C. S. Lewis, *Letters to Malcolm: Chiefly on Prayer* (London: Geoffrey Bles, 1964), pp. 151-53.

with each other. Small wonder, then, that Anglo congregations generally are shrinking, and that 'continuing' Anglican splinter churches
have begun to appear. In the circumstances, it would be strange it they
did not.

In black Africa, where persecution and evangelism flourish together, the question, what do Anglicans stand for, can be answered
without ambiguity, but in the Anglo West it is not so, and the bewilderment that this brings to Africans who visit, as to watchers nearer home,
is painful to contemplate. The pleasing fantasy of Anglican comprehensiveness within secure structures of discipline and worship has
metastasised into the scandalous fact of Anglican ambiguity within
constant structural adjustments prompted less by Christian principle
than by managerial pragmatism. Which leads on to my last preliminary
observation.

Agony

Third, let us observe that world Anglicanism is currently *agonised*, in
the sense of being racked by internal tensions that are tearing it apart
emotionally and could tear it apart organisationally as well. On the one
hand, great numbers of Anglicans in the older churches are struggling
with the perception that truths, strengths, disciplines and missional
tasks that belonged to the Anglicanism they were reared in are being
contradicted and abandoned by persons at the top, and replaced by
falsities and laxities of various kinds, which they are now asked to
accept as divinely sanctioned. On the other hand, some are avowedly
aiming to alter the Anglican belief- and value-system, and are ready to
ride roughshod over any who hold out against the changes. And some
at the top, it seems, are in a state of what counsellors would call denial
regarding all this: confident that change means progress and gain every
time, they are impatient of pleas for stability and take amiss any recall
to the old paths, or any suggestion that our chief need at present is
contemporary application of time-tested truths that show the grace and
power of Jesus our Lord, the unchanging Christ of the Bible. Such a
recall was recently attempted in Canada through the conference *Essentials '94* and the book that accompanied it, *Anglican Essentials: Reclaiming
Faith within the Anglican Church of Canada;* the strength of the negative

reactions was striking.[4] Organisations of recall in the Church of England and the Episcopal Church of the USA constantly meet, it seems, with similar reactions. So, for believers nurtured in the historic Anglican mainstream, the agony goes on, and the psalmist's cry, 'How long, O Lord?' is constantly echoed in their hearts.

Unity

Our theme, now, is Anglican unity, a question which in light of the facts reviewed we must tackle in practical form. Anglican churches, seeking to adjust to the post-Christian relativism that has flooded the modern world, are as we see losing some of the unity that once they had. The encouraging of liturgical variation and experiment in place of liturgical uniformity has reduced unity in worship. The sanctioning of a plurality of theological thought-systems in place of Anglicanism's agreed orthodoxy has reduced unity of faith. The ordination of women in some provinces, against the conscientious judgement of sizeable minorities, has reduced unity at ministerial level and produced a state of impaired communion within and between particular dioceses. The yielding of some to pressure from the gay lobbies to put homosexuality and heterosexuality on a par has reduced unity in ethics. The disrupting of unity in all these ways continues. We ask, therefore: how can Christian unity in the Anglican communion be strengthened, starting from where we are? To help us answer this question, we turn for guidance to the Bible.

The first thing we note, as we survey the Scriptures, is that the entire New Testament affirms the unity of all Christian people as a divinely given fact, a direct consequence of our redemption by Christ, and our conversion to him. Jesus Christ, the living Lord, the one mediator, 'Jesus, my shepherd, husband, friend, my prophet, priest and king, my Lord, my life, my way, my end', as Newton's hymn puts it, is the focus of this unity, because it is through direct, supernatural, new-creational union with him that it comes about. Those who are linked to Christ by faith from the human side, and by incorporation

---

4. See now the reply to *Anglican Essentials*, in John Simons (ed.), *The Challenge of Tradition* (Toronto: Anglican Book Centre, 1997). See p. 303 below.

into his dying and rising, through the power of the Holy Spirit, from the divine side, are one in him: one, through him, in union and communion with the triune God: one vine, one bride, one body, one temple, one new man; one family, one flock, one people, and so on. 'You are all sons of God through faith in Christ Jesus, for all of you who were baptised into Christ have clothed yourselves with Christ. There is neither Jew nor Greek, slave nor free, male nor female, for you are all one in Christ Jesus' (Gal. 3:26-28, NIV).

In Ephesians 4:3-6, as part of the initial point in his exposition of what it means to live as befits one's calling in Christ, Paul speaks of the new solidarity as 'the unity of the Spirit' (that is, the unity created and sustained by the Spirit), and he offers a seven-strand analysis of what constitutes it. Basic to it is the tripersonal unity of God himself — one life-giving Spirit; one Spirit-giving Lord; and 'one God and Father of all, who is over all and through all and in all'. It is through the personal faith-relation of each believer to the Father, the Son, and the Holy Spirit that the unity of God's people becomes the given reality that it is.

The fourth strand of unity is the one faith itself: which surely means a shared belief, corresponding to Paul's own belief, about the Father, the Son, and the Holy Spirit, our Creator, our Redeemer, and our Sanctifier, plus a matching commitment in penitence and trust to the Three-in-One who is, or you can equally well say, are, the One-in-Three: a commitment that is modelled archetypally on Paul's own. Paul's 'imitate me' is first and foremost a call to faith like his.

The fifth strand of unity is the one baptism, the rite all undergo that proclaims the reality of our being made sharers of Christ's risen life through identification with him — his with us, as well as ours with him — in his atoning death.

The sixth strand of unity is the reality of the one body, intricately unified, controlled, and directed in ministry, by Christ its head, and manifested in microcosm every time Christians meet to do together things that the church does.

Then the last strand of unity is the hope of glory in and with Christ, a hope that includes happy togetherness with all Christians to all eternity. This unity, says Paul, is not to be created, as if it did not already exist; it is, rather, to be acknowledged, preserved, and lived out in peace, through humility towards each other, patience with each other, and love for each other (Eph. 4:2).

We further note that Jesus' high-priestly prayer for the church that was to be, centred on a request for its unity. Having identified that church as the apostolic community, 'those who will believe on me through (the apostles') message', Jesus asks 'that all of them may be one, Father, just as you are in me and I am in you. May they also be in us so that the world may believe that you have sent me. . . . May they be brought to complete unity to let the world know that you sent me and have loved them even as you have loved me' (John 17:20-23, NIV).

Jesus' words reveal four things about the unity he has in view. First, it is a goal to be aimed at. Second, it is modelled on the relation between the Father and the Son. Third, it will be a fruit of God's grace to all who are 'in' — that is, in union and communion with — the Father and the Son. Fourth, it will be a more-than-human reality, giving credibility and persuasive power to the gospel. We see, then, that what Jesus' mind is focused on is not a unity of essence, as between the persons of the Godhead, nor a unity of organisation, as in the coalescing of congregational and denominational structures, but a quality of believers' life in company: namely, a Spirit-empowered togetherness of mutual love and honour, and of co-operation in ministry and mission. These are matters that John's gospel in particular sets before us as central in the perfect relationship of the incarnate Son and his divine Father to each other,[5] and they are matters in which the people of God on earth must always be seeking to do better than they have done thus far — matters, in other words, that constitute for us a constant goal.

For each generation of the church on earth to move into the divinely wrought togetherness that Jesus envisages means that love, honour, and active co-operation must not be restricted by racial, social, tribal, sexual, educational or economic distinctions, but rather that believers must constantly labour to transcend these factors, in ways appropriate to each culture. To embrace the dynamics of this new sort of human community, which must ever be on display in the church, will in fact be the living out of that given unity of which Paul spoke in Ephesians.

5. See John 3:35; 4:34; 5:19-23, 36; 6:31-40, 57; 7:16-18; 8:16-18, 26, 49, 54-55; 10:25-30; 12:49-50; 14:10-11; 17:1-4; etc.

Truth

So far, so good; unity as such is not, after all, a controverted theme among Anglicans; we favour it, as we favour motherhood and apple pie. We are used to thinking of each congregation, diocese, province and national church, and indeed of the entire Anglican communion, as a visible outcropping of the one universal church to which this seven-fold unity belongs. But now we must face again the wrenching question of truth — specifically, the truth of theological statements, biblical, con-fessional, and revisionist — and here the tensions cannot be masked. Are we entitled to affirm our internal unity as we do, when our diver-gences regarding God's truth are so acute? Is there a way to reduce existing tensions? Those are the questions we must discuss now.

What is truth? A clear answer can be given to jesting Pilate's question. Truth, essentially, is a relation of correspondence between statements, or beliefs, and how things actually are. This is a way of saying that statements and beliefs are true, and express truth, and so are trustworthy, when they are factually correct. They are verified, or falsified, by appeal to appropriate evidence, and by argument based on the results of that appeal. Such is truth in every department of study and thought.

It is the nature of truth to be public: that is to say, what is true for anyone is true for everyone. Granted, some today dispute this. Popular post-modernism has recently caused a stir by seeming to affirm that there is no such thing as public truth, only personal, private truth that differs for each individual. But if this affirmation itself is offered as public truth, it can only be true by being false, and thus it refutes itself; and if it is offered as the personal truth of the offerer, there is no reason why anyone who already has a different idea of truth should take any notice of it. Again, popular relativism, widely spread in North American universities,[6] affirms that there can be no decisive evidence for any assertion involving moral or religious values, and that to speak defini-tively in this sphere is to misuse your mind: all you can do with integrity is note the similarities and differences of one view as compared with another. But such relativism is really dogmatic agnosticism, and it may

6. See Allan Bloom, *The Closing of the American Mind: Education and the Crisis of Reason* (New York: Simon & Schuster, 1987).

fairly be met by urging that the real misuse of the mind is to assume without evidence the universal impossibility of verifying any single moral or religious assertion. That in the realm of matters of fact you cannot prove a universal negative was pointed out by Aristotle a very long time ago. The truth is that the public nature and availability of truth is assumed by the very act of speaking in public against it, so that denials of it can never get very far.

Now, the New Testament writers make an unambiguous public truth-claim for the gospel of Jesus Christ, and the letters of Paul, Peter, John and Jude to churches make agreement on the truth of the apostolic message the first requirement for churchly fellowship. Denial of the incarnation of God's Son (1 John 4:2-3; 5:6-12) or of Jesus' bodily resurrection (1 Cor. 15:12-17) or of the universal need and availability of justification by grace through faith on the grounds of Christ's atonement (Gal. 2:15-21), is seen as destroying the gospel, and meriting personal exclusion of its exponents (Rom. 16:17; 2 John 10). The same view is taken of obsessive and obtrusive harping on notions of one's own that leads people away from the Christ-centeredness of true Christian faith and life (Titus 3:9-10). How, we ask, do these principles apply to contemporary Anglicanism?

As we have in part seen already, some latter-day Anglicans, flying the flag of liberalism or modernism or radicalism, have recast Christian doctrine in such a way that the Father-Son-Spirit relationship in the Godhead, the identity of Jesus as the incarnate divine Son, his atoning achievement of reconciliation on the cross, his bodily resurrection, and our new birth through the Holy Spirit, are negated in their New Testament sense. These revisionist negations have been tolerated, not because many Anglicans agree with them (most have in fact thought them false as factual information and misleading as spiritual icons), but because the established Anglican way is to wait for the discipline of debate to expose the falsity of well-meant error, rather than to make martyrs by coming down on the error with a big stick. One may still wonder whether this tolerance is not pastorally irresponsible to a degree, but maybe the Anglican habit of pointing, when pressed on the subject, to the historic Prayer Books and Articles as embodying Anglican faith should be seen as a way of evading this censure — even though saying this while not restraining the errorists makes Anglicans seem to talk out of both sides of their mouth, and to be suffering from doctrinal indifferentism at a deep level. But tolerance, even of what some find intolerable, is certainly the Anglican way, and since we cannot change it by criticising it we may as well move on.

Revisionist hypotheses that ride high at present, not just among Anglicans but among biblical scholars generally, are in essence last-century ideas that have been given a new lease of life through a new interest in Jewish studies. They are, first, that the Jesus of history was different from the Christ of the New Testament; second, that the theology of Paul, which in any case (so it is claimed) is commonly misunderstood, differed from original Christian teaching; and, third, that the New Testament throughout is shaped much more by non-Christian factors than Christians can comfortably admit. These hypotheses are typical products of the characteristic liberal axiom that secular studies yield wisdom which makes necessary some scepticism about the Bible and some adjustments in Christian belief.

Nor is this all. A latter-day hermeneutical axiom (that is, a view about understanding the Bible) also rides high: namely, that the real burden of the Bible is liberation from jeopardy, and that a first-hand experience of the appropriate form of jeopardy is a necessary precondition of insight into what God through Scripture is communicating. Applications of this axiom have produced Latin American liberation theology, where the jeopardy is economic and liberation means social restructuring; also, feminist theology, where the jeopardy is male oppression, and liberation means eliminating male supremacy and, for some at least, feminising the Father, the Son, and the Holy Spirit. Also, applying this axiom has produced gay theology, where the jeopardy is the threat of ostracism and the liberation is freedom from fear as one 'comes out', 'acts out', and leaves the closet behind. Since these theologies impress some as reading into the Bible what is not there and failing to read out of it what it actually affirms, tensions about the methodology and conclusions of liberation theologies are deep and sharp.

This is particularly so with regard to homosexual behaviour. Scripture condemns it, treating it as one of the many forms of perverse conduct that cannot please God. Attempts to relativise or redirect the Bible's negative assessments and prohibitions appear on examination as unsuccessful special pleading. But in the modern West, with its sharply honed sensitivity to minority rights, freedom to behave homosexually without being penalised has been treated as a justice issue, and this freedom has now been entrenched in civil law. Against this background, in various parts of the Anglican world pressure builds up to see homosexual inclination as a created condition on a par with heterosexual inclination, and on this basis to ordain confessedly practising homosexuals just as the church ordains heterosexual persons who are sexually active within their marriages. But those who advocate such action face other Anglicans who see it as quite incompatible with biblical teaching on the image of God in man, on the nature and effects of sin, on God's purpose in redemption, on the meaning of the holiness to which all Christians are called, and on the duty of clergy to be an example to their people, particularly to young people. It is not homophobic hostility, but biblical loyalty and theological conviction that makes these Anglicans so firm in their refusal to sanction homosexual behaviour in any context, and it seems clear that no section of the Anglican communion could legislate for the ordination of practising homosexuals without triggering a major split.[7]

The question we posed was: how can Christian unity within the Anglican communion be strengthened, starting from where we are — that is, significantly less united in agreed truth than Anglicans used to be. The main factors eroding internal Anglican unity have been noted already. There is the recent dominance in the West of liberal theology, with its ideology of sanctified worldliness and its retreat from the conscientious biblicism, reformational Augustinianism, and moral absolutism of the first four reformed Anglican centuries. There is the offence to many consciences and the impairing of inter- and intra-provincial communion that the ordination of women has brought. There is the ongoing presence of theologies that avowedly adjust the teaching of Scripture about God and godliness in the interest of secular ideas and

---

7. See for further confirmation of this the following extracts from the Kuala Lumpur Statement unanimously adopted by eighty delegates representing the Anglican Churches of the South, which contain between 80 and 90 per cent of the Anglicans in the world. (6) 'The Holy Scriptures are clear in teaching that all sexual promiscuity is sin. We are convinced that this includes homosexual practices, between men or women, as well as heterosexual relationships between men and women outside marriage'. (9) 'We are deeply concerned that the setting aside of biblical teaching in such actions as the ordination of practising homosexuals and the blessing of same-sex unions calls into question the authority of the Holy Scriptures. This is totally unacceptable to us'. See Appendix I for full text, p. 295 below.

particular minority groups. There is the disruptive pressure to stop calling the first two persons of the Trinity Father and Son, and to start feminising them, and there is the disruptive pressure to ordain practising homosexuals. There is everywhere an abundance of permitted liturgical variants, within which significant doctrinal shifts are sometimes encased. There is the spreading sense that bishops and bureaucrats no longer seek consensus for change, provided they can ram their agendas through on a bare majority vote. Nobody wants division, but the dynamics of our situation seem to be driving us towards the brink, and there is a real risk that Anglicanism's internal tensions, like the Canadian national debt, will escalate to the point of ultimate disaster.

Large-scale optimism about the Anglican future, and denial that our internal problems are really serious, is part of our traditional ethos, but such optimistic denial would be very much out of place today. Says Samuel Edwards:

> One might be forgiven for asking whether the term 'Anglican Communion' is still meaningful, when the fundamental conditions for sacramental communion between churches — namely, common faith and a mutually recognised ministry — no longer exist within it. The Anglican Communion may well have become an Association of the descendants of the English Reformation, having the same basic standard for membership as a genealogical society in which legitimate descent from the ancestral group rather than fidelity to its principles is the determinative qualification.[8]

Unhappily, he has a point. The Anglican family is in a state of internal schism, and there can be no recovery of biblical unity among us further than there is a recovery of the biblical truths that are unity's basic bond.

Hope

Is there hope for Anglicanism, particularly for Anglo-Anglicanism, as it struggles with the headaches and heartaches that we have described?

8. Samuel L. Edwards, 'A Light at Nightfall', in Robert Hannaford (ed.), *The Future of Anglicanism* (Leominster: Gracewing, 1996), p. 145.

There could be. The light at the end of the tunnel does not have to be the light of an oncoming train. Three things, under God, would surely help to rebuild the unity that is currently under threat.

The first thing would be an agreed moratorium on hasty constitutional change — hasty in the sense of making it on the basis of a bare majority in synods while anything approaching consensus is as yet lacking. It was wisdom when in 1969 England's Anglican-Methodist union scheme was shelved because it mustered less than a seventy-five per cent vote in the Church of England; we need more of that wisdom today, for where moral consensus is lacking we ought to conclude that the Holy Spirit is not leading.

The second thing would be a theological development. Thought leaders of the world church are today freshly aware that the Trinity and the incarnation are the central Christian truths, from which all others flow. Anglican scholars firmly maintained this awareness before others recovered it; now that is has become general, Anglicans should be leaders in applying it. And critical application of this insight will quietly expose and correct all the shortcomings of Anglican liberal theology.

The third thing would be a pastoral move. Conservative Anglicans have excelled in producing catechetical and evangelistic materials within a mainstream incarnational and trinitarian frame. (The Alpha course is a recent example.) If Anglicans of all sorts will consent as of now to practise outreach together, drawing on these materials, we shall be realising straight away one dimension of the unity for which Jesus prayed, namely oneness in God's mission, and we shall be giving outreach priority over the preoccupations of our domestic pluralism, as we ought to have been doing throughout the whole Decade of Evangelism. This unitive process, rather than further doses of rapid structural change, is what the Anglican world needs at present.

But none of this may happen; so I think it is well for me to sign off with one of Chesterton's golden jingles:

> The men of the East may spell the stars
> And times and triumphs mark,
> But the men signed by the cross of Christ
> Go gaily in the dark.

Go gaily in the dark! Yes: we can at least pledge ourselves to do that.

Questions

1. What has been your experience of Anglicanism's internal tensions? Do you agree with Packer's analysis of the roots of tension today? Why or why not?

2. What do you see as the non-negotiable fundamentals of the Christian faith? Do you have problems with Packer's view of them?

3. Do you think that the three remedial courses of action recommended at the close of this chapter are realistic? If so, how could they be promoted?

251

Refusing Division: Advances and Setbacks

JOHN FENWICK

Summary

The years since the last Lambeth Conference have seen ecumenism advance in some areas and slow down in others. The present chapter looks primarily at three areas of particular significance: (1) ecumenical methodology; (2) defining the goal of visible unity; and (3) the acceptance of ministers not in a tactile historic episcopal succession. Specific dialogues are used to illustrate these. The chapter then draws attention to the way in which ecumenical dialogue is not isolated from issues of anthropology, language and culture.

Introduction

Of the sixty-eight resolutions passed by the 1988 Lambeth Conference, fourteen are directly concerned with ecumenism (evangelism, by contrast, is only mentioned in the title of two resolutions). These fourteen resolutions relate to a vast amount of ecumenical activity at many different levels and on every continent.

A comprehensive review of all that has happened in this area since the 1988 Lambeth Conference is clearly not possible in the confines of the present chapter. What follows is merely an attempt to identify some significant advances and failures and to explore the issues raised by them.

Methodology: The Roman Catholic Church

Expectations for a significant leap forward in relations with the Roman Catholic Church were high at Lambeth '88. The bishops voted overwhelmingly in favour of the ARCIC I agreements and could have been reasonably confident that there would have been a substantial breakthrough by the time the Lambeth Fathers met again. Many, no doubt, hoped that the shadow of *Apostolicae Curae* which had lain across Anglican/Roman Catholic relations for nearly a century, would have been lifted by 1998.

That hope was indeed fulfilled. The judgement of Pope Leo in his *Apostolicae Curae* in 1896 that Anglican Orders were 'absolutely null and utterly void' now stands modified. The absolute is no longer an absolute. The circumstances that produced that apparent break-through, and the grounds on which the decision was made were not, however, those envisaged by the bishops who endorsed ARCIC I. The situation is all the more ironic, for the relaxing of Rome's absolute judgement (something for which many Anglicans had longed, worked and prayed for decades) was accompanied by what was felt to amount to a virtual rejection by Rome of the ARCIC process. The outline of the events is told here briefly as questions are raised which it is vital that the bishops preparing for Lambeth 98 consider.

The first Anglican-Roman Catholic International Commission (ARCIC) was set up in 1967 following the meeting between Archbishop Michael Ramsey of Canterbury and Pope Paul VI the previous year. Its brief was to engage in serious dialogue 'founded on the Gospels and the ancient common traditions'.[1] Over the years the Commission produced a series of Agreed Statements on Eucharist, Ministry and Authority. These were published for international comment and a further explanatory document, *Elucidations*, was produced in 1979 to clarify a number of issues. The reports were formally commended to the provinces of the Anglican communion and responses requested. These proved generally favourable to the agreements reached on eucharist and ministry, and accepted the report on authority as a useful beginning in that area. Furnished with the responses from the provinces, the

---

1. 'Common Declaration' (24 March 1966), in *ARCIC — The Final Report* (London: 1982), p. 118.

bishops in 1988 passed the following resolution: 'This conference: (1) recognises the Agreed Statements of ARCIC I on *Eucharistic Doctrine, Ministry and Ordination,* and their *Elucidations,* as consonant in substance with the faith of Anglicans and believes that this agreement offers a sufficient basis for taking the next step forward towards the reconciliation of our Churches grounded in agreement in faith' (Resolution 8).[2]

The report *Authority in the Church* was welcomed as 'a firm basis for the direction and agenda of the continuing dialogue on authority . . .' (Resolution 8.3).

The expectation was that, now that the Lambeth Conference had endorsed doctrinal statements agreed by Rome's official representatives in the dialogue, the way was cleared for a major reassessment by the Vatican of its judgements on Anglicanism. Probably no one expected full communion within the decade, but a radical adjustment to Roman Catholic attitudes and approaches seemed a real possibility.

While the ARCIC I Agreed Statements had been going around the provinces of the Anglican communion, they were also being examined by the Bishops' Conferences of the Roman Catholic Church. There was, therefore, an expectation that the official responses of both churches would appear at about the same time. There was some disappointment that the Roman response was not out in time for Lambeth '88. It was nevertheless expected shortly. The present writer remembers September 1988 being discussed as a likely time. In fact Anglicans had to wait over three years before the official Roman Catholic response to ARCIC I was published.

The delay — which itself felt discourteous to a partner in dialogue — gave rise to speculation that the response was going to be a negative one. That expectation was fulfilled. The official Roman Catholic Response to the Final Report of ARCIC I was published on 5th December, 1991. It was anonymous, which suggested that neither the Pope nor any particular department of the Vatican wished to take public responsibility. It consisted of a 'General Evaluation' of less than one page, followed by eight pages of 'Explanatory Note'. The essential conclusion was that 'The Catholic Church judges . . . that it is not yet possible to state that substantial agreement has been reached on all the questions studied by the Commission'.

2. Text in *The Truth Shall Make You Free* (London: 1988).

The Anglican response was one of bitter disappointment. 'The publication of this judgement has led to widespread dismay', wrote Bishop Colin Buchanan.[3] Even the Anglican Co-Secretary of ARCIC I, Canon Christopher Hill (now Bishop of Stafford), abandoned his normally measured, diplomatic style to write, 'Anglicans, of no matter what school, will at best be able to raise one cheer out of three at the long awaited publication of the official Roman Catholic *Response* to the *Final Report* of ARCIC I'.[4]

The Archbishop of Canterbury's official comments published on the same day as the Roman Catholic Response, while seeking to be positive in tone, nevertheless pointedly identified the root of the problem as a crucial difference in approach and methodology. He made the point that the 1988 Lambeth Conference had recognised that the ARCIC agreements were not all expressed in the terms, language, thought-forms and even theology of the Thirty-nine Articles and Book of Common Prayer. Since the whole point of the ARCIC methodology, as Anglicans understood it, was to get behind the language of the era of division, the Anglican provinces had, instead of looking for old familiar words and formulae, sought to ascertain whether the agreements expressed were 'consonant' with the faith of the church as expressed in the Anglican communion despite being expressed in new terminology. This, said the Archbishop, the Lambeth Conference had been able to do in the case of the documents on Eucharist and Ministry and Ordination. The Archbishop continued: 'In the case of the Roman Catholic Response, however, the question to our two communions appears to have been understood instead as asking: "Is the Final Report *identical* with the teaching of the Roman Catholic Church?" The argument of the Response suggests that a difference in methodology may have led to this approach. If either Communion requires that the other conforms to its own theological formulations, further progress will be hazardous'.[5]

The question is clearly a crucial one for all ecumenical dialogues. In the case of the Anglican/Roman Catholic dialogue it remains, as far

3. *News of Liturgy* 204, Nottingham (Dec. 1991).
4. 'Response to a Response', in *Anglican and Roman Catholic Response to the Work of ARCIC I* (GS Misc 384), Council for Christian Unity of the General Synod of the Church of England (London: 1992).
5. 'Comments of the Archbishop of Canterbury on the Official Roman Catholic Response', in GS Misc 384.

as the present writer can see, totally unresolved. It is difficult to see how any further progress is possible until Rome addresses the apparent differences in method and authority between the different dicasteries, and faces the fundamental challenge of acknowledging truth expressed other than in her own formularies.

In view of this dashing of so many hopes, it seems ironic that one of the Lambeth '88 bishops should appear to have single-handedly succeeded where the combined resolutions of that Conference failed. On 6th April, 1994 the Right Reverend Graham Leonard, the recently retired Bishop of London, was received into the Roman Catholic Church and on 23rd April was ordained conditionally to the priesthood by the Cardinal Archbishop of Westminster, Basil Hume. Since then it has emerged that there have been other such conditional ordinations, but that of Graham Leonard furnishes the most public example of Rome's thinking. (Another interesting feature of the event is that it was *per saltum:* there was no prior ordination, conditional or otherwise, to the diaconate.) The grounds for the conditional nature were stated by Cardinal Hume to be (1) the involvement of Bishops of the Old Catholic Church 'who are validly ordained' in the lineage of the Anglican bishops who ordained Graham Leonard to the priesthood and episcopate; (2) the fact that documentary evidence of the Old Catholic succession and the intention of the Anglican bishops in it existed; and (3) Dr. Leonard's own Catholic understanding of his ordinations. Much has since been written on the event and the significance of the explanations that accompanied it. The methodology used by Rome in addressing the issue had not only been abandoned in ecumenical dialogue for decades, but has also been questioned by some of her own theologians.[6] Should Anglicans now look at it seriously again? Furthermore, the circumstances which occasioned the event are inevitably an embarrassment to Anglicans. The bishops who gather for Lambeth 1998 will have to come to terms with an apparent breakthrough directly occasioned by divisions within their own communion.

It is little wonder that the first modification of the judgement of *Apostolicae Curae,* which in other circumstances might have been expected to be a cause of heartfelt celebration, has brought so little joy.

---

6. See, for example, Edward Yarnold, 'A New Context: ARCIC and Afterwards', in R. W. Franklin (ed.), *Anglican Orders* (London: 1996), p. 72.

Its accompaniment by Rome's apparent rejection of a generation of painstaking dialogue, leaves its value very uncertain. Even those Anglicans who derive some comfort from the fact that Rome may judge that there is prudent doubt about the invalidity of their orders, are left asking 'So what?' What use is formal recognition (or the hint of it) if it is not accompanied by a release of ecumenical energy sufficient to transform the local situation? The apparent gain has so far proved sterile.

Defining the Goal: The Moravian Church in England

If conversations with Rome have apparently foundered through lack of agreed *methodology*, the failure of the Church of England to reach a breakthrough with the Moravians, seems to illustrate the problem of the lack of an agreed *goal*.

The Moravian Church, heirs to the ancient Unitas Fratrum, first appeared on the agenda of a Lambeth Conference in 1878, though contact between Anglicans and Moravians went back at least to the seventeenth century. Conversations with this episcopally-ordered church have taken place throughout the twentieth century. (It should be noted that Anglican-Moravian relations take on different forms in other parts of the world, especially East Africa. The present section is merely a reflection on developments in England.) The most recent set of such conversations is that between the Church of England and the Moravian Church in Great Britain and Ireland which lasted from 1989 to 1995. The report, containing *The Fetter Lane Common Statement,* is a clear and welcome statement of substantial agreement between two churches which seem to be comfortable with the methodology they are using. The surprise, therefore, is that it takes the two churches very little closer than they were before. After three hundred years of contact and decades of mutual exploration, it is surprising that the joint Declaration can do no more than 'look forward to the time when our churches are united and our ministries are interchangeable'. Even the 1908 Lambeth Conference went further and produced specific proposals for creating an interchangeable ministry! Here, too, the Archbishop of Canterbury had to express himself 'profoundly disappointed' that a reconciliation had not been achieved, when commenting on the report in the General Synod.

The report itself gives no explicit explanation for such an apparent failure. However, its section on 'Issues still to be faced' is full of statements about not involving a loss of identity of either partner, nurturing the distinctive 'ethos' of both traditions, safeguarding diversity, and sustaining particular gifts. Such phrases suggest that a major difficulty was the lack of an agreed goal: what would the co-existence of two churches in the same place with mutually recognised and interchangeable ministry and sacraments look like? No doubt for the small British Moravian Church there was the danger of absorption and the ultimate loss of any distinctive contribution. On the Anglican side the issue of parallel jurisdictions no doubt loomed. This, as Colin Podmore points out, had been an Anglican concern as far back as 1908.[7] For complex historical reasons Anglicanism, particularly in England, has been unhappy (some would say paranoid) about acknowledging parallel jurisdictions. At one level, such a 'purist' approach is attractive: the ancient ideal of one bishop in one place. The question that has to be honestly asked is whether holding to the ideal is being used to protect a privileged position and to stave off adjustments that would threaten that position. The accusation is sometimes made that Anglicanism uses this position at its own convenience: parallel jurisdictions in fact already exist in the Anglican world (Europe and South Africa are often cited). Why are we so adamantly opposed to accepting them to facilitate ecumenical progress (or to ease the tensions caused by the ordination of women)? The Methodist and Reformed Churches in England, for example, find it hard to understand how the Church of England can make agreements with European Protestant churches which it seems unwilling to make with its Protestant neighbours at home. The Orthodox church, which holds even more strongly to an ecclesiology based on the local bishop, is nevertheless much more flexible on this matter. Parallel jurisdictions (usually created by the different ethnic origins of the congregations — Greek, Russian, Serbian, etc.) are accepted by *economy* — the exercise of flexibility.

Anglicans perhaps need to learn something here. Ecumenical partners in the same geographical area are not, in the short term at least, going to accept takeover or absorption by us. Unless our medium-term

7. C. Podmore, 'Essays in Moravian and Anglican History', in *Anglican-Moravian Conversations* (London: 1996), p. 81.

goal involves the acceptance of some measure of parallel jurisdiction, it is difficult to see progress being made.

Breaking the Log-jam: The Lutheran Churches

A more promising area of ecumenical progress has been with the Lutheran churches. Lambeth '88 recognised 'the high degree of consensus reached in international, regional and national dialogues between Anglicans and Lutherans' and urged that this recognition 'prompt us to move towards the fullest possible ecclesial recognition and the goal of full communion' (Resolution 4).

In the European context at least a substantial move forward has been achieved. The Anglican provinces within Britain and Ireland have reached a comprehensive agreement with the Lutheran churches of Sweden, Norway, Iceland, Finland, Estonia and Lithuania. Called *The Porvoo Agreement* (after the name of the place in Finland where the Commission worshipped prior to the final sessions) it is arguably the boldest ecumenical step that the Church of England has ever taken.

Ever since discussions which led to the formation of the Church of South India in 1947 the question of the reconciliation of episcopal and non-episcopal ministries has continued to prove an impasse. To put it another way, was it possible to recognise a church before its ministry was in the historic succession? The Nordic/Baltic churches provided a halfway house. They are churches of pre-Reformation foundation. All of them are episcopal in structure in that episcopate is exercised among them by individuals set aside to exercise that ministry. In many of them the dioceses and externals of worship that had existed prior to the sixteenth century continued. In the case of some of them, however (Denmark, Norway, and Iceland), the continuity of laying on of hands in episcopal consecration had been broken. Agreements between the Church of England and most of the churches concerned had been reached in the first half of the twentieth century. What was now achieved was a comprehensive act of recognition which placed all the participating churches on an equal footing.

Consequently, the churches stated in the Porvoo Declaration that: '. . . we acknowledge one another's churches as churches belonging to the One, Holy, Catholic and Apostolic Church of Jesus Christ and truly

259

participating in the apostolic mission of the whole people of God'.[8] Following on from this basic recognition of each other as churches came a recognition of a common confession of the apostolic faith, and of one another's ordained ministries as given by God. This in turn led to an acknowledgement that 'the episcopal office is valued and maintained in all our Churches as a visible sign expressing and serving the Church's unity and continuity in apostolic life, mission and ministry' (para. a[vi]).

The basic premise is thus a recognition that apostolicity is not located solely in a chain of episcopal consecrations, but more widely in the life and continuity of the church. 'Apostolic tradition in the Church means continuity in the permanent characteristics of the Church of the apostles: witness to the apostolic faith, proclamation and fresh interpretation of the Gospel, celebration of baptism and the eucharist, the transmission of ministerial responsibilities, communion in prayer, love, joy and suffering, service to the sick and needy, unity among the local Churches and sharing the gifts which the Lord has given to each.'[9]

The tactile succession of bishops, it is argued, is merely one strand in the many-stranded rope of apostolicity. To ordain bishops in the historic succession is a sign of the church's intended continuity in this wider apostolicity. 'Resumption of the use of the sign does not imply an adverse judgement on the ministries of those Churches which did not previously make use of the sign. It is rather a means of making more visible the unity and continuity of the Church at all times and in all places' (para. 53).

The breakthrough is thus a recognition by Anglicans of the fullness of churches without bishops in the tactile succession. Two things made this possible: (a) the willingness of the other participating churches to take the sign into their systems; (b) the fact that the churches involved were already episcopal in foundation, structure and organisation.

While there is a sense in which the Nordic/Baltic Lutherans were 'an easy case', nevertheless Porvoo remains a significant achievement. Already under its provision Lutheran ministers ordained by bishops

8. *The Porvoo Declaration*, para. a(i). Full text in *Together in Mission and Ministry* (London: 1993), pp. 30-31.

9. *The Porvoo Common Statement*, para. 36, in *Together in Mission and Ministry*, p. 23.

not in the historic succession, have been licensed by a Church of England diocesan bishop, perhaps the first time that this has happened since 1662. Those evangelicals who remember how vehemently it used to be denied that something similar had ever happened in the sixteenth century, will marvel at how quietly and naturally it is now happening.

As mentioned above, at the time of the acceptance of the Porvoo Agreement, English Protestants asked why the agreement could not be applied to themselves. Certainly, in the present climate, the acceptance that such churches are part of the 'One, Holy, Catholic and Apostolic Church' seems perfectly possible (and is already envisaged in the proposed Church of England/Methodist talks.[10] However, the British Free churches differ markedly from the Nordic/Baltic churches in that they have never been episcopal in structure or intent. In addition the fact that they overlap geographically with existing Anglican provinces means that it is inevitable that they will encounter the same reluctance that the Moravians have had to face.

There are signs, however, that other provinces of the Anglican communion are able to move faster on this one. In November 1995 the Church of the Province of South Africa entered into a mutual recognition of ordained ministries with the Methodist Church, the Presbyterian Church of South Africa and the United Congregational Church of South Africa. There is now the opportunity for a free interchange of ministers between the participating churches, and even the acceptance of appointment in another church. It has been described as 'a most far-reaching breach by Anglicans in the provision of the 1662 Preface to the Ordinal'.[11] Now that the log-jam has been broken, progress in some areas could be very rapid indeed.

The Ticking Time Bomb: Whose Culture?

Behind the successes and failures of the decade since the last Lambeth Conference there looms a set of questions, the resolution of which is likely to be crucial for the future of the Anglican communion, if not for

10. *Commitment to Mission and Unity: Report of the Informal Conversations between the Methodist Church and the Church of England* (London: 1996), para. 36, p. 14.
11. *News of Liturgy* 265 (Jan. 1997), p. 9.

the Christian faith itself. Ecumenism is not done in a vacuum. It takes place in the context of a whole host of unfolding issues.

Buried deep in the 1988 Lambeth Conference Section Reports — in that on Ecumenical Relations — is a statement which identifies the problem: 'The Gospel and Church may be radically distorted by adaptation to a particular culture, so that the Church in that place becomes heretical or schismatic, and no longer witnesses to the truth of the reconciliation of all people to God in Christ'.[12]

In a time of rapid change and communication the question which has to be faced (not of course just by Anglicans) is whether the gospel and church are currently being radically distorted by adaptation to Western culture.

This has implications for practically every area of the life of the church, as the other chapters of this volume explore. In the ecumenical field it relates, for example, to the language of dialogue. To some degree the impasse in Anglican/Roman Catholic dialogue discussed earlier in this chapter could be said to be about the extent to which late mediaeval European terminology should be normative. Both the Anglican communion and the Roman Catholic Church are world-wide bodies yet insist on 'doing theology' in languages which are not the mother tongues of perhaps the majority of their members. In a different arena, the present writer remembers a lively debate at the Anglican/Orthodox Joint Doctrinal Discussions about the appropriateness or otherwise of conducting the dialogue substantially in Greek patristic terminology.

The issue of language relates closely to that of *anthropology*, a subject which is one of the four major themes for the 1998 Lambeth Conference. There is no space here to explore this vast issue and the particularly high profile dimension of feminism. But Anglicans have to ask to what extent the phenomenon is a product of the way the English language has been interpreted (and misunderstood?) in recent decades. The re-writing of liturgy to exclude an inclusive use of 'masculine' forms (he, his, king, etc.) for both the worshippers and, increasingly, for God, is an obvious and highly contentious example.

But the question of anthropology goes much deeper. It is about what it means to be human. Whole new ethical areas (for example, cloning) are opening up, to which a measured Christian response is

12. *The Truth Shall Make You Free*, p. 133.

needed. Being human necessitates interaction with others. To what extent are there God-given patterns for this? Is patriarchy, for example, part of the divine 'givenness'? To what degree are the frameworks of male/female interaction in the Bible non-negotiable? Or, if they are no longer normative, with what should they be replaced? Western Christians seem on the one hand to be acutely critical of some aspects of their tradition (*e.g.*, an involvement with the slave trade) which they now see as a distortion of the gospel, while appearing totally incapable of applying the same critical eye to many of their current assumptions and practices. Thus, the ordination of women, which crops up frequently in ecumenical debate, is not simply a *ministerial* issue, it is an *anthropological* issue. Furthermore, it incarnates the rejection of much that is normative in the thought-world of the Bible and the embracing of a set of very recent assumptions that are dominant in current Western culture. Yet, when one considers the breakdown of family and community life, and the immense environmental and social problems which are the hallmarks of many parts of the Western world, it seems astounding that so many Western church leaders are so insistent on the rightness of their perspectives.

The assumptions which lie behind Anglican responses to such issues also pervade ecumenical dialogue. Given that the more radical approaches look like a redefining of Christianity itself, the chance of finding common ground with some at least of our ecumenical partners looks increasingly remote.

The bishops gathering for the 1998 Lambeth Conference will do a great service to the Anglican communion and to the ecumenical endeavour if they have the courage to ask to what degree the gospel and the church are being radically distorted by adaptation to Western culture.

Questions

1. How (if at all) can churches distinguish between the faith they hold and the language in which that faith has traditionally been expressed?

2. In the pursuit of visible unity, is it better to insist on an all-embracing tidy settlement, or to accept an interim situation which may

have anomalies, but whose anomalies are less than the existence of Christian dividedness?

3. In recognising the ministry of those not ordained in historic tactile episcopal succession, what has Anglicanism gained and lost?

4. Whose culture and language are to be normative in ecumenical dialogue? Those of the patristic era, the sixteenth century or of the modern English speaking West? Can serious ecumenism proceed much farther without addressing the extent to which Western culture is a distortion of the gospel?

The Universality of Christ

VINOTH RAMACHANDRA

Summary

From its inception, the social inclusiveness of the Christian movement and its missionary character flowed out of the conviction that God has accomplished, in Jesus Christ, something decisive for his entire creation. The impetus to mission sprang from the very logic of the life, death and resurrection of Jesus. The gospel was *for* the world because it had to do with the world's future. It revealed both the tragic alienation of the world from its Creator and the glorious hope of its reconciliation and re-creation. The church is that particular community, drawn from all communities, which is called to embody and communicate this subversive message.

Introduction

In his enthronement as Archbishop of Canterbury during the bleakest days of the war in 1942, William Temple referred to 'the great new fact of our time' — namely, that the church of Jesus Christ had become a truly global society for the first time in history. Today, as the most brutal and barbarous century known to humankind draws to a close, more than half the world's Christians live in the countries of the South, many experiencing persecution or discrimination as minorities. Christianity is no longer the 'white man's religion', and to be a Christian (whether in the South or the North) is once more to be on the political periphery.

265

Along with the changing face of the church, the character of mission has undergone a remarkable transformation. In the wake of anti-missionary sentiments in the post-colonial era and the increasing captivity of the older denominations to the secularist mind-set, many clergy climbed on board the 'development/liberation' bandwagon as their sole *raison d'être* in a predominantly non-Christian world. Evangelism in the older sense has, however, reverted to the laity (as it was from the beginnings of the Christian movement). For instance, Russian university students were enthusiastically evangelised by African room-mates in the pre-*Glasnost* era; and Filipino housemaids 'gossip the gospel' with their affluent mistresses in the repressive feudal states of the Persian Gulf. Sudanese and Chadean Christians take the gospel as refugees into 'unreached' parts of north Africa and beyond, just as did the Christians who were scattered following Stephen's martyrdom (Acts 11:19ff.). In the past two decades, thousands of university graduates in India have crossed socio-economic and linguistic barriers to serve, in the name of Christ, as health workers, teachers, engineers, agricultural advisors and evangelists to marginalised and underprivileged peoples across that great subcontinent. Mission, in our generation, is indeed moving towards the fulfilment of the adage 'the whole Church taking the whole gospel to the whole world'.

Jesus Christ and the World of Religion

The first major critic of the Christian movement in the Graeco-Roman world was the Greek philosopher, Celsus, whose book *True Doctrine*, written around AD 170, was considered sufficiently influential to require detailed refutation by the mighty Origen some eighty years later. Celsus wrote at a time when Christians were not numerous enough to pose a threat to the cohesion and stability of the Roman empire. But he was deeply disturbed by what he saw of its subversive potential. If this sect continued to attract people from different nations and social classes, detaching them from their fundamental loyalties to emperor and city, insisting on exalting the man Jesus over local deities and promoting a distinctive social behaviour, then it would not be long before the very foundations of Roman society collapsed.

Anglican Christians in the modern West may be surprised to find the terms *revolution* and *sedition* occurring repeatedly in Celsus' description of the Christian church; for Celsus saw Christians as severing the ancient bond between religion and the particular *Nomos* (the accumulated wisdom and practices) of a city or local community. Christianity represented a new and disturbing phenomenon — a people without a traditional homeland, knit together by a religious allegiance with its own peculiar beliefs and a way of life that sat loose to the *Nomos* of the city and nation they inhabited. By revolting against the religious *Nomos* of Judaism, the ancient tradition from which it sprang, Christianity threatened to undermine the traditions of Hellenism. What was important, in Celsus' view, was not so much the specific doctrinal content of these 'local narratives' as the fact that they were local and inherited. 'It is impious to abandon the customs which have existed in each locality from the beginning.'[1]

There is an ironic 'political correctness' in Celsus' fear of causing offence and his suspicion towards anything smacking of universalism. But, of course, he did believe that there was one supreme deity who watched over the fortunes of the empire. He recognised that the social inclusiveness of Christians and their missionary thrust was linked to their disgusting habit of worshipping 'to an extravagant degree this man who appeared recently'.[2] If you elevate Jesus to the status of the most high God, says Celsus, you effectively abandon the teaching that there is one king to whom God has given power; and there is 'nothing to prevent him from being abandoned, alone and deserted, while earthly things would come into the power of the most lawless and savage barbarians . . .'.[3]

It is here that the resonances with our own age appear most clearly. Christians, by refusing to see their 'founder' as one among a number of equally praiseworthy heroes or divine men, threatened the harmony of the social and political order. The latter was not, of course, religiously 'neutral', anymore than the 'secular' state in the modern age is religiously neutral (in the sense of not promoting any beliefs about the nature of ultimate reality and of what constitutes human well-

1. Origen, *Contra Celsus,* translated by Henry Chadwick (Cambridge: Cambridge University Press, 1953; paperback edn., 1980), 5.26.
2. Origen, *Contra Celsus,* 8.12.
3. Origen, *Contra Celsus,* 8.68.

being). In Celsus' world view — the world view of classical Graeco-Roman paganism, and shared by much of the population of the Indian subcontinent — the foundational category of *divinity* was extremely flexible. It could be stretched down from the one high God (single, solitary, timeless and changeless) to embrace the several Olympian deities (Zeus, Hermes, Hera, *et al.*), the Capitoline gods (Jupiter, Juno, Minerva), the invisible gods of the stars and other heavenly objects, the *daimones* who mediated between the earth and the higher gods, and, on the lowest level, heroes who had been elevated to divine status by their outstanding acts (Heracles, Orpheus *et al.*). The supreme God ruled the world through the lesser deities, so that the worship of the latter, in locally prescribed ritual, did not run counter to the worship of the high God. Such worship did not threaten the unity of God.

The worship of Jesus could readily take its place within this divine pantheon. But the obstinate Christian refusal to comply with such a reasonable pluralism meant that the unity of God was being compromised. If there are now two high Gods, there must be a more transcendent source which stands 'behind' them. The political implication (as Celsus saw so clearly) was to call into question the benevolent providence of that God as expressed in the rule of the one emperor (and how much more galling to Roman ears would have been the reminder that this Jesus was a criminal executed by the Roman state!).

Jesus Christ as the Story of Israel[4]

The New Testament writers relate the story of Jesus' life, ministry, death and resurrection, not as a sudden and bizarre eruption of divine power into history, but as the climax to a much longer story — the story of Israel. The latter, in turn, is the pivotal focus of the story of the Creator's caring involvement with his disfigured world. The Christian movement began when a group of frightened Jews came to the conclusion that all of Israel's hopes had come true in the death and resurrection of Jesus of Nazareth. The apostles never understood themselves to be founding

---

4. For a more detailed argument see my *The Recovery of Mission: Beyond the Pluralist Paradigm* (Carlisle: Paternoster/Grand Rapids: Eerdmans, 1996), chs. 6 and 7. This section and the next are heavily dependent on ch. 7.

a 'new religion'. The story of Jesus and the experience of his Spirit in the life of the Jesus-community is proclaimed as the final phase of Israel's story, a story that begins with the divine calling of Abraham and the divine word of promise concerning the nations.

This call of Abraham and the emergence of the people of Israel is set, in the Hebrew Bible, against the dramatic background of the story of creation and the alienation of all the 'families of the earth' from their Creator. All human beings share in the solidarity of sin and death. Sin has disfigured and corrupted all human relationships — with God, with the earth, and with one another. The covenant that God makes with Abraham is ultimately for the blessing of 'all the families of the earth' (Gen. 12:3b). The effects of sin are universal, but God's redemptive purpose is equally universal. God works with the one man and his family while his gaze, so to speak, is on all the families of the earth.

The God of the biblical revelation, then, is the God of universal history. But he brings that history to its goal (salvation) through the particular history of a particular people. This interplay between the universal and the unique runs right through the Old Testament narrative. One striking example is given in the early chapters of the book of Deuteronomy. That Yahweh is not Israel's tribal deity but the sovereign God of the whole earth, actively involved in the histories of nations other than Israel, is the axiomatic framework within which the uniqueness of Israel is repeatedly emphasised (note, for instance, the tantalising glimpses the narrator gives of Yahweh's sovereignty in the migrations and conquests that marked the pre-Israelite history of Canaan, 2:9-12, 20-23). But it is only within Israel that Yahweh works in terms of a redemptive covenant, initiated and preserved by his grace. The people of Israel had experienced something unparalleled 'from the day God created man on the earth' and 'from one end of the heavens to the other' (4:32): a unique revelation of Yahweh and a unique experience of his redemptive power (4:7-8, 32-38). This was all of sheer grace, never to be construed as favouritism (*e.g.,* 7:7-8), to which the only appropriate response was to imitate Yahweh's awesome love towards the weak and the alien (*e.g.,* 10:14ff.).

Israel existed as a nation at all only because of Yahweh's intention to redeem people from every nation. While Yahweh works in all nations, in no nation other than Israel did he act for the sake of all nations. Israel's unique experience of Yahweh issues in a unique socio-political witness to Yahweh among the nations, for their covenantal obedience to Yahweh now takes the form of imitating Yahweh's dealings with Israel. The distinctiveness of Israel's social, political and economic structures was an integral part of their theological significance in God's saving purpose for his world.[5] To choose to respond to the true God was to choose the truly human as well. This distinctiveness was the means by which God would attract the nations to himself, so that ultimately all the earth would acknowledge and experience the gracious rule of Yahweh as the only true and living God.

But in the meantime, where the universal eschatological vision impinges on the present historical situation, there is spiritual and social conflict — between Yahweh and every other claimant to deity. This is a conflict that ran through Israel's national life as well as in her dealings with her pagan neighbours. The great temptation Israel faced, and to which she repeatedly succumbed, was to think of Yahweh too as simply another tribal deity and to worship him in terms derived from an alien religious framework, thus betraying the revelation entrusted to them for the sake of the nations. Such betrayal robbed Israel of her self-identity and any claim to uniqueness. 'The whole Old Testament (and the New Testament as well) is filled with descriptions of how Yahweh-Adonai, the covenant God of Israel is waging war against those forces which try to thwart and subvert his plans for his creation. He battles against those false gods which human beings have fashioned from the created world, idolized, and used for their own purpose . . . the Baals and the Ashteroth, whose worshippers elevated nature, the tribe, the state and the nation to a divine status. God fights against magic and idolatry which, according to Deuteronomy, bend the line between God and his creation. He contends against every form of social injustice and pulls off every cloak under which it seeks to hide.'[6]

As the Old Testament scholar, C. J. H. Wright, perceptively reminds us, 'The calling of Israel to bear faithful witness to the revelation of the living God entrusted to her was not a matter of Israel's flaunting their privilege in an attitude of "our religion is better than yours" — as

5. *E.g.*, Deut. 10:14ff.; Lev. 19:1-2; Lev. 25.
6. J. Verkuyl, *Contemporary Missiology, An Introduction* (Grand Rapids: Eerdmans, 1978), p. 95, quoted in C. J. H. Wright, 'The Christian and Other Religions: The Biblical Evidence', *Themelios*, Vol. 9:2 (1984), p. 9.

if Israel's faith was one among many brands of a commodity, "human religion." Rather what was at stake, what was so threatened by Israel compromising with the gods and worship of other nations, was the continuity of the redemptive work of the Creator God of all mankind within the unique historical and social context which he himself had chosen'.[7]

Wright notes that Israel's mission was to be a holy (distinctive) and priestly (representing God) nation (Exod. 19:3-6), and in the light of this calling 'for Israel to have accepted Canaanite and other religions as equally valid and acceptable alternatives to their own faith would have been no act of tolerance, kindness or maturity. It would have been an utter betrayal of the rest of mankind, for the sake of whose salvation they had been chosen and redeemed'.[8]

Biblical teaching about election can only be grasped when seen as part of the characteristically biblical way of understanding human reality. Human life consists in mutual relationships: a mutual interdependence that is not simply a temporary phase in the journey towards salvation but one that is intrinsic to the goal of salvation itself. If God's way of blessing 'all the families of the earth' is to be addressed to those families in their concrete situations, and not to unreal abstractions such as 'immortal souls' or 'autonomous selves', then it must be accomplished through election — calling and sending some as vehicles of that blessing for all — so that human community may be freed from fragmentation and re-created in communion with God.

For the disciples of Jesus, that divine promise, first bequeathed to a nation, had seen the dawn of its fulfilment in an individual human being. They were now witnesses of that promise, in continuity with Old Testament Israel but now in fellowship with other men and women drawn from all nations. The promise had come into brilliant focus now in the crucified and risen Christ. The re-telling of the story of Israel in the story of Jesus, and the radical transformation of the traditional Jewish symbols, meant that the Jewish world view was subverted from within.

This is evident in all the New Testament writings, and especially in the epistles of Paul and the epistle to the Hebrews. Paul understood

---

7. Wright, 'The Christian and Other Religions', p. 7.
8. Wright, 'The Christian and Other Religions', p. 8.

his own vocation, to be the apostle to the Gentiles, as part of a wider gospel framework according to which the creator God was fulfilling his promise to Abraham. Although his preaching of the gospel subverted the narrative world of his Jewish contemporaries no less than it did the pagan stories, his claim was that it actually reinstated the true sense of the covenant promises.[9] The end of exile and the restoration of Israel are not now future events to be experienced in terms of a cleansed land, a rebuilt temple, an intensified Torah. N. T. Wright expresses it like this: 'The exile came to its cataclysmic end when Jesus, Israel's representative Messiah, dies outside the walls of Jerusalem, bearing the curse, which consisted of exile at the hands of the pagans, to its utmost limit. The return from exile began when Jesus, again as the representative Messiah, emerged from the tomb three days later. As a result the whole complex of Jewish expectations as to what would happen when the exile finished had come tumbling out in a rush. Israel's God had poured out his own Spirit on all flesh; his word was going out to the nations . . .'.[10]

Jesus Christ as the Story of God

But the story of Jesus is also presented in the New Testament as the story of God. He embodies the identity and mission of Israel by embodying the identity and mission of Israel's God. In the light of their experience of the resurrected Jesus and the unique authority with which he spoke and acted in the days of his public ministry, the early Christians underwent a radical transformation in their understanding of God: they gave to Jesus the worship that, in their Jewish context, was due to God alone. They unconditionally ascribed universal dominion to him. Whenever the New Testament writers speak of Jesus Christ, in the rich diversity of ways they do, it is to point to his theological significance: in some way or the other he is the presence of the eternal, infinite God in time and space.

In the apostolic church this christological focus finds its most

---

9. *Cf.*, esp. Rom. 4; Rom. 10:1-4; Gal. 3:1–4:7.

10. N. T. Wright, *The New Testament and the People of God* (London: SPCK, 1992), p. 406.

famous expression in the Johannine prologue: 'The Word became flesh and made his dwelling among us. We have seen his glory, the glory of the One and Only, who came from the Father, full of grace and truth.' (John 1:14). Similarly, Paul writes of Christ that 'in him all the fullness of the Deity lives in bodily form' (Col. 2:9); that 'God was pleased to have his fullness dwell in him and through him to reconcile to himself all things whether on earth or heaven, by making peace through his blood shed on the cross' (Col. 1:19-20); and, in the setting of a discussion on sacrifices to idols, affirms that 'there is no God but one' and only 'one Lord, Jesus Christ, through whom are all things and through whom we live' (1 Cor. 8:4ff.).[11]

Even more striking are the many passages where these truths are implied, rather than explicitly stated. The very early Christian hymn which Paul uses in Philippians 2:6ff. not only confesses the incarnation and exaltation of Jesus Christ but applies to him an Old Testament text which affirmed the uniqueness and supremacy of Yahweh.[12] Similarly the prophet Joel's injunction 'to call on the name of Yahweh' for salvation now becomes 'to call on the name of Jesus' (Rom. 10:13, *cf.*, Joel 2:32). The 'Spirit of God' and the 'Spirit of Christ', the 'love of God' and the 'love of Christ' are used interchangeably, for example in Romans 8.

In his important book on christological method entitled *Yesterday and Today*, Colin Gunton points out that the movement in early Christian

11. See Gordon Fee who comments bluntly: 'Although Paul does not here call Christ God, the formula is so constructed that only the most obdurate would deny its Trinitarian implications. In the same breath that he can assert that there is only one God, he equally asserts that the designation "Lord," which in the OT belongs to the one God, is the proper designation of the divine Son. One should note especially that Paul feels no tension between the affirmation of monotheism and the clear distinction between the two persons of Father and Jesus Christ. As with other such statements in the NT, Jesus is the one through whom God both created and redeemed. Thus together the two sentences embrace the whole of human existence', *The First Epistle to the Corinthians*, NICNT (Grand Rapids: Eerdmans, 1987), pp. 375-76. James Dunn has made a brave attempt to see only Adam christology, stemming from the resurrection (and not pre-existence), and no incarnational christology in the Pauline corpus in *Christology in the Making: A New Testament Inquiry into the Origins of the Doctrine of the Incarnation* (London: SCM, 1980), esp. pp. 125-28, 254-56. For a refutation of Dunn's arguments, see, *e.g.*, S. Kim, *The Origin of Paul's Gospel* (Grand Rapids: Eerdmans, 1982), pp. 137-268.

12. Isa. 45:21-23. Interestingly, both Old and New Testament texts are voiced against a backdrop of religious pluralism.

thought was not from an abstraction called 'the Jesus of history' to the unity of Jesus with his Father. It was rather a movement whose understanding of Jesus' eternal significance and reality was expanded. 'What begins by seeing him oriented to the future ends by conceiving him as also the incarnation of a pre-existent Word of God'.[13] Gunton wryly observes: 'That a particular human being should, in the past, have been a unique spatio-temporal instantiation of the divine, is the most intellectually offensive of all Christian claims. Yet that is the burden of both New Testament and orthodox patristic Christology in its various forms'.[14]

Gunton recognises the apparent absurdity of the claim: 'That our lives should be measured and healed by this lonely and suffering figure is the real reason why the ascription of uniqueness is difficult. But it is also the reason why it should be made'.[15]

Jesus is unique because he is the way by which God restores his human creation — and, along with it, his whole creation — to a wholeness of relationship with him. This does not mean that God is met with nowhere else than in Jesus, but that Jesus confronts us with the reality of God in a manner that is unique.

'It is only when we appreciate that it is in and through Jesus of Nazareth that God meets humanity where it is, in its alienation and fallenness, and so liberates it for an imitation of that love, that we shall begin to understand that the assertion of Jesus' uniqueness, far from being immoral or illogical, is the presupposition for an understanding of the love of God for all of his creation.'[16]

If human sin is such that only God can deal with it, the incarnation is good news because it teaches that he deals with sin in a way that respects human dignity. The incarnation enables us to assert the radical corruption of humankind without denying that it was created good and intended for fellowship with its Creator. 'Theology can thus be true to moral realities, falling neither into a life-denying pessimism nor a naive and counter-intuitive optimism.'[17] In other words, the relevance of

13. C. Gunton, *Yesterday and Today: A Study of Continuities in Christology* (London: Darton, Longman and Todd, 1983), p. 70.
14. Gunton, *Yesterday and Today*, p. 132.
15. Gunton, *Yesterday and Today*, p. 165.
16. Gunton, *Yesterday and Today*, p. 164.
17. Gunton, *Yesterday and Today*, p. 180.

Christian teaching for human life depends upon what it is able to say in its christology.

Conclusion

The universalism of the Christian story is unlike the 'totalising metanarratives' (to use the contemporary jargon) of modernity (*e.g.*, narratives of Progress, Evolutionism, Science, Marxist teleology, etc.), in that it is a story rooted in the concrete particularities of space-time events but 'owned' by a people who are truly global. Moreover, the truth of the gospel is 'cross-shaped'. Such a message of vulnerable, self-humbling, self-sacrificial love for the unlovable can only be communicated by a people who embody that message in their corporate lives. It rules out all methods of manipulation and coercion, and subverts all our feelings of moral or cultural superiority.

The church itself is a particular community among other particular communities in the world. But it has a universal mission: to be the bearer of God's saving purpose for God's world. Moreover, such a calling affirms cultural specificity while remaining universal in its scope. From the point of view of the gospel, no human culture is inherently unclean in the eyes of God, nor is any culture the exclusive norm of truth. The events of Pentecost served to 'sanctify' vernacular languages as adequate channels of access to the truth of God. This commitment to a christocentric pluralism (which endorses cultural diversity) is no mere tolerance. It is to recognise that, in God's plan of salvation, the heritage of the nations, purged of all their idolatrous accretions, will ultimately serve his kingdom (*e.g.*, Isa. 60; Rev. 22:24). Such a vision prevents the church from lapsing into the role of a domesticated chaplain to the nations, and frees it to be a prophetic agent of transformation.

What this means is that the particular body of people who bear the name of Jesus through history, 'this strange and often absurd company of people so feeble, so foolish, so often fatally compromised with the world, this body with all its contingency and particularity',[18] is the

18. L. Newbigin, *The Gospel in a Pluralist Society* (Grand Rapids: Eerdmans/London: SPCK, 1989), p. 87.

body which has been entrusted with the 'open secret' of God's kingdom at work through human history. As Lesslie Newbigin puts it succinctly: 'God's purpose of salvation . . . is that in and through history there should be brought into being that which is symbolized in the vision with which the Bible ends — the Holy City into which all the glory of the nations will finally be gathered. But — and of course this is the crux of the matter — that consummation can only lie on the other side of death and resurrection. It is the calling of the church to bear through history to its end the secret of the lordship of the crucified'.[19]

Questions

1. In your own local church context, how is the universal Christ challenging and transforming culture?

2. How socially inclusive is your church? How is the diversity of human cultures enriching your worship and witness as a church?

3. What may it cost the church in your nation to share in a truly global, missionary partnership with churches in other nations?

---

19. Newbigin, *The Gospel in a Pluralist Society*, p. 87.

EPILOGUE:
TOWARDS THE MILLENNIUM

Memory and the Millennium: Time and Social Change at the Fin de Siècle

DAVID LYON

Summary

Today's Western cathedrals attract more tourists than worshippers, illustrating the erosion of cultural memory and its transformation into curiosities for tourist interest. Cultural memory is apparently eroded. This affects the church, which must connect memory of God's past with hope. Secularisation may be partly to blame, but that is now under attack. Communications and consumerism mark this era, with fluidity and flux. Its icon is Disney virtual history, not linked to the living past of a community. We can deny the past or present: go with the flow or retreat to fundamentalism. The response of faith is to retrace the promises of God and take our bearing into the future accordingly. Our part in God's great story is to remain faithful, to listen to the stories of others and take advantage of genuine plurality.

Once, you rolled grandly into Toronto on the train, stopping at Union Station, that marvellous marble-clad monument to the age of the railway. As you looked out of the window beyond the Royal York Hotel, the skyline was dominated by steeples and church towers. Between them, you knew, were the workshops, markets and homes of daily life. Today, as you circle to land at Pearson International, all you see is the soaring CN Tower, the Skydome sports arena, and the shining glass,

279

steel and cement bank buildings. Beyond, strung around endless sub-urban perimeters, you can pick out the mysteriously named 'centres' dedicated to shopping.

Very often, venerable worship edifices are still visible in the an-cient cities of Europe and the Americas. But they frequently find their most faithful visitors are tourists. Cathedrals are under new manage-ment. Such church buildings stand as symbolic sentinels, museums marking the sites of old practices, quaint relics of a bygone era. Memory has succumbed to nostalgia. If camera-clicking pilgrims do find some service in progress, they could be forgiven for thinking, from the dress and language, that they have stumbled into a 'living museum' where old ways are dramatically reproduced by seasonal staff, acting parts. Except that Disney does it better.

Hardly surprising, then, that to many Western Christians at the end of the twentieth century, the future looks bleak. While the same cannot necessarily be said for churches in other parts of the world, they too confront many of the same conditions that cause concern in the West. Little confidence is left that 'time like an ever rolling stream' just flows continuously onward. Rather, to hear them, one suspects that 'the sands of time are sinking'. It is harder to imagine how 'God is working his purpose out, as year succeeds to year'. Millennial hopes and dreams, that once animated generations of Christians, give way to fears for the millennium. The twenty-first century holds fewer attractions than anxieties for the faithful.

If correct, this is bad news indeed for a 'historic' religion like Christianity, in which the dynamic of future hope depends on an ap-propriation of past events. Continuity is crucial — 'Do this,' says Jesus of the Eucharist, 'until I come'. Yet that sense of unbroken continuity is under strain. The steeples behind the skyscrapers are in poor shape. Institutional churches in the West seem sickly, having lost members, social influence and public credibility. Many worry about the prognosis for such patients; haemorrhage and diminution of powers often por-tends a terminal condition. Even where growth is strong, such as in some Latin American and African countries — the latter now account for one quarter of all Anglicans in the world — conditions have changed. Most obviously, colonialism has collapsed, and diversity flourishes. Memories that sustain true hope are weakening.

Why is this? While the very idea of millennium has obvious Christian connotations, it is often greeted with more gloom than gladness by Christians. Delighted dreams of millennium have been appropriated by the weird and the wacky. The age of Aquarius excites more popular interest than the progress of salvation history. Could it be that a sort of collective amnesia afflicts many Christians? If so, what causes such memory-loss? In what follows, I suggest that among the reasons for this state of affairs is the high-modern social and cultural context in which an increasing proportion of the world's population finds itself. This corrodes our 'chronotopes' — our frameworks for thinking about history and time. Perhaps ours is not so much a time of crisis as a crisis of time.

Until a few years ago, the popular account of all this was summed up in one word, 'secularisation'. This concept was called on to do much work in explaining what happens to religion in the modern world. It is also a chronotope, that organises our sense of religious time, hinting strongly that eternal concerns steadily give way to temporal. By and large, secularisation was taken to be a negative process, whereby beliefs became implausible in an age of science, religiously rooted social action became irrelevant in an era of state involvement, and religion withdrew to the social margins, leaving the real world to pursue its business without the benefit of divine direction. The secularisation story was stimulated in part by the growth of the modern story of progress, which was itself — ironically — a secularised version of Christian salvation history. Where God once held centre stage, Reason, and faith in unaided human capacities, took over. Today, techno-science has pride of place in the drama.

At the same time, confidence in this secular story has been eroding. Modernism itself, as a false-faith, is secularising. The definitional problems plaguing 'secularisation' as much as 'religion' refuse to go away. Older forms of religiosity also seem to persist and sometimes revive. Evidence accumulates of fresh and fast growth of conventional religion in some modernising parts of the world (another paradox — does not modernity deny religion?), and also of the flowering of many new religious movements. The world beyond religious institutions and movements is clearly undergoing profound changes.

The old secularisation thesis referred to the modern world of heavy industry and the rise of working classes, urbanisation, the growth of administrative power in the nation-state, of reliance on the findings of science and dependence on technological development. Each of these was thought to affect negatively the fortunes of the faithful. Time accelerated, cosmologies altered. The world itself, and the word 'secularisation', lived under the sign of progress. This sign both promised to provide satisfaction for all human needs and simultaneously showed how the churches, and religion in general, were superfluous to human fulfilment, scarcely-mourned casualties of the forward thrust of change.

Today's world, however, is one of high technology — computers to clones — of an explosion of electronic media, of a pervasive consumer culture, and of globalised relations of all kinds. Whether or not this world is rightly described as 'post-modern', it certainly exhibits characteristics that warrant thinking of it as high modern, hyper-modern or meta-modern. It is not the same world as that described by the earlier secularisation theories. The world of cyberspace and consumerism lives under the sign of fluidity and flux, in which institutional churches may continue their dreary decline, but where the religious is reborn as a cultural resource.

To read the signs of the times, to grasp some dimensions of the massive changes taking place at the fin de siècle, attention must be paid to these shifts in modernity, and to the new chronotopes they have generated. This in turn helps to put millennial turbulence in context, and yields some of the vital clues for the urgent task of reconnecting memory and hope.

Modernity in Question

Although questions about modernity are as old as modernity itself, at the end of the twentieth century the debate became central and unavoidable. Anti-modernists, such as Britain's brilliant socialist craft designer William Morris, have made their views felt since Victorian times. But doubts about the life-expectancy of the modern project — completely to conform the world to human design and desire — did not make the headlines until well after the Second World War. Even then, post-war reconstruction and the consumer boom in the West lent a certain confidence to commerce and manufacturing. The warning bells sounded by automobile safety critic Ralph Nader or big-is-beautiful dissident Ernst Schumacher largely went unheeded until the early

1980s. Since then, of course, movements such as Greenpeace have gained a global hearing, and disasters such as Chernobyl or Challenger have drastically raised the profile of risk.

Some have suggested that the debate over modernity is itself a symptom of millennial angst. Environmentalism invokes apocalyptic dread, while recurring genocide hints that Hitler's holocaust was no mere blip on the chart of civilised progress. But while there may be some exacerbation of the debate's intensity, there are good grounds for thinking that the debate over modernity relates to real changes occurring within modernity. The debate over modernity is not merely intellectual or aesthetic anti-modernism reappearing. It is a debate over the ongoing viability of the modern project itself. That millennialism emerges alongside the seismic shifts of modernity is hardly surprising. But it is more consequence than cause.

What are these transformations of modernity? At risk of oversimplifying, one can say that two factors are crucial — communications media and consumer markets. More broadly, these relate to the dominance of technoscience in general and the intensification of the global capitalist enterprise. It is not so much that technological change or modes of consumption on their own are upsetting the old patterns of modernity. Rather, these two key factors are implicated in all contemporary currents of change. On the one hand, information and communications technologies (CITs) help to connect the local and the distant as never before. On the other, those connections have to do, more often than not, with consuming, whether of TV shows, exotic fruit or running shoes.

A historian of the mid-twenty-first century may well look back on our own and locate the invention of the silicon chip as the turning point towards the high- or post-modern world. The 'chip' enabled the incredible miniaturisation and power-magnification of electronic devices, that made possible both widespread computer applications, and enabled their marriage with telecommunications. Those applications encouraged the growth in other areas such as genetic engineering and the world of virtual realities created through simulation and modelling. The marriage with telecommunications ensured that global traffic in information would be central to future developments.

In their turn, changes in CITs are involved in the growth of consumerism. Without the technological changes, today's customised products — from cars to clothing to kitchenware — would be unthink-

283

DAVID LYON

able. But this is to focus on the supply side. While the massive machinery of corporate power is used to lure and seduce consumers, there is little doubt that their subjects are unwilling. Consumerism has become the milieu of modern social life, and as it does so, has challenged the nature of that life. A major fault line has appeared, dividing between those with the means to consume and those shut out of the market. Once it was 'common sense' to save. Now it is 'common sense' to spend. Failure to consume becomes a moral flaw, subject to sanctions.

Where once, in modern times, Westerners might have found their identity, their social togetherness and the ongoing life of their society in the area of production, these are today increasingly found through consumption. It's not that companies are producing less, or that people no longer work. Rather, the meaning of these activities has altered. We are what we buy. We relate to others who consume the same way that we do. And the overarching system of capitalism is fuelled by, and geared to stimulating, consumption. It is important to grasp this, not least because it has the signs of becoming a global phenomenon. Simultaneously, consumerism affects the most mundane human experiences, especially our bodily lives. Consumer choices are expressed through the body, now the site of regimes of fitness, cosmetic alteration and exhibition through trade-named clothing. The malleability of the body is taken to its logical conclusion in the current body-piercing and tattooing trends, that caricature as well as conform to consumer culture.

Image and style are now central to identity. Nike running shoes, Levi jeans, Coca-Cola — these and more — all help to give shape to who we are. This is different from binding our identity to work or paid employment, characteristic of modernity — and it raises shopping skills to the level of virtue. Likewise our social circle, our peer-group, is likely to share consuming patterns in common, more than anything else. So North American database marketers cluster the country according to type. Sure enough, postal code areas coincide with 'pools and patios' or 'furs and station wagons' (among forty other groups). As for the grand economic system that circles the globe, this too has switched from mere efficient mass production to making things or selling services specifically for each niche, each type.

This is why we now live under the sign of fluidity and flux. Things turned this way with the systematic undermining of tradition that began two centuries ago and more. The Enlightenment philosophers

284

questioned the old regime of monarchy and religion, replacing it with a focus on human capacities to transform the world. More significantly, capitalism, always striving to find new and better ways of doing things, put aside traditional ways of work and exchange. Without doubt, Christianity was also implicated in this transformation. But these forces are now rampant, and affect all of life. Detraditionalisation is carried along by communications and consumerism. In exchanging regimes of virtue for those of virtuality, we rub electronic shoulders with strangers and are socially classified by credit-rating.

The CITs, even more than modern transport, have brought the world together, in the sense that we all have far more culture-contact than before. The old world of empires and of Christendom, where lines of authority were clear, has cracked and splintered. When many voices can be heard, who is to say that one should be heeded more than another? When one person's creed is another's curse, we are subject to what Peter Berger calls the 'heretical imperative'. When the only criteria left for choosing between them are learned in the marketplace, then truth as well as authority appears as a commodity. We hear that people 'buy into' a belief or that, rather than rejecting a dogma as false, they 'can't buy' this or that viewpoint.

Not only truth and authority are fuzzy and fluid. The old categories of time and space, that served modernity so well, also evaporate in present conditions. In the most obvious case, 'cyberspace', the only 'spaces' are virtual ones. There is no place to this space — yet cyberspace has 'sites' that are 'visited' and many other ersatz reminders of physical space. The one that interests us particularly here, however, is time. When the idea of global time-zones is only a century old, and chronotopes have had to adjust to the possibility of communication without transportation (with the invention of the telegraph, messages no longer had to be physically carried), we now have a dizzying range of chronotope shifts. In the world of electronic communications, distinctions must be made between 'real time' and the asynchronous experiences of e-mail and the Internet.

Time is also transfigured in the confluence of consumerism and communications known as Disneyland. Take 'Main Street' — a common feature of Disney's colonies in Europe and Japan as well as in the American home-base. Here, not only are some of the world's most famous places available within walking distance, but their connections in time are also confused. Past, present and future appear, not as a line, but as a melange, a collage. Disney's planned 'Historyland' park would take this even further. Recently, in a public discussion, the authenticity of Disney's America was affirmed in these words: 'Disney always does things first-class, and . . . they'll hire the best historians money can buy . . . to create a completely plausible, completely believable appearance of American history'.

The details don't matter, it seems. Mere dates and actual locales are incidental to Disney's 'history'. If nostalgia can be generated and tourism stimulated, then history can be created, customised and consumed. Ironically, many of Disney's narratives echo and imitate Christian themes of suffering and redemption, now cosmetically retouched and digitally imaged. Such secular chronotopes reorganise the past in ways that sever it from its original co-ordinates. But the idea easily catches on that the past was some rosy Christian idyll, and, lo and behold, Christian heritage is born again! But I am anticipating.

Torn from tradition, the modern world looks wistfully for replacements, and finds them in heritage, in the invention of pasts. Hope, once linked to history, now moves from its moorings, drifting with the currents, very vulnerable to winds and storms. The 1990s precede not just a new century but a millennial encounter. What was once a spur to faith and action is now a controversy, a conundrum, and possibly a cul-de-sac. Today's TV version is both apocalyptic and comic, gloomy and fun. While some are gearing up for Armageddon, and others anticipate the arrival of a higher plane of human consciousness, yet others just prepare for the party.

The Millennium: History's End?

Pre-millennial tension abounds, throughout the West at least. Millennial anxieties are attached to events such as the Oklahoma government building bombing and Sarin gas attacks on the Tokyo subway. Crackpots and con-artists of all kinds are cranking out claims to be the antichrist or to have powers of foretelling the final doom. UFO sightings and alien abductions are on the increase, not to mention the active Madonnas. In one celebrated case, of the Little Madonna of Civitavecchia, in Italy, the Virgin's statue was first seen to weep bloody tears on February 2, 1995.

This last is a particularly interesting case because it illustrates a number of significant themes. Checks on the authenticity of the bloody tears include time-tested modern methods, including DNA analysis. The sceptics, including church authorities, are careful. Not long after the first sighting, a church-state controversy broke out, in which the attorney confiscated the statue for inspection, while the Bishop objected that it was church property. Who decides on the genuineness of the 'miracle'? It seems to be a contest between science and the state.

This controversy does little to curb interest in the matter, however. Contemporary telecommunications ensure that such 'news' is instantly available across the world. Others besides religious believers pay attention to the story. Nor does DNA testing and the like serve to stop visitors arriving to see the Madonna for themselves. Probably the reverse. Knowing that the approaching millennium would cap all holy years for some time to come, the Mayor of Civitavecchia immediately channelled funding into the church and its surroundings — benches, water fountains, portable toilets — to cope with the expected tourist trade. If millennium pilgrims to Rome could be temporarily diverted to Civitavecchia, think of the boost to the local economy!

Apart from the forgivable cynicism that might attend such happenings, what more can be learned from them? Curiously enough, one millennialogist, Mike Dash, notes that millennial fever may have more to do with broader cultural currents than the mere mystery and magic of a triple 000 turning on the calendar. He sees an 'authority vacuum' opening as faith fades in government, in science as a vehicle of progress, and in religion. Politicians are suspect, science seems to create as many problems as it solves, and churchgoing has dropped off drastically. Without the older authorities, people are credulous, '. . . because they would rather believe in something than nothing.' Thus, he argues, 'The millennium provides a focus for that general feeling of malaise.' It also produces a range of responses, from anger to apathy.

The coming of the millennium spawns both dire warning and confident assertion. Or at least, these symptoms appear coincidentally with the millennium. On the one hand, history is viewed as being volatile, ready to blow in some apocalyptic blast. The 'millennium rage' exponents expect something pretty explosive. Their evidence? The ac-

287

tivities of the Sons of Gestapo, the Unabomber, Waco, and so on. On the other hand, Francis Fukuyama's version of the 'end of history' is much nearer a whimper than a bang. For him, the collapse of the Berlin Wall and the close of the Cold War usher in an era in which battling ideologies are no more. So-called liberal democracy has triumphed, he claims, as the 'final form of human government'. From henceforth, relentless calculation, problem-solving, and consumer satisfaction will bring boredom to all.

The controversy surrounding the Fukuyama thesis has been out of proportion to the technical significance of his work, but it clearly struck a chord. A number of factors leave his ideas open to serious question. His notion of liberal democracy leaves little room for the massive — and frequently bloody — upsurges of nationalism appearing throughout the world. Neither does it account for the so-called Asian values that have risen to prominence on the Pacific rim — Singapore and Korea hardly count as 'liberal democracies' in the sense that Fukuyama intends. More left-wing oriented versions of liberal democracy also continue to be available, throwing down a gauntlet to the free market version espoused by Fukuyama. And, lastly, this thesis does not account for those events that may break into history, such as ecological disaster or genocide and refugee migrations.

Notably, Fukuyama has little to say about religion. This is odd, given the role that, say, Augustine has in forming at least Western ideas of history (and of which Hegel and Marx were in part legatees), not to mention the huge and ongoing influence of religion in world history. Whether conventional or otherwise, religion will still be implicated in changes occurring on both sides of the millennium. How could Fukuyama not discuss fundamentalisms at least? Such movements have taken on tremendous — if sometimes exaggerated — political importance at the end of the century. Gilles Kepel, for instance, calls revivals of Jewish, Islamic and Christian fundamentalism 'the revenge of God'.

For Christian people, understanding the contemporary directions of religion is of crucial significance. To stand back and examine such directions gives the chance to see the context of, and therefore the meanings assigned to, any form of religious activity in high-modern and post-modern situations. Here, the focus is on the 'time' dimension, and what today's religious trends 'do with history'. We are back with our chronotopes.

Apart from the die-hard date-plotters of the end-of-the-world minority, it is hard to find much evidence of strong future orientation in these religious trends. Of course, that minority, especially in its pre-millennial fundamentalist forms, is fairly vocal. Sinister signs and por-tents are discerned everywhere, and often linked to fear of crime (even in countries like Canada, where crime rates are falling) and a call for more 'law and order'.

In general one could characterise the primary alternatives — at least in North America and Europe — as denying the present and ac-cepting the past or accepting the present and denying the past. Both tendencies are fairly familiar — more or less so depending on one's location in a global context. In Canada, for instance, denying the past and accepting the present is prevalent, at least within the mass media and academe. The abuses reported in residential schools that were established for First Nations peoples by both Catholics and Protestants are today almost synonymous with those schools' names. 'Missionary' activity in general, whether at home or abroad, is often assumed to be a form of cultural imperialism, and the teachings of the churches on matters such as sexuality or life-and-death, a barrier to tolerant attitudes and policies.

A mood of strong scepticism also pervades much fin de siècle academic writing. 'Christian' chronotopes are viewed as distorting the true diversity of the world, and denying the rights of others to a legit-imate voice. If Fukuyama complacently ignores religion, at the other extreme Donna Haraway deplores its ongoing effects — at the heart of the American technoscience enterprise. She argues that incarnation, suffering, redemption and fulfilment are still potent motifs, seen for instance in the 'Human Genome' project. Books and TV programmes on this theme include 'In the Beginning Was the Genome', 'Genetic Ark', and 'Decoding the Book of Life'. Haraway seeks liberation from such secularised Christian chronotopes. Change the story! she urges. Embrace the present, with its kaleidoscope of narratives.

The present may be seen as acceptable, even though not much contentment about it is expressed. To 'go with the flow' is to adapt and accommodate to present conditions. This can take many forms. Among those dissatisfied with conventional churches, it may mean exploring spiritualities that have long been excluded from the range of options, centring possibly on goddesses or witches, or, more likely, on the sacralised self. It may involve new forms of syncretism, such as

289

churches in Korea that combine soccer with the Spirit in their Sunday programmes. Within mainstream denominations, it may mean 're-imaging' God, such as occurred at the Minneapolis conference in 1993, when 'Sophia' turned out to be the new deity. This is now reflected in the 'God of many names' who has made an appearance in the new United and Anglican Church Hymnbook in Canada. But equally, the attempt to adapt to the times could be of the Sheffield UK 'Nine O'clock Service' variety, a highly successful post-modern experimental worship venture that in 1996 failed tragically at the leadership level.

Just as visible, in parts of the Western world at least, is the denial of the present and the acceptance of the past. As Chris Swain, a hand reading consultant and millennium watcher, observes, 'We are not happy with the present situation in society. . . . I have noticed a growing dissatisfaction with people generally'. Some are unhappy because of what they discern to be moral decay and decline, a drift away from what they refer to as 'objective truth' and 'absolute morals'. Others are disturbed for more mundane but no less real reasons, the overwhelming choices of a consumer society, where deciding between multiple alternatives affects much more than mere shopping.

All this makes the (idealised) past seem very attractive. Let's turn the clock back and revive old ways. Most prominently, and fearfully, this occurred in Iran, whose fundamentalistic Islam has also had repercussions in the West, such as the fatwa against novelist Salman Rushdie. This is anti-modern malaise tinged with violence and repression. But the fringe of the 'Christian right' in the USA is clearly not above such tactics either. However much others might dissociate from their actions, people claiming Christian justification attack abortion clinics, defend the carrying of handguns, or denounce AIDS sufferers. Margaret Atwood's harrowing novel about the patriarchal Republic of Gilead (*A Handmaid's Tale*), formed after a righteous right wing coup, may not be so far-fetched after all.

Without going to those extremes, some Christian churches offer forms of certainty and guidance far beyond that warranted by the newer testament. True, relief for the troubling surfeit of choice may well be found in handing life's decisions over to a pastoral team, or in making a clear, across-the-board judgement about anything from AIDS to refugee policy. But this could also be seen to deny the basic frailty of human wisdom and the precariousness and complexity of human life. These tendencies have as much to do with the malaise of modernity, and a wish to return to the false certainties once offered by science, as they do with faithful Christian commitment in an inherently ambiguous and risky world.

The millennium is not the end of history, even if doubts about history are exacerbated by anxious millennial anticipation. But that anxiety, in turn, has more to do with the fading fortunes of modernity than with anything intrinsically millennial. And one aspect of this is our disturbed sense of time. Modernity twisted Providence — which connects past-present-future under God — into Progress, and then discovered that Progress is not automatic or assured. Paradoxically, in the process, the open horizon of Providence was turned into a closed system of Progress. Only recently, and reluctantly, has it been accepted that modernity has other faces than the so-called Western model.

So rather than seeking a different future, a choice is offered between living for the present or living in the past. Thus deprived of a full-orbed sense of time and history, many religious people, too, feel caught between present and past. Either way Christians, and especially Anglicans, are in a quandary. Fundamentalism's future is apocalyptic; judgement looms large. Only the past holds hope. By contrast, consumerism — our quotidian context — focuses on the present — permanently. Its 'future' is more-of-the-same, and it has little or no sense of the past.

Reconnecting Memory and Hope

This is the current 'crisis of time'. Perhaps we should call it 'chronotope fatigue'? The focus of the foregoing, on the ways that communication technologies and consumerism are contributing to a high- or post-modern world, raises this as a serious question. Zapping with the TV remote control and fast-food may sound like trivial examples, but they are symbolic signs of our times. While the word 'cyberspace' suggests location, one could equally argue that drastically reduced communication time is what the Internet is all about. The lure of the instantaneous has seduced us. We are prisoners of the immediate, trapped between past and present. As the African joke says, 'All the whites have watches, but never have the time'.

All this helps to create an unwelcoming environment for the religious life. If, as Daniele Hervieu-Ledger has argued, religion operates within 'communities of memory' then disruptions to memory, through collective amnesia and, for that matter, selective amnesia — the Disneyfied collage approach to history — pose a challenge of some magnitude. Maintaining a living memory as a source of meaning for the present and hope for the future is difficult, to say the least. Yet in biblical terms, this is exactly what goes on, as the most ancient records show. The Jews of Nehemiah's time, for instance, found again their future hope in God through re-tracing the line of collective memory back to promises made to Abraham, and beyond, right back to creation.

In the modern world, memory and hope are steadily uncoupled. Disney culture plays tricks with both. A sense of history is often reduced to commodified heritage, while the future is in the high-tech hands of EPCOT (the Disney future technology exhibition), the idol of silicon-simulated worlds. Here again is a 'Christian-influenced chronotope' that emphasises the story of a good past and a rosy future, but where the redemptive dynamic is in human hands. Communities of memory, among which the religious are the strongest and the longest lasting, have been dominated in the West by detraditionalisation and deinstitutionalisation. Religious symbols and stories are, like so much else in contemporary culture, cut-loose, free-floating, fluid. They don't disappear. Rather, they reappear as a cultural resource. Little surprise then, that such surrogates tend towards the bricolage, the smorgasbord, the mixing and melding of once different elements. With religion deregulated, it seems, anything goes.

Or does it? In fact, one still finds patterns of belief, some sense of memory, a quest for coherence. In some Latin American churches, for instance, where conventional Christian commitments mingle cheerfully with worship and post-modern pastiche-style patter, there is marked growth (and no sense of incongruity). The deinstitutionalisation and deregulation of religion allows for fresh growth, new directions and sometimes surprising strategic alliances. This raises the awkward question posed by Jesus himself — how far, in times past, have believers mistaken mere human traditions for the demands of God? This challenge is particularly acute for Anglican churches, which sometimes hold as many attractions for heritage hunters as for would-be disciples.

Challenges confronting churches that prioritise faithfulness to Christ in high- or post-modern contexts are manifold and complex.

There are no easy answers, no risk-free zones. To seek these is to abdicate responsibility for the world as we find it today. Tradition that will not negotiate with modernity fuels fundamentalism. Equally, to accept as 'all there is' the slippery surfaces of a commodity-saturated world is to succumb to lifestyle levels well below the calling of Christ. This is as feckless as fundamentalism is futile. Is there any faithful way forward? Can Christians find ways of reconnecting memory and hope; of recalibrating our chronotopes?

Recognising the signs of the times and cross-referencing them with the stories of Scripture is a good start. Against the backdrop of modernity's malaise, these stories show up as good news indeed. Where, culturally and politically, questions of the body and identity are so frequently raised, opportunities are presented for offering alternatives that speak to just these questions. If full humanity is compromised by consumer-constructed identities, or if bodies are devalued into mere meat, or denied in cyber-solipsism, let those who hear the voice of the 'incarnate one' live a different way.

Where full humanity is threatened by fractured relationships and broken bonds, let us live and teach another way. Hurting people cry out for guidance, and more, role models of how to maintain that marriage, how to nurture those children into responsible and mature adulthood. Where full humanity is subverted by the idolising of a global market economy, that overlooks local needs, let us turn again to building community and resisting remote capital. These are all authentic ways of living and proclaiming good news.

Returning to stories is also significant. Not only the stories of Jesus — though, God knows, they could bear repeating more often, in fresh and incisive ways — but also the stories of communities of faith. Revitalising the repositories of memory is crucial in an era when the crumbling institutional churches of the West can no longer be relied upon to tell the story. In house-groups, families, and in church-events, the big story of God's grace from creation, through the cross, to the new heavens and new earth, can be told and retold. So too can the stories woven into that big story, as the drama of redemption is populated by new actors in every generation, playing out in practice the incarnated gospel. 'As the Father sent me, so I send you. . . .' To connect our bit parts with the divine megadrama is to re-weave the threads of memory into the tapestry of hope.

293

This too is part of faithfulness in a plural world, and of unity with other believers. To know and live our own story is also to be able to hear without fear the stories of others, and to find ways of co-existing and, where possible and appropriate, collaborating with those whose narratives are different. Care is also called for. Christians have sometimes been over-eager to appropriate (for instance Jewish) or to deny (for instance North American aboriginal) beliefs and practices of others.

Too much time has been wasted — and too much blood shed — in a world where others have been defined by their differences rather than loved as neighbours. Christians, again, have a unique — and terrifying — calling, to be in, but not of, this world. Particularly in places where pluralism amounts to a denial of distinctives, in law, education, or sexuality, for instance, the calling is critically hard to maintain. But bluff can always be called. Christians would do well in many situations to be for, not against, pluralism. A true and full-blooded pluralism, that respects and protects difference, is surely worth seeking.

At the time of millennium, modernity's malaise is given voice. But so, too, is the Good News, in rule of Christ, the Servant-Leader. Old institutional structures of regulated religion may well be under threat, but new networks are emerging, within which memory can be maintained and reasons for hope rekindled. Communities of faith, capable of telling and living the story in faithful and contemporary ways, will only survive if nourished and encouraged. If they fail, the twin dangers of fundamentalism and hedonism/nihilism will only loom larger.

In the end, however useful the sociologist's account of cultural change within a consumerist and communicative world, the real resources for faithful living are yet to be found where they have ever been available, in the goodness and grace of God.

Questions

1. Why does the impending millennium cause 'turbulence' in Western culture, and how should Christians use this phenomenon?

2. In what ways can the biblical stories provide models for recovering the past in order to negotiate with modernity, under God?

3. Discuss ways in which a genuine pluralism in culture can be used by Christians. Is pluralism in our culture in fact truly plural?

Kuala Lumpur Statement, 1997
Trumpet II: The Encounter Statement

From 10-15 February 1997, eighty delegates representing the Anglican Churches of the South gathered in the beautiful city of Kuala Lumpur, to meet, know and encourage one another, in our Christian life and mission; to follow up on the first Encounter in the South and specifically to seek God's light and wisdom as we reflect on the place of Scripture in the life and mission of the Church in the twenty-first century. Because the Lambeth 1998 Conference was in view, many of the delegates were Bishops or Archbishops.

We listened to a major address from the Encounter Chairman, the Most Revd Joseph A. Adetiloye, Archbishop of Nigeria, on the Encounter theme, 'The Place of Scripture in the Life and Mission of the Church in the 21st Century', and to one another's 'witnesses', as to how Scripture impinges on the life and mission of the Church in our different cultures and contexts.

Several common issues emerged and a number of resolutions were reached as we prayed together, studied the Bible together, talked together and listened to God and one another. There was the consciousness of the presence of the Spirit of God and an awareness that people around the world were praying for us.

In every way, we sensed a spirit of commitment as we set ourselves to the task before us with a due sense of seriousness. We recognised the importance of our chosen theme for the Church at a time of difficulty and confusion in some provinces and of growth, martyrdom, dynamic missionary encouragement and quiet but powerful witness in others.

There was a significant move towards self-reliance and missionary vision as most of the delegates sponsored themselves to this Encounter. This suggests that the Churches of the South are beginning to take seriously the challenges that came to them during their first Encounter that, as a result of the current demographic shift in the world Church, the future of Christianity and the hope for the fulfilment of the Great Commission now lies with them.

The following concerns were highlighted from the keynote address, regional 'witnesses' and stories, Bible studies and discussions, as we listened to God to ascertain what place Scripture should have in the life and mission of the Church as we move into the third millennium:

1. Scripture and Our Common Experience and Concerns in Society

A call to prophetic and redemptive witness. We are learning again at this Encounter, that we share of a common experience of life overshadowed by ethnic hatred, political instability and neo-colonialism, social injustice and marginalisation, crippling international debt and spiralling inflation, environmental damage and pollution, religious strife and intolerance, unbridled materialism and pervasive corruption.

We find ourselves in situations overflowing with refugees as a result of war and sometimes natural disaster; where hunger, poverty and recurrent debt combine to dehumanise our people.

In view of all this, especially the crippling effect of international debt, we call on the churches of the West to put pressure on their governments and on the World Bank and the IMF to respond to the many appeals coming from various quarters world-wide, to make the year 2000, a year of Jubilee, to remit the Two Thirds World debt.

We further challenge the Anglican Consultative Council and the Primates of the Anglican Communion to set up a body to be co-ordinated by the South, named 'Anglicare' which can respond quickly with aid to crisis situations around the Communion.

2. Scripture and Mission

We believe that Scripture teaches that the Church exists for mission and that any Church which fails to engage in mission is a disobedient Church. Therefore:

a. We call on our Communion to return to mission as the pivot of our life and ministry in the world.
b. We re-affirm that our understanding and practice of mission as taught by Scripture is holistic and includes an intention to make new Christians.
c. We reassert that mission includes engaging in dialogue with secular authorities, where possible, on the one hand, and commitment to prophetic witness as the conscience of society and the voice of God in the world, on the other, no matter what this may cost.
d. We further believe that our baptismal call to Christian life is a call to discipleship and mission. We therefore call for the empowerment of all the people of God for mission and for the prioritisation of mission in our budgets.
e. We call the Church to return to faithfulness and to reliance on the Holy Spirit in the interpretation and application of Scripture.

3. Scripture and Other Faiths

a. We have learned in the course of this Encounter that many of us are called to live and witness to the love of God in Christ in contexts of religious pluralism. In some of these contexts, the local church is an insignificant minority. We affirm our solidarity with and prayers for those who suffer or pay the ultimate price for their faith in those situations. We thank God for those nations and governments where, because of wise leadership, people of different religions co-exist peacefully, practise and propagate their faiths without being inhibited. We praise the courage of those Christians, whose constancy in faith and witness in some cases involving martyrdom, has resulted in exciting growth of the church in their context. This confirms to us that 'the blood of the martyrs is the seed . . .'.

b. We praise the wisdom and courage of those who work to preserve the faith and maintain a faithful witness in situations where the Christian presence is threatened with extinction. We commend and encourage the witness of those who, through service of love, human compassion and other aspects of social care and advocacy, seek to draw others to experience the love of the Saviour of the world.

c. We have been learning in this Encounter that mission not only includes proclaiming the Gospel and converting men and women to faith in Christ, but also learning to live at peace with all persons, and being faithful to the Saviour. We encourage all Christians therefore wherever they are, to remember the words of our Lord Jesus, 'blessed are the peace makers for they shall be called the children of God.'

4. Scripture and the Youth

a. We have learnt again that the youth are the Church of the present and the future, and observed that in many provinces of the South, youth form an overwhelming majority of Church membership as well as of society. We therefore, call for empowerment of the youth through training and involvement, and by trusting them with responsibility.

b. We encourage Anglican youth to be in fellowship with one another across the Communion for mutual encouragement and envisioning. We urge the youth of the South at this Encounter to link up with those who organised the 1995 Anglican Youth Encounter as well as with the Inter-Anglican Youth Network, with a view to exploring the possibility of another Anglican Youth Encounter in the South and participation in the Inter-Anglican Youth Network events.

c. We urge the South to South Co-ordinating Group to ensure that the next Encounter in the South include a significant input from the youth. In an age when many young people live in search of models and direction, we challenge the leadership of the Church to exemplify the ideals they proclaim. We equally challenge the youth to take their cue from the theme of this Encounter to make

Scripture their rule of faith and conduct and to submit themselves to God for missionary service through the Church at home and abroad.

5. Scripture and the Church in Context

We have learned from experience in rich diversity of situations and cultures that:

a. The life and witness of the Church can be enriched through the unique contribution of each member.
b. In order to be fully and effectively 'Church' in any given context our local congregations need to be freed from the trappings of the colonial past.
c. While theology, worship and liturgy need to be rooted in Scripture, the Churches of the South are challenged to contextualise and make them relevant.
d. The life of the Communion is impoverished by the lack of direct input from the South. We therefore urge the Communion to explore ways of intentionally encouraging direct South input for the enrichment of the life and mission of the whole Church.

6. Scripture, the Family and Human Sexuality

Reflection on our Encounter theme has helped further deepen our resolve to uphold the authority of Scripture in every aspect of life, including the family and human sexuality. Therefore:

a. We call on the Anglican Communion as a Church claiming to be rooted in the Apostolic and Reformed Tradition to remain true to Scripture as the final authority in all matters of faith and conduct;
b. We affirm that Scripture upholds marriage as a sacred relationship between a man and a woman, instituted in the creation ordinance;
c. We reaffirm that the only sexual expression, as taught by Scripture, which honours God and upholds human dignity is that between a man and a woman within the sacred ordinance of marriage;

d. We further believe that Scripture maintains that any other form of sexual expression is at once sinful, selfish, dishonouring to God and an abuse of human dignity;

e. We are aware of the scourge of sexual promiscuity, including homosexuality, rape and child abuse in our time. These are pastoral problems, and we call on the Churches to seek to find a pastoral and scriptural way to bring healing and restoration to those who are affected by any of these harrowing tragedies.

7. Scripture and Church Unity

a. Aware of the scriptural teaching on the significance of unity among Christians, we challenge our Churches to examine their relationship with Christians of other denominations in their contexts.

b. We further challenge our Anglican Churches to recognise the missionary and pastoral implications, as well as guard the internal unity, of our Communion. Even though some of us may feel marginalised, pushed out and not recognised, yet we must also recognise our integral inter-relatedness and that we need each other. Among other things this calls for greater sensitivity to the effects of our local policies and pronouncements on those of our members who are called to witness in situations of martyrdom and religious pluralism.

c. We therefore call on the Primates, the Anglican Consultative Council and the Lambeth Conference to take the necessary steps to establish such new structures (or reinforce old ones) that will strengthen the bonds of affection between our provinces, and especially, make for effective mutual accountability in all matters of doctrine and polity throughout the Communion.

Special Resolutions

a. This Encounter in the South, meeting in Kuala Lumpur 10-15 February 1997, unanimously endorsed the Statement on Human Sexuality (which is appended to this report).

Statement on Human Sexuality

1. God's glory and loving purposes have been revealed in the creation of humankind. (Rom. 1:18, Gen. 1:26, 27) Among the multiplicity of his gifts we are blessed with our sexuality.
2. Since the Fall (Gen. 3), life has been impaired and God's own purposes spoilt. Our fallen state has affected every sphere of our being, which includes our sexuality. Sexual deviation has existed in every time and in most cultures. Jesus' teaching about lust in the Sermon on the Mount (Matt. 5:27-30) makes it clear that sexual sin is a real danger and temptation to us all.
3. It is, therefore, with an awareness of our own vulnerability to sexual sin that we express our profound concern about recent developments relating to Church discipline and moral teaching in some provinces in the North — specifically, the ordination of practising homosexuals and the blessing of same-sex unions.
4. While acknowledging the complexities of our sexual nature and the strong drives it places within us, we are quite clear about God's will in these areas as expressed in the Bible.
5. The whole body of the Scripture bears witness to God's will regarding human sexuality which is to be expressed only within the lifelong union of a man and a woman in (holy) matrimony.
6. The Holy Scriptures are clear in teaching that all sexual promiscuity is sin. We are convinced that this includes homosexual practices, between men or women, between men and women outside marriage as well as heterosexual relationships.
7. We believe that the clear and unambiguous teaching of the Holy Scriptures about human sexuality is of great help to Christians as it provides clear boundaries.
8. We find no conflict between clear biblical teaching and sensitive pastoral care. The call to repentance precedes forgiveness and is part of the healing process. We see this in the ministry of Jesus, for example his response to the adulterous woman, 'neither do I condemn you. Go and sin no more.' (John 8:11)
9. We are deeply concerned that the setting aside of biblical teaching in such actions as the ordination of practising homosexuals and the blessing of same-sex unions calls into question the authority of the Holy Scriptures. This is totally unacceptable to us.

10. This leads us to express concern about mutual accountability and interdependence within our Anglican Communion. As provinces and dioceses we need to learn how to seek each other's counsel and wisdom in a spirit of true unity, and to reach a common mind, before embarking on radical changes to Church discipline and moral teaching.

11. We live in a global village and must be more aware that the way we act in one part of the world can radically affect the mission and witness of the Church in another.

Anglican Encounter in the South, Kuala Lumpur,
10-15 February 1997

APPENDIX II

The Montreal Declaration of
Anglican Essentials, June, 1994

'In essentials, unity;
in non-essentials, liberty;
in all things, charity.'

St. Augustine

As members of the Anglican Church of Canada from every province
and territory, and participants in the Essentials 1994 Conference in
Montreal, we unite in praising God for his saving grace and for the
fellowship we enjoy with our Lord and with each other. We affirm the
following Christian essentials:

1. The Triune God

There is one God, self-revealed as three persons, 'of one substance,
power and eternity', the Father, the Son, and the Holy Spirit. For the
sake of the Gospel we decline proposals to modify or marginalise these
names and we affirm their rightful place in prayer, liturgy, and hym-
nody. For the Gospel invites us through the Holy Spirit to share eternally in the divine fellowship, as adopted children of the God in whose
family Jesus Christ is both our saviour and our brother. (Deuteronomy
6:4; Isaiah 45:5; Matthew 28:19; 2 Corinthians 13:14; Galatians 4:4-6;

2 Thessalonians 2:13-14; 1 Peter 1:2; Jude 20-21. *Cf.* Article I of the 39 Articles, Book of Common Prayer [BCP], p. 699.)

2. Creator, Redeemer and Sanctifier

The almighty triune God created a universe that was in every way good until creaturely rebellion disrupted it. Sin having intruded, God in love purposed to restore cosmic order through the calling of the covenant people Israel, the coming of Jesus Christ to redeem, the outpouring of the Holy Spirit to sanctify, the building up of the church for worship and witness, and the coming again of Christ in glory to make all things new. Works of miraculous power mark the unfolding of God's plan throughout history. (Genesis 1-3; Isaiah 40:28; 65:17; Matthew 6:10; John 17:6; Acts 17:24-26, 28; 1 Corinthians 15:28; 2 Corinthians 5:19; Ephesians 1:11; 2 Timothy 3:16; Hebrews 11:3; Revelation 21:5. *Cf.* Article I.)

3. The Word Made Flesh

Jesus Christ, the incarnate Son of God, born of the virgin Mary, sinless in life, raised bodily from the dead, and now reigning in glory though still present with his people through the Holy Spirit, is both the Jesus of history and the Christ of Scripture. He is God with us, the sole mediator between God and ourselves, the source of saving knowledge of the Godhead, and the giver of eternal life to the church catholic. (Matthew 1:24-25; 1:14; 17:20-21; Acts 1:9-11; 4:12; Romans 5:17; Philippians 2:5-6; Colossians 2:9; 1 Timothy 2:5-6; Hebrews 1:2; 9:15. *Cf.* Articles II-IV; the Nicene Creed, BCP.)

4. The Only Saviour

Human sin is prideful rebellion against God's authority, expressing itself in our refusing to love both the Creator and his creatures. Sin corrupts our nature and its fruit is injustice, oppression, personal and social disintegration, alienation, and guilt before God; it destroys hope and leads to a future devoid of any enjoyment of either God or good. From the guilt, shame, power, and path of sin, Jesus Christ is the only Saviour; penitent faith in him is the only way of salvation. By his atoning sacrifice on the cross for our sins, Jesus overcame the powers of darkness and secured our redemption and justification. By his bodily rising he guaranteed the future resurrection and eternal inheritance of all believers. By his regenerating gift of the Spirit, he restores our fallen nature and renews us in his own image. Thus in every generation he is the way, the truth, and the life for sinful individuals, and the architect of restored human community. (John 14:6; Acts 1:9-11; 2:32-33; 4:12; Romans 3:22-25; 1 Corinthians 15:20-24; 2 Corinthians 5:18-19; Philippians 2:9-11; Colossians 2:13-15; 1 Timothy 2:5-6; 1 Peter 1:3-5; 1 John 4:14; 5:11-12. *Cf.* Articles II-IV, XI, XV, XVIII, XXXI.)

5. The Spirit of Life

The Holy Spirit, 'the Lord, the Giver of life,' sent to the church at Pentecost by the Father and the Son, discloses the glory of Jesus Christ, convicts of sin, renews the sinner's inner being, induces faith, equips for righteousness, creates communion, and empowers for service. Life in the Spirit is a supernaturalising of our natural existence and a true foretaste of heaven. The loving unity of Spirit-filled Christians and churches is a powerful sign of the truth of Christianity. (Genesis 1:2; Exodus 31:2-5; Psalm 51:11; John 3:5-6; 14:26; 15:26; 16:7-11, 13-15; 1 Corinthians 2:4; 6:19; 12:4-7; 2 Corinthians 3:18; Galatians 4:4-6; 5:22-26; Ephesians 1:13-14; 5:18; 1 Thessalonians 5:19; 2 Timothy 3:16. *Cf.* Article V; the Nicene Creed.)

6. The Authority of the Bible

The canonical Scriptures of the Old and New Testaments are 'God's Word written', inspired and authoritative, true and trustworthy, coherent, sufficient for salvation, living and powerful as God's guidance for belief and behaviour.

The trinitarian, Christ-centred, redemption-oriented faith of the Bible is embodied in the historic ecumenical creeds and the Anglican foundational documents. To this basic understanding of Scripture, the Holy Spirit leads God's people and the church's counsels in every age through tradition and reason prayerfully and reverently employed.

The church may not judge the Scriptures, selecting and discarding from among their teachings. But Scripture under Christ judges the church for its faithfulness to his revealed truth. (Deuteronomy 29:29; Isaiah 40:8; 55:11; Matthew 5:17-18; John 10:35; 14:26; Romans 1:16; Ephesians 1:17-19; 2 Timothy 2:15; 3:14-17; 2 Peter 1:20-21. *Cf.* Articles VI-VIII, XX.)

7. The Church of God

The supernatural society called the church is the family of God, the body of Christ, and the temple of the Holy Spirit. It is the community of believers, justified through faith in Christ, incorporated into the risen life of Christ, and set under the authority of Holy Scripture as the word of Christ. The church on earth is united through Christ to the church in heaven in the communion of the saints. Through the church's ministry of the word and sacraments of the Gospel, God ministers life in Christ to the faithful, thereby empowering them for worship, witness, and service. In the life of the church only that which may be proved from Scripture should be held to be essential to the faith and that which is non-essential should not be required of anyone to be believed or be enforced as a matter of doctrine, discipline, or worship. (Ephesians 3:10-21; 5:23, 27; 1 Timothy 3:15; Hebrews 12:1-2; 2 Timothy 3:14-17. *Cf.* Articles XIX, XX and XXI.)

8. The New Life in Christ

God made human beings in the divine image so that they might glorify and enjoy their creator forever, but since the Fall, sin has alienated us all from God and disorders human motivation and action at every point. As atonement and justification restore us to fellowship with God by pardoning sin, so regeneration and sanctification renew us in the likeness of Christ by overcoming sin. The Holy Spirit, who helps us practice the disciplines of the Christian life, increasingly transforms us through them. Sinlessness, however, is not given in this world, and we who believe remain flawed 'in thought, word and deed' until we are perfected in heaven. (Genesis 1:26-28; 3; John 3:5-6; 16:13; Romans 3:23-24; 5:12; 1 Corinthians 12:4-7; 2 Corinthians 3:17-18; Galatians 5:22-24; Ephesians 2:1-5; Philippians 2:13; 2 Peter 3:10-13. *Cf.* Articles IX-XVI; Book of Alternative Services, p. 191.)

9. The Church's Ministry

The Holy Spirit bestows distinctive gifts upon all Christians for the purpose of glorifying God and building up his church in truth and love. All Christians are called in their baptism to be ministers, regardless of gender, race, age, or socio-economic status. All God's people must seek to find and fulfil the particular form of service for which God has called and equipped them. Within the priesthood of all believers we honour the ministry of word and sacrament to which bishops, priests and deacons are set apart by the Ordinal. (Romans 12:6-8; 1 Corinthians 3:16; 6:11; 12:4-7, 27; 2 Corinthians 5:20; Galatians 2:16; Ephesians 4:11-13; 1 Timothy 3:1, 12-13; 5:17; Hebrews 2:11; 1 Peter 2:4-5, 9-10. *Cf.* Articles XIX, XXIII.)

10. The Church's Worship

The primary calling of the church, as of every Christian, is to offer worship, in the Spirit and according to truth, to the God of creation, providence, and grace. The essential dimensions of worship are praise and thanksgiving for all good things, proclamation and celebration of the glory of God and of Jesus Christ, prayer for human needs and for the advancement of Christ's kingdom, and self-offering for service. All liturgical forms — verbal, musical, and ceremonial — stand under the authority of Scripture.

The Book of Common Prayer provides a biblically-grounded doctrinal standard, and should be retained as the norm for all alternative liturgies. It should not be revised in the theologically-divided climate of the contemporary church. The Book of Alternative Services meets a widely-felt need for contemporary liturgy, and brings life and joy to many Anglican worshippers.

No form of worship can truly exalt Christ or draw forth true devotion to him without the presence and power of the Holy Spirit. Prayer, public and private, is central to the health and renewal of the church. Healing, spiritual and physical, is a welcome aspect of Anglican worship. (John 4:24; 16:8-15; Acts 1:8; 2:42-47; Romans 12:1; 1 Corinthians 11:23-26; 12:7; 2 Corinthians 5:18-19; Ephesians 5:18-20; Colossians 3:16; 1 Thessalonians 1:4-5; 5:19. *Cf.* The Solemn Declaration of 1893, p. viii, BCP; Articles XXV, XXXIV.)

11. The Priority of Evangelism

Evangelism means proclaiming Jesus Christ as divine Saviour, Lord, and Friend, in a way that invites people to come to God through him, to worship and serve him, and to seek the empowering of the Holy Spirit for their life of discipleship in the community of the church. All Christians are called to witness to Christ, as a sign of love both to him and to their neighbours. The task, which is thus a matter of priority, calls for personal training and a constant search for modes of persuasive outreach. We sow the seed, and look to God for the fruit. (Matthew 5:13-16; 28:19-20; John 3:16-18; 20:21; Acts 2:37-39; 5:31-32; 1 Corinthians 1:23; 15:2-4; 2 Corinthians 4:5; 5:20; 1 Peter 3:15.)

12. The Challenge of Global Mission

Cross-cultural evangelism and pastoral care remain necessary responses to the Great Commission of Jesus Christ. His command to preach the gospel world-wide, making disciples and planting churches, still applies. The church's mission requires missions.

Christ and his salvation must be proclaimed sensitively and energetically everywhere, at home and abroad, and cross-cultural mission must be supported by praying, giving, and sending. Global mission involves partnership and interchange, and missionaries sent by younger churches to Canada should be welcomed. (Matthew 28:19-20; Mark 16:15; Luke 10:2; Romans 15:23-24; 1 Corinthians 2:4-5; 9:22-23; 2 Corinthians 4:5; 8:1-4, 7; Ephesians 6:19-20; Philippians 2:5-7; 1 Thessalonians 1:6-8.)

13. The Challenge of Social Action

The gospel constrains the church to be 'salt' and 'light' in the world, working out the implications of biblical teaching for the right ordering of social, economic, and political life, and for humanity's stewardship of creation. Christians must exert themselves in the cause of justice and in acts of compassion. While no social system can be identified with the coming Kingdom of God, social action is an integral part of our obedience to the Gospel. (Genesis 1:26-28; Isaiah 30:18; 58:6-10; Amos 5:24; Matthew 5:13-16; 22:37-40; 25:31-46; Luke 4:17-21; John 20:21;

2 Corinthians 1:3-4; James 2:14-26; 1 John 4:16; Revelation 1:5-6; 5:9-10. *Cf.* Article XXXVIII.)

14. The Standards of Sexual Conduct

God designed human sexuality not only for procreation but also for the joyful expression of love, honour, and fidelity between wife and husband. These are the only sexual relations that biblical theology deems good and holy.

Adultery, fornication, and homosexual unions are intimacies contrary to God's design. The church must seek to minister healing and wholeness to those who are sexually scarred, or who struggle with ongoing sexual temptations, as most people do. Homophobia and all forms of sexual hypocrisy and abuse are evils against which Christians must ever be on their guard. The church may not lower God's standards of sexual morality for any of its members, but must honour God by upholding these standards tenaciously in face of society's departures from them.

Congregations must seek to meet the particular needs for friendship and community that single persons have. (Genesis 1:26-28; 2:21-24; Matthew 5:27-32; 19:3-12; Luke 7:36-50; John 8:1-11; Romans 1:21-28; 3:22-24; 1 Corinthians 6:9-11, 13-16; 7:7; Ephesians 5:3; 1 Timothy 1:8-11; 3:2-4, 12.)

15. The Family and the Call to Singleness

The family is a divinely ordained focus of love, intimacy, personal growth and stability for women, men and children. Divorce, child abuse, domestic violence, rape, pornography, parental absenteeism, sexist domination, abortion, common-law relationships, and homosexual partnerships, all reflect weakening of the family ideal. Christians must strengthen family life through teaching, training, and active support, and work for socio-political conditions that support the family. Single-parent families and victims of family breakdown have special needs to which congregations must respond with sensitivity and support.

Singleness also is a gift from God and a holy vocation. While single, Christians are called to celibacy and God will give them grace to live in chastity. (Psalm 119:9-11; Proverbs 22:6; Matthew 5:31-32; Mark 10:6-9; 1 Corinthians 6:9-11; Ephesians 5:21–6:4; Colossians 3:18-21; 1 John 3:14-15.)

The New Beginning

Together we reaffirm the Anglican Christianity that finds expression in the historic standards of the ecumenical creeds, the Thirty-Nine Articles, the Solemn Declaration of 1893, and the 1962 Book of Common Prayer. Respect for these standards strengthens our identity and communion. In humility we recognise we have often been ashamed of the gospel we have received and disobedient to the Lord of the Church. God helping us, we resolve to maintain our heritage of faith and transmit it intact. This fullness of faith is needed both for Anglican renewal and for the effective proclamation of the good news of Jesus Christ in the power of the Holy Spirit.

We invite all Anglicans to join us in affirming the above as essentials of Christian faith, practice, and nurture today. In this declaration we believe that we are insisting upon only what is genuinely essential. In regard to non-essentials, we should recognise and respect that liberty and that comprehensiveness which have been among the special graces of our Anglican heritage.

Participants in Essentials '94, with the Sponsoring Bodies:
Anglican Renewal Ministries of Canada
Barnabas Anglican Ministries
The Prayer Book Society of Canada

21 June 1994, Montreal, Canada

A Prayer
for the Church

Merciful Lord, we beseech thee to cast thy bright beams of light upon thy Church, that it being enlightened by the doctrine of thy blessed Apostle and Evangelist Saint John may so walk in the light of thy truth, that it may at length attain to the light of everlasting life: through Jesus Christ our Lord. *Amen.*

(Prayer for Saint John the Evangelist's Day,
Book of Common Prayer, 1662)

311